FORMATION

The Making of Nigeria from
Jihad to Amalgamation

FORMATION

The Making of Nigeria from
Jihad to Amalgamation

FOLA FAGBULE
FEYI FAWEHINMI

First published in Nigeria 2020 by Cassava Republic Press
Abuja – London

First published in the UK & USA in 2021 by Cassava Republic Press

A CIP catalogue record for this book is available from the National Library of Nigeria and the British Library.

ISBN 978-1-913175-09-2
eISBN 978-1-913175-10-8

Editor: Bibi Bakare-Yusuf
Copy editor: Layla Mohamed
Proofreader: Uthman Adejumo
Book design by Adekunle Adebisi
Cover & Art Direction by Wilna Combrinck

Printed and bound in the UK by Bell & Bain Ltd, Glasgow

Distributed in Nigeria by Yellow Danfo
Distributed in the UK by Ingram

Worldwide distribution by Ingram Publisher Services International

CONTENTS

INTRODUCTION

How Did We Get in Formation?

Nigeria is the largest Black country in the world. Formed around two mighty rivers and made up of a stunning diversity of peoples and lands, there is no shortage of stories about the history, politics and culture of Africa's most populous nation. But how did the country come to be in the first place? A combination of factors has ensured that this is not as easy a question to answer as it should be.

Many official versions of Nigeria's creation story do exist. Yet, as with all official histories, these stories are often coloured by the lenses of politics and agenda worn by the narrators. This has not always been for lack of carefully preserved records and credible eye-witness accounts, certainly not in the one-hundred-year period immediately preceding formation. Nor has it always been on account of a dearth of rigorous academic work by indigenous and foreign historians. A lot of great history books and research studies have been written about Nigeria. It has not even been so much the result of popular disinterest in the subject. Quite the contrary, Nigerians are as passionate about their history as any people anywhere in the world. We might never all agree on what version of history is the 'correct' one, but we share an abiding interest in the subject.

So how did Nigeria come to be in the first place? And why is there not a deliberately apolitical, nuanced and coherent origin story available for our modern generation to grapple with? Our objective with *Formation: The Making of Nigeria from Jihad to Amalgamation* is to answer the former question, and in doing so occupy the vacuum described by the latter. *Formation* is a work of popular history. Neither of us have been trained as historians; we both work in financial services. But we share a belief that history is too important to be left to historians alone. We also believe that a story this fascinating only needs careful narrators for it to shine on its own merits. So, this is how we got into *Formation*.

We hope that you will have an answer to many questions about Nigeria's formation by the time you finish this book. Even though we offer a coherent narrative, we do not purport to tell the *entire* story of Nigeria's formation. That would be a bold claim for any single work of history to make in any country, let alone in one as complex as Nigeria. What we hope is to leave you better informed about the origins of what we know today as Nigeria, and perhaps also with some ideas on what this rich history teaches us about the future. One historian, whose work we have relied on describes an effort like this as a 'brick for our common house.'[i] *Formation* is our brick for the construction of the common house that is Nigeria's origin story.

Our narrative begins with a description of the great, muddy, contorted water bodies that we consider to be the raison d'etre for Nigeria in the first place: The River Niger and its sister, the Benue. In A "River Runs Through It," we trace the history of the Niger, which is the central setting for much of the events retold in the rest of our narrative. We also explain why the rivers are so important to the structure of the country, and we introduce our ideas as to how these mighty water bodies served at once to attract and divide the humans of Nigeria. We also describe some critical adjacent river roads, which combine with the great rivers to complete the tapestry into which our narrative is intricately woven.

Next, our story properly begins with a stunning revolution at a place called Gobir. This successful revolution and its unlikely leader, known as the "Son of the Jurist" would turn out to be the landmark event that fired the starting gun on the series of actions leading to *Formation*. We proceed to assess the resulting Caliphate in Session following the Gobir revolt, and very early in our narrative begin to chronicle some of the successes and failures that would come to

---

i [i] See Professor Robert Tombs' *The English and their History,* Page 891.

define the character of Nigeria to the present day. From here, the pace of our story quickens considerably because we have to catch the Oyo Empire at its dramatic moment of disintegration, triggering a devastating civil war from which a group of hardy survivors would emerge at a settlement called Abeokuta, the ray of "Sunrise within the Tropics." The remarkably astute geopolitical and foreign policy posturing of this small settlement and its accomplished civil and military leaders would prove to be our second most important milestone, crystallising another series of events leading to *Formation*.

From Abeokuta, our story takes on an even more multinational colour, as the foreign adventurers whom we term "Mad Men and Missionaries" arrive on the scene with their unique agenda. We describe their agenda in detail and retell the story of their successes and failures, which will also come to greatly shape the character of the future country, Nigeria. A few short decades later, our tale of *Formation* becomes even more complex. As we show in "Exit the Bible, Enter the Gun," the global Industrial Revolution, which began in the eighteenth century in Britain, arrived on the scene in pre-colonial Nigeria with force and determination. Next to the Gobir revolution and the clever survival strategies at Abeokuta, the Industrial Revolution would prove to be the third most significant event, triggering another series of actions leading to *Formation*. We show how the Industrial Revolution led to a shift in the terms of export trade from stolen human bodies to palm oil and other commodities, dramatically altering the state of affairs in the still inchoate country.

With this change, the arrival of "The Glorious Incompetents" on the scene was portentous for the future country, which was to be forcibly formed from a combination of imperial vision and capitalist zeal. We chronicle some of the more destructive consequences of this irresistible combination for the existing indigenous ruling classes. We continue with this theme in "Game of Thrones in the Niger Heartland," retelling the story of what happened when an unstoppable force met with an immovable object.

Finally, with the benefit of all the preceding colourful background stories, we can arrive at the more popular modules of Nigeria's pre-colonial history. The detestable as well as remarkable actions of "Frederick Lugard, The King in the North" can now be understood in their proper context, challenging the outsized significance that has been placed on them in the official versions of Nigeria's history. With proper context, we demonstrate how Lugard's revolution was in many ways the completion and expansion of the work started by the Son of the Jurist. With nuance and balance, we illuminate the brief period of "Conquest and Discontent" which followed the emergence of Lugard on the scene.

Ultimately, we end our narrative by reopening the story of the expulsion of Frederick Lugard from Nigeria, centering the work of overlooked indigenous protagonists in that crucial event. With that, the prequel to the colonial creation of modern Nigeria is complete. We end our *Formation* story just as the First World War is wrapping up, a seminal catastrophe that did not exclude the newly amalgamated country of Nigeria in its ramifications.

From start to finish, covering roughly the century and a decade from 1804 to 1914, *Formation* is written from the viewpoint of a curious observer, centering the perspectives of indigenous peoples, and retelling Nigeria's origin story in a way that is accessible and enjoyable to a modern audience. We deliberately avoid broad conclusions as much as possible. This is not because we lack opinions, as we are both very opinionated men, but because we wish the readers to draw their insights and conclusions from our story.

Our sincerest hope for *Formation* is that it will trigger the beginning of many more delightfully nuanced journeys into the history and culture of Nigeria, undertaken by Nigerians themselves. We hope that the insights and conversations that this book will spark are of the kind that will lead to a more advantageous future for the humans of Nigeria.

CHAPTER 1

A River Runs Through It

River of Rivers

In the last quarter of the eighteenth century, few rivers still held as much international fascination and mystery as the great, muddy, contorted Niger; draining as it did an incredible expanse of land over a more than a 4,000-kilometre course, which was home to a stunning diversity of peoples and places. The tenth longest waterway in the world, the river had for more than 2,000 years been the primary source of livelihood for the many peoples and groups that had come to live all along its banks and shores. Even for nations further inland in its immediate and distant hinterland, the river was for centuries the most effective means of transportation and communication with their neighbouring countries, for trade and commerce as much as military conquest, leisure and politics.

Originating in mountains close to the west coast of Africa, the Niger arches 'like a question mark'[1] through a spectacular corridor, 2,500 kilometres of which is navigable - irrigating barren steppes into fertile land, before reaching its ultimate terminus at a convoluted delta feeding into the Atlantic Ocean. The river's course is an epic one, rising and falling as it does through mountains, valleys, cataracts and other geographical obstacles. A geological wonder, the river was probably formed by the joining of at least two distinct waterways following the drying up of the Sahara Desert, itself historically fertile and irrigated with multiple large inland water bodies. This might be one of the reasons why it was given several names by the native populations living in and around it. The river was known to some as *Joliba*, to others as *Kworra*, and yet others as *Orimili*, and *Oya*, and *Torubeni*. In all cases, the name appears to have meant 'Great River' or 'Great Water', and so the reverence and importance of the river to local culture and tradition are clear in all the various languages. Even Juba the Second, the Rome-educated scholar and Berber king of Numidia in present-day Algeria, who gave the river its current name, identified the waterway by its greatness, calling it the 'Niger,' derived from the Tuareg expression 'N'ger-n-n'gero,' meaning 'River of Rivers.' Herodotus, the father of Hellenic history, mainstreamed the later European fascination with the river in his ancient fifth century BC writings, while his modern successor Pliny the Elder continued the tradition and popularised the name 'Niger' in his *Natural History*, written in the first century AD.

The river is somewhat peculiar on account of the storage limitations of its basins, combined with the irregularity of rainfall over its course, which is the ultimate determinant of the water volumes available to be drained into those basins. For these reasons, on some sections of its journey, the river is broad and expansive with several kilometres between both banks. Here, it is allowed to flow fast and furious, undisturbed by sandbanks and rocky islands midstream. In other sections, however, the Niger is perilously narrow and muddy, slowing to barely a mud swamp, constrained by geological obstacles upon and beneath it. The river flows over large mountains sitting right in its path, mangrove swamps, numerous subterranean formations, limited only by the climatic conditions of the countries it flows through. Perhaps the deepest mysteries, myths and legends of the river have arisen from the sheer diversity of the many lands it traverses - desert, prairie, savannah, mountainous, hilly, and tropical forest - and the myriad geological structures that it flows over, above, or through.

From an immense outpouring around the Fouta Djallon mountains in present-day Guinea, the river struggles determinedly upwards into the Sahara Desert, attaining its northernmost position near a point where the ancient city of Timbuktu was located in present-day Mali. Timbuktu was founded here as a dry season camp by Tuareg merchants trading between the rich Mediterranean world and the ancient countries like Songhay and Mali down the river. From here, the Niger commences a slow descent back through still more arid desert, into equatorial Africa. North of Bamako, the present-day capital of modern Mali, the river forms an interior delta, made up of swampy lakes and tributaries that are flooded during the wet season. Continuing southwards, the river bends and arches its way through broad plains, thick tropical forest, and across several lakes and reservoirs as it makes its way towards a rendezvous with its sister waterway, the Benue. Both bodies then drain further southwards, making a crooked beeline for the Atlantic Ocean via several hundred kilometres of tropical vegetation. In the event, the muddy, merged, and messy mass of twin waters arrive at a confusing maze of inhospitable creeks, streams, and swamps that form their common Atlantic delta.

Difficult Road to Master

Wide here, deep there, narrow here, lake-like there, the river drains into large lakes and reservoirs at several key points. But the River Niger has been a difficult road for its inhabitants to master, never mind visitors and curious explorers from afar. This has not stopped the human communities living on and around the Niger from attempting to dominate it, given its critical importance for commercial interaction everywhere it flows. Before mechanised travel, waterways had always provided a cheaper means of moving goods and humans than land transport, and things were no different in the Niger area. Many wars were fought over the river, and Sonni Ali, a mighty ruler of the fifteenth century Songhay Empire famously drowned in 1492 while attempting to cross a small tributary of the Niger on a military raid. The great Sonni Ali would not be the first or last traveller to meet his end on the river. By the time we pick up our story in 1804, the Niger-Benue river road may have already become one of the most contested highways in the world, divided as it was into controlled lots, held, exchanged, and fought over by empires far away, and by national or commercial groupings and communities indigenous to the area. In all of the lands covered by the great river that are relevant to our narrative, the entire length of both water bodies had been revered, studied, travelled, hunted, farmed, and lived upon for centuries.

Around 1469, Portuguese settlers had already arrived at Cape Verde, off the coast of West Africa; and followed through from there to a less important waterway near the mouth of the Niger in 1486. A man named João Afonso d'Aveiro undertook the tortuous journey into the hinterland of the then great Benin empire, where he met with Ozolua, the Oba of this ancient kingdom. Ozolua ruled over a rich and proud nation with a long-standing monarchical structure, inherited from the king's 17 predecessors prior to his establishing relations with Europeans. D'Aveiro had been preceded to the coast by another Portuguese merchant-sailor named Ruy de Sequeira, during the reign of Oba Ewuare in 1472. These were some of the first White men ever to be seen near the Niger's delta. Images of these strange visitors were captured and preserved in brass plaques made by Benin artists at the royal court. The Portuguese arrival heralded the great Atlantic slave trade from the inner realms of the Niger area, and the river began to serve as a leading transport corridor for human cargo. Further inland, in 1526, a Spanish-Muslim traveller named Al Hassan Ibn Mohammed but better known as Leo the African published the first popular eyewitness account of life on and around the Niger. Titled *History and Description of Africa and the Notable Things Contained Therein*, this ancient travel journal contributed to later European fascination with the Niger, as it included tales of a roaring gold trade, as well as of great and prosperous cities like Timbuktu, which were then centres of trade and learning.

To understand the state of affairs at the dawn of the nineteenth century when our story commences, our earliest eyes and ears reporting sights and sounds of the river at the time are those of intrepid and stubborn glory-seekers visiting the area from Britain. They had heard and read vague accounts of this geological and geographic mystery and were determined to settle once and for all the controversies in the modern scientific world as to its origin, course and termination. Their successes and failures in this endeavour form an important part of our narrative, and the subsequent history of the area.

A Labyrinth of Kingdoms

The hinterland of the Niger and Benue rivers in 1800 was already diversely populated by a significant number of indigenous and migrant peoples[2]. The rivers served at once to unite these neighbouring countries but also, to divide the area into multiple geopolitical entities. Set immediately north of the Benue were a multiplicity of independent communities, most notable for their focus on agriculture in this fertile tropical valley, and their intense resistance to being incorporated into any broader imperial nationalities. Further inland above these groups lay precisely one such imperial nation, Bornu, a Mediterranean facing empire with its provenance in southern Arabia (Yemen). An ancient kingdom, Bornu once extended its imperial reaches far northwards across the great Sahara to include inland territories of present-day Libya but was by this time more constrained in its extent to the areas around and below the great Lake Chad. This now vanishing oasis was itself at the time still a magnificent inland ocean, at a great distance above and unconnected to the Benue.

In the more central and western Sahelian area situated just beneath the fringes of the arid Sahara lay the confederation of loosely associated, nominally Muslim merchant and agrarian Hausa city-states. Within these famed trading-states lived a great diversity of people, particularly in the main metropolitan cities. There were autochthonous indigenes melded with migrants from the Middle East and all over Sahelian Africa. One prominent group among the latter was an enlightened class of itinerant preachers, teachers, pastoralists and traders that we will soon learn more about. These long-standing Hausa city states had a thousand-year history of alternating self-governance, war, peace, and submission to the rule of imperial Songhay, then Bornu, and eventually, each other. They were located some distance away from the upper Niger, which flowed through the territory held by Kebbi, one of the richest and oldest of the city states. The Hausa city-states were outwardly oriented in commercial and political outlook, towards the powerful Ottoman world in the Mediterranean Sea, Arabia and the Middle East. From there, the dominant religious, trading, cultural and military influences in the old world had acted on them for centuries. For example, Kano, a great inland metropolitan emporium, was the centre of all the important trade, learning and communications south of Tripoli on the Mediterranean coast. So great were the connections between these two key entrepots that it was said that even unimportant events which happened in either city were known in the other within three months[3].

Directly north of the Niger lay another diverse collection of independent nation-states, including the dominant Nupe country. Famed for its diverse enterprise and ownership of Bida, later to become the inland port city of the Sokoto Caliphate, Nupe was at the time the most powerful country in its neighbourhood. Westwards from here, protected on either side by a tropical forest and the great lakes in the Niger, lay the Borgu kingdom and its associated imperial city-states like Bussa and Kaiama in the present-day Kwara state of central Nigeria, and Nikki, which is now in northern Benin Republic. To the east was the beautiful and temperate Jos-Bauchi plateau, later famous for significant deposits of tin, and the discovery of the nearby ancient Nok civilisation. Below the western banks of the Niger lay the country now known as Yoruba, an extensive collection of people speaking a similar language and consolidated into the declining Oyo Empire.

More centrally on the lower Niger and its hinterland were still more diverse groups of independent nations and kingdoms, including notable empires like the Ijebu, the Benin (by now already in decline, relative to its heyday), and multiple coastal trading states like Bonny, Brass, and Itsekiri. These city-states were situated in the Niger's delta as well as on the quite separate Cross River, where Calabar was already established as an important metropolitan capital. The Igbo country was situated east of the lower Niger, hemmed in by the Cross River, the coastal trading states, and the independent agrarian nations south of the Benue. Here, the inhabitants lived in relative self-sufficiency and autonomy from much of the rest of the world, as culturally affiliated but independent groups of towns and villages[4]. Later to be known as Lagos, a small but increasingly important island, established by Benin in the seventeenth century, on the western coast, but separated from the Yoruba country by a large inland lagoon, was now on the ascendancy. Its rise was on account of being a leading depot for trading in slaves with European vessels calling on the Gulf of Guinea.

Down and across the crooked stems of the Niger and Benue were numerous independent communities and mini kingdoms, controlling inland territories on either bank, with an astonishing diversity of languages and customs, given their proximity to one another. With a few exceptions, the most common theme consistent with the communities, settlements, kingdoms, and groupings on and around the Niger and Benue at the start of the nineteenth century was the aspiration for political independence and self-regulation or put differently: a mistrust for collaboration with strangers. An important backdrop to this mistrust, diversity, and fragmentation was the destructive political economy resulting from multiple centuries of violent trade in human bodies down the rivers, at the coast, and across the Sahara by all of the main peoples living in these areas. It was quite unusual to find an early nineteenth century nation or community in the Niger-Benue area that was not engaged in some form of slave trading. The domestic and international trade in humans had become by this time the single most important and definitive driver of all military, social, political, diplomatic, and economic decisions by the nation-states and peoples of the area.

To Kill or Be Killed

In those circumstances, the primary organising principle of all relevant groupings in the area was either offensive, often for the capture and trade of humans, or defensive - for protection from defeat, capture and plunder. The natural geographical boundaries and separations between the various locations - including the rivers - were optimised for those goals, to the detriment of commerce in goods and services, or political and cultural collaboration. Additional non-natural barriers and defences were erected by all of the organised communities on the banks of the rivers and in the hinterland, including everything from ramparts, moats, and ditches, to city walls, crude landmines, and booby traps[5]. Also, all major inland roads were policed and tolled at various intervals. Despite this, trading caravans were frequently attacked by armed bandits and safe travelling was not to be taken for granted. In addition, the flow of the rivers was also unpredictable, making them hard to navigate by larger trading vessels outside of the wet season. As a consequence, already hard-to-conquer natural obstacles such as the broad rivers served to create divisions and separations (turfs) to be protected at all costs by the leading commercial and state actors.

It must not be surprising therefore that the rivers remained shrouded in mystery from the outside world for so long. Firstly, it would have been the rare person or group of individuals that had managed to safely travel the entire length of the rivers at the turn of the century. Because, quite apart from the treacherous and unpredictable terrain for river navigation, the social, political, military, and economic conditions in the countries along the banks and the interior did not lend themselves to safe passage. Trade was transacted at key entrepots and port-cities up and down the Niger in particular, and passage between those trading centres was regulated and invariably conducted with armed escorts. In addition, startling differences in languages spoken by many of the people doing business on the Niger rendered much of the most accurate available information on its course either lost in translation or obscured from written records exported to the rest of the world. For these reasons more than any other, the available information to most of the world on the life, customs, and conditions of the people; and the mapping of the rivers remained limited up to the end of the eighteenth century.

Best Kept Secret of the Tropics

From the time of the Romans, until the early nineteenth century, competing theories remained afloat internationally as to the source, course and terminal point of the Niger. Accurate information about the Niger and Benue remained elusive and unknown to the world, except for the local people who lived upon the banks and islands, and who controlled trade and intercourse up and down their relevant turfs and lots. Some ambitious European theorists even speculated that both rivers emptied into Lake Chad, or the Nile or the Congo, those other well-known rivers of Central and Eastern Africa. This was despite the fact that centuries of communication and interaction had been ongoing between the coastal peoples and the daring European traders who had joined the Portuguese and spread out from Benin across the entire mouth and delta of the river. Similarly, the nations of the upper Niger hinterland had engaged for centuries in active trans-Saharan interaction with the Ottoman-Arabian and Mediterranean worlds but had managed to keep the secret of the Niger's course unrevealed or forgotten internationally.

It was not until the late 1700s that European adventurers began to commit capital, technology and their lives to understand, and broadcast abroad, accurate information about the rivers and their surrounding countries. These new arrivals in the Niger-Benue country were spurred by Victorian era curiosity and by the desire to achieve fame and fortune as explorer-celebrities. By this time in history, these muddied, seasonal, rock-and-island-studded maritime highways had been fully mastered as the primary natural corridors for transmission of commerce and information between hinterland kingdoms and communities. Our story will later follow the earliest travellers from Europe whose manic insistence forced open the secrets of the rivers.

Adjacent River Roads

Inland from and adjacent to the Niger-Benue river complex lay other important water highways worth mentioning for their similar impact on commercial and political interaction between the peoples of the pre-European Nigerian hinterland. For example, the rivers Hawal and Gongola drained large areas and connected the Benue to the northernmost point accessible from that main waterway system, at Nafada, a river port town in present-day Gombe, in North-East Nigeria. Flowing into the later great lake terminus at Shiroro - where a modern hydroelectric dam is now installed - the Kaduna river connected the upper Niger to central areas within a less than 300 kilometre range from the most populous settlements below the Sahara. And the important Cross River system provided an independent coastal outlet from the Niger-Benue system, dipping south-eastwards into present-day Cameroon where it connected a vast tropical area to the Atlantic world.

More important for our narrative, proximity to and control of commerce on the Cross river allowed the emergence of critical political, economic and military powers on the coast such as Calabar and in the hinterland, Arochukwu, the revered, itinerant Igbo martial-cultural, mercenary and merchant non-state institution and confederation[6]. In a very similar manner, the Imo river provided the natural transport corridor that led to the emergence of Opobo as a short-lived independent merchant kingdom, unconnected to the river Niger. As we have seen, control by the Benin monarchy of its eponymous river with its coastal access, acting through their

Ijaw and Itsekiri allies and subsidiaries - as much for reasons of superstition as for specialisation - was critical to the emergence of that prestigious kingdom in antiquity[7].

The rest of the West African coastline from Cape Verde to the Cameroon mountains is notorious for its dearth of natural harbours, Dakar and Freetown being the locations of two excellent exceptions. Hence, port sites were few and far between for the earliest arriving large vessels, hindered by the presence of estuarine bars, heavy surf, shallow lagoons, marshes and mangrove swamps. This natural deficiency would seal the importance of the Lagos lagoon and the Badagry creek system in our narrative, as well as for the future evolution of the countries lying behind their shorelines. Deep and eminently navigable, as well as provisioned with perilous openings to the Atlantic Ocean and connectivity to nearly 200 kilometres of unobstructed hinterland landing points, the lottery of geography ensured the emergence of Lagos and Badagry as the twin future entrepots of Nigeria.

With the benefit of this background to the area, we may now begin our narrative, which starts in the countries around the upper Niger and then proceeds downriver and across to other neighbouring lands connected by the great rivers. While the rivers provided the critical transmission mechanism for the flow of ideas and information across these historical lands, it is to the actions and agency of human beings that we owe our story. To these stories we must now turn, beginning at a place called Gobir.

---

1.   De Gramont S. *The Strong Brown God: The Story of the Niger River.* Houghton Mifflin; 1975.

2.   Kemper S. *A Labyrinth of Kingdoms: 10,000 Miles through Islamic Africa.* W. W. Norton & Company; 2012.

3.   Orr CWJ. *The Making of Northern Nigeria.* Macmillan and Company, Limited; 1911.

4.   Basden GT. *Among the Ibos of Nigeria.* Seeley, Service & Co.; 1921.

5. Bacon R. *Benin, the City of Blood*. Creative Media Partners, LLC; 2018.

6. De Gramont S. *The Strong Brown God: The Story of the Niger River*. Houghton Mifflin; 1975.

7. Kemper S. *A Labyrinth of Kingdoms: 10,000 Miles through Islamic Africa*. W. W. Norton & Company; 2012.

CHAPTER 2

Son of the Jurist

In the Beginning at Gobir

The history of the country formed around the Niger river began on 21 February 1804. It was on that day that the long-running tensions between Uthman Dan Fodio and Yunfa dan Nafata came to a head. That Tuesday, the popular preacher, Dan Fodio led his followers away from Degel, a town in the old Hausa city-state of Gobir straddling today's Nigeria and Niger Republic, to Gudu, 48 kilometres North-East, in a migration replaying the Hijra by the Holy Prophet Muhammad nearly a dozen centuries before. Once there, the jihad that kicked off the Nigerian story was inevitable.

For much of its history, Gobir had been an independent city-state located on the southern fringes of the Sahara Desert. Gobir was sustained in wealth and military relevance by its trade and interaction with its six Hausa-speaking sister states (Biram, Daura, Kano, Katsina, Rano and Zaria - collectively the Hausa Bakwai), its imperial and often hostile neighbour Bornu, and the broader Sahelian hinterland of the Mediterranean Sea. Gobirawa were traders and farmers, with human bodies being a primary commodity and transaction currency. Domestic slavery existed as an important institution to maintain the economic vitality of the state. Successive rulers of Gobir had engaged in periodic armed conflicts and outright wars with neighbouring states; and its fortunes had risen or ebbed, depending on the quality of military and political leadership at various points in its long history. By the late eighteenth and early nineteenth century, Gobir was past its glorious prime, weakened as much by constant warfare on multiple fronts, as by internal politics.

Among the Gobirawa lived an enterprising group of foreigners called the Fulani. These were a migrant nation of people living across multiple states in West Africa. The Fulani at Gobir could be classified into three socio-economic categories: metropolitan merchants, Islamic educationists (referred to as Mallams) and itinerant pastoralists. Among the metropolitan Fulani party were some of the most influential and wealthiest citizens of Gobir, long integrated into the fabric of local society, as had often happened with many other outside groups, including slaves, who assimilated into the welcoming Hausa language and culture. The Fulani lived in fragile harmony within their adopted countries, maintaining their own strong linguistic and cultural homogeneity, while also becoming important contributors to trade, education, political and military matters in Hausaland. The biggest factor affecting the state of life for the Fulani within Gobir and in the many other nation-states they occupied was the personal relationships between their leadership elite and the ruling party at the royal court.

For their part, the kings of Gobir had not always known what to do with the Fulani. Their attitudes over the decades had ranged from warmth to outright hostility. Bawa Jan Gwarzo, the powerful warrior-king of Gobir who reigned from 1768 to 1790, had been friendly towards Dan Fodio and even appointed him to his court as an adviser. He also permitted Fulani Muslims to dorn their distinctive turbans, a significant concession as we shall see. All this was despite the fact that Gwarzo himself was only a nominal Muslim and was constantly being heckled by Dan Fodio to take Islam a lot more seriously than he was willing to. Perhaps it was because of Gwarzo's advancing age that the king venerated in praise song as the 'Iron chieftain, causer of terror'[1] allowed Dan Fodio a free hand to proselytise as he liked. For his part, Dan Fodio responded to Gwarzo's friendliness by never assuming open hostility towards the ruling Gobir party in his preaching. This fine balance continued long after Gwarzo's death in 1790 and through the reign of his successor, Yakubu.

Not for the first or last time in the history of the area that will become known as Northern Nigeria, a charismatic and revolutionary Islamic preacher had risen up, and built a following of people who were disaffected by the excesses of the ruling elite. It just so happened that on this occasion, the intellectual and spiritual leader of this revolutionary movement arose from among the Fulani society at Gobir and found his strongest early support within the merchant-preacher set of this elite. Islamic proselytisation - from its very origins - had leaned heavily into political revolution and social justice. Ideological consonance was as fundamental to the spread of the religion as was moral instruction and supernatural belief. The adherents to the Holy Prophet's message and traditions were religious followers who accepted not just the sovereignty of a spiritual lord of all the worlds, and almighty ruler on the day of reckoning, but also in the directives relayed through his servant and messenger, as to the mode of life and government that must exist in the temporal.

Many of Dan Fodio's followers were not even Muslims yet, but they liked the sound of what the wise preacher had to say about oppression and injustice. Arbitrary taxes and - where it existed at all - insecure land tenure were just two of the most relevant concerns to citizens of Gobir. That the Hausa ruling elite could take their land with impunity was as much a problem for the indigenous Gobirawa as it was for the Fulani immigrants. Quite apart from their racial and linguistic affinity, Fulani followers were drawn to Dan Fodio's teaching on account of his strident criticism of the jangali cattle tax. This was imposed arbitrarily like other taxes – such as the kudin ghari which was levied on townspeople and the kudin salla which was levied at festival times - in Gobir and across Hausaland. It was written that if a Fulani man's cattle so much as strayed close to the herd of a member of the Hausa ruling elite, that was enough to cause seizure of the erring animal, until compensation - typically a proportion of the herd - was paid[2].

As with any society that held a significant proportion of

its inhabitants in disenfranchised bondage, an in situ body of oppressed people also existed within the kingdom, constituting another potent source of discontent waiting to be unleashed. To make matters worse, the nominally Islamic rulers of Gobir and the broader Hausa kingdoms had no qualms about enslaving other Muslims, which infuriated the devout Dan Fodio who argued in line with proper Islamic doctrine that only infidels could be enslaved. As Dan Fodio and his followers did enjoy some level of protection from enslavement, many of the persons held as slaves would have readily made the simple calculation that rallying to the preacher's standard might extend the same protections to them. Mohammed Bello, Dan Fodio's son, would later list ten different groups of people who were drawn to the Shehu (or Sheikh) and his message. These supporters ranged from socially-conscious intellectuals who found his message fashionable, to people who simply wanted to fight for fighting sake[3]. As we shall see, holding such a disparate coalition together once the dust had settled would prove difficult.

Flight to Gudu

Sometime in 1796, Nafata became king at Gobir and decided that he had to do something about the growing Islamist threat to his authority. The hitherto finely balanced relationship between Dan Fodio and the Gobir ruling house came to a disharmonious end when Dan Fodio withdrew from the King's court on account of Nafata's increasing loyalty to the practises of his polytheist ancestors, and general disregard for resolutely monotheistic Islam. This court withdrawal freed Dan Fodio from his previous reticence in not directly attacking the government in his preaching. The gloves were now off. Nafata on his part settled on a strategy of squeezing the movement's membership, after unsuccessfully trying to get them to disband. Towards the end of his reign, he issued a decree designed to finish off Dan Fodio and his followers. This iniquitous law banned the jama'a - followers of a learned man - and stipulated that no one other than Dan Fodio himself was permitted to preach to people. He then went after Islam itself by decreeing that no one was allowed to be a Muslim except if he had inherited the religion from his father - in effect prohibiting conversions. All converts were mandated to return to their original faiths. But that was not all. The Muslims were easily distinguishable by their appearance, and so he banned the wearing of turbans. The wearing of veils by women was further declared contra legem.

In fairness to Nafata and his advisers, they had more than a few reasons to be worried. Not long before Nafata's decree, Dan Fodio had composed and published important propaganda via a poem, which contained more than a hint to his followers that it was perfectly okay for them, as Muslims, to acquire weapons and wage a holy struggle. It may well have been a case of the tail wagging the dog, as his followers had started demanding that he lead them into war against their Hausa rulers and to establish an Islamic caliphate. In that sense, the entirety of Dan Fodio's actions leading up to the armed struggle might be interpreted as a coordinated effort by his most ardent Fulani elite merchant-mallam followers to utilise the fiery preachers' convenient mass popularity for the explicit purpose of overturning the prevailing social order and establishing a new state. Whatever the underlying motivations, Nafata knew of the poetic call to arms and reacted aggressively, as would be expected of any self-respecting autocrat.

Nafata died not long after issuing his anti-Islamic decree and was succeeded by his son, Yunfa. The new king initially attempted a truce with Dan Fodio and the Muslim party, but he quickly abandoned this course of action when it became clear that they were not going to be appeased by anything short of total allegiance to Islam. Thus, he doubled down on his father's policies and began to implement the anti-Islamic edicts energetically. But even this hardly worked, as it drove the Muslims underground or out of his immediate jurisdiction. One of Dan Fodio's disciples, Abdus Salam, took some followers and left for Gimbana, in present-day Nigeria's

Kebbi state. Yunfa thought this retreat presented an opportunity to teach an isolated group of Muslims a lesson, and so he sent an expedition to Gimbana in December 1803.

The town was destroyed, and all the Muslims were either killed or captured as slaves. These captured unfortunates were being caravanned back to Alkalawa, the capital of Gobir, when they passed by Dan Fodio's base, Degel, where they were spotted by their co-religionists. The pitiable sight of enslaved Muslims was unacceptable to the Degelians, and they launched a spontaneous attack on Yunfa's posse, freeing their captured brethren in the process. This infuriated King Yunfa, who ordered Dan Fodio and his followers to release the freed captives to him. For two months, his order was ignored, and so the inflamed ruler raised the stakes by threatening to do to Degel what he had done to Gimbana - raze it to the ground. He also asked Dan Fodio to abandon his followers and proceed on exile. The revolutionary leader refused this order, proclaiming that he was going nowhere without his followers - 'I will not forsake my community, but I will leave your country for God's earth is wide!'[4] was his reply, influenced by the Quranic exhortation to believers living among apostates: 'Was not the earth of Allah spacious enough for you to migrate therein?'.

Thus, began the hijra to Gudu. Seeing this retreat as another opportunity, Yunfa approved armed forces under his control to go after the Muslims in his kingdom, a task to which they took with relish. Yet, this also backfired as it underrated the preacher's popularity and caused many more Muslims to flee to Gudu and team up with Dan Fodio. This exodus continued for months, with Yunfa and his forces unable to stop it. Dan Fodio quickly set about organising his followers, who in turn chose him as Amir al-Mu'minin - Commander of the Faithful. The Islamic flag was hoisted in Gudu for the very first time in what is now Nigeria's North-West, and the outcome which Yunfa and his predecessors had long feared finally came to pass. There was now a rising Islamic state right on their doorstep.

Unleashing the Sword

A religion-fueled ideological movement against social, political and economic oppression, led by a revolutionary itinerant preacher, had morphed into a full-scale popular military insurrection. An armed conflict based on this uprising would soon consume much of present-day northern Nigeria and culminate in the evolution of an entirely new political order, which would last for 100 years. Who was this Dan Fodio that started the revolution which was soon to permanently change his country and kickstart the coalescing of the modern Nigerian nation as we know it? He was Usman, Uthman, Usuman or simply, the Shehu to different people. Some would also call him Sheikh later in life. But formally, his name would be written as Uthman bin Muhammad bin Uthman bin Salih.

Born in December 1754, he came from what we would call an aspiring middle-class family in Maratta, very close to modern Nigeria's border with Niger Republic. Uthman's family was of the Fulani Toronkawa clan who had adopted Islam quite early in their history and had thus moved away from the rural, nomadic lifestyle to a more sedentary and urban existence. A well-sized community of similarly successful merchant or preacher class of immigrant Fulani existed in all of the Hausa states and beyond; trading and communicating with each other regularly, as well as keeping well informed of developments in the broader Ottoman Mediterranean world and farther. Uthman's father, Muhammad ibn Salih was popularly known as Fodio, meaning 'The Jurist,' reflecting the family's scholarly tradition. While the Son of the Jurist was still young, the family moved to Degel, which is located near where the Rima river road joins the Sokoto river and flows down south into the Niger.

The Fulani in those days were distinct from their Hausa neighbours in their way of life and even physiognomy. Typically tall, slim and fair-skinned, members of these close-knit immigrant families kept to themselves and spoke their own inscrutable Fulfulde language. They carried themselves quite formally and proudly, with an innate sense of superiority, which further entrenched their separateness from their Hausa hosts. They also described themselves as being like birds - 'If one is touched, all the others fly away'[5]. Members of the aristocratic, urbanised and settled Fulani class, a distinct group from the pastoral nomads, were known for their knowledge gained from literacy in Arabic as well as regular study and communication with the rest of the world. This meant that even though they lived apart from their Hausa rulers, there was a long tradition of appointing them to the ruling court as advisers, imams and judges going back at least to the fifteenth century. Most substantial (and even some less important) nations or settlements in the sub-region would usually have some resident learned Fulani living in their community, with at least one knowledgeable Mallam sitting regularly and advising at the royal court.

The import of this is that, by the eighteenth century, after various waves of Fulani migration from the east and west, many Hausa towns boasted some kind of Fulani settlement, usually away from the capital. Dan Fodio's ancestors had themselves migrated from present-day Senegal to Degel, which was one such settlement. While the nomadic Fulani paid no attention to formal education, and literacy was almost non-existent among them, the settled Fulani continued the tradition of literacy and Islamic education they had brought with them from Timbuktu. Parents and relatives were a child's first teachers, and life went the same way for the Son of the Jurist. Young Dan Fodio first recited the Quran with his father before taking a deeper dive into Islamic texts with his uncles and several other scholars. But perhaps the single biggest teaching influence on the future Shehu was a fiery fundamentalist preacher known as Sheikh Jibril dan Umar. 'If there be said of me that which is of good report, then I am but a wave of the waves of Jibril' Dan Fodio himself once said[6].

Early Waves of Revolution

Sheikh Jibril wanted jihad, and with it the establishment of an Islamic Caliphate, and he wanted it *now*. This fiery forerunner openly preached against the Hausa kings and may have even tried to launch his own revolution without much success. So extreme was Jibril that Bawa Jan Gwarzo, who later tolerated Dan Fodio, kicked him out of Gobir[7]. The failures of Sheikh Jibril likely taught his young disciple the value of patient reform, something which stayed with him for a long time. Dan Fodio spent a year with Jibril learning Islam, reading voraciously, and travelling as far as Agadez (in present-day Niger Republic). While the master carried on to the holiest city of Islam, Makkah al-Mukarramah for the pilgrimage, young Dan Fodio had to return to Degel as he did not have his father's permission to undertake the journey. This failure to make the obligatory pilgrimage to Mecca would prove to be a lifelong regret for the later Caliph.

By the time he was around 20 years old in 1774, Dan Fodio was ready to strike out on his own as a preacher. He started at home in Degel, which would become a sort of regional Islamic intellectual mecca, attracting adherents from far and wide, but soon took his message on the road - to the neighbouring countries of Zamfara and Kebbi where his jama'a greatly increased. The Son of the Jurist shrewdly surmised that his popularity was putting him on a collision course with the Hausa ruling establishment, and so, in 1780, he embarked on a trip to the metropolitan capital of Gobir, Alkalawa, for talks with King Bawa. There, he asked the nominally Muslim Bawa to reject polytheism and move towards the proper practise of Islam, a demand that Bawa could not accept in its entirety, considering its political consequences. Bawa's reticence was understandable, given the still important contribution of traditional religious beliefs to social cohesion and political stability among his fellow ruling Hausa elite. Still, both men found a way to accommodate each other and Bawa even offered Dan Fodio some gifts of gold, which the future Sheikh rejected.

Much as Dan Fodio had come under the sway of the fiery Jibril, he was still his own man. He railed against injustice but believed that persuasion was the correct course of action, as opposed to violence. Even where he imposed some of the stricter edicts of Islam such as segregating women and insisting on face veils for them (purdah), he did this in ways that were generally seen as compassionate. He openly disagreed with the more conservative Jibril on at least one major point of Islamic teaching. Where Jibril had preached that disobedience to the Islamic legal code, Sharia was enough to invalidate the faith of a Muslim, Dan Fodio took the more humanitarian view that ordinary folk could not possibly be condemned for flouting laws they did not even fully understand. Sins were sins and no more than that.

Dan Fodio also led by example, most especially with his austerity - he was said to be so frugal as to own only one pair of trousers and one turban[8]. And whatever he thought about the segregation of women, this did not extend to denying them an education. He condemned the men who 'shut up their wives, their daughters, and their captives in the darkness of ignorance while they daily impart knowledge to their students.'[9] When he taught his followers, he only demanded that the men and women sit separately and then he delivered the message to them jointly. Sheikh Dan Fodio's liberal attitude to women's education would lead to at least four of his daughters becoming renowned for their scholarship - Mariyam, Khadija, Fatima and the most famous of them, Nana Asma'u.

The global history of Islamic revivalism is one of successive periods in which popular preachers emerge in different parts of the globe, calling for a renewed commitment to the fundamental principles of the religion, while demanding social reconstruction according to the teachings and traditions of the Holy Prophet. Contemporaneous with the life of Jibril and Dan Fodio's birth in the middle of the late eighteenth century, there was at least one such movement afoot. This even more conservative religious revolution occurred in the domains of the then mighty Ottomans and was inspired by another itinerant preacher called Muhammad ibn Wahhab who lived from 1703 to 1792. Wahhab was the founder of the eponymous Wahhabist movement which later underpinned the formation of modern Saudi Arabia. This was the intellectual milieu in the late eighteenth-century Arabic and the trans-Saharan world just across the Red Sea from the Sahel, within which Dan Fodio was developing his thoughts, ideas and ambitions.

The turning point towards the armed revolution for the future Shehu began around 1790 when Dan Fodio began to delve deeper into Islamic mysticism by way of Sufism. The Sufi community regarded the manifestation of visions and supernatural experiences as the mechanisms by which Allah spoke to his faithful disciples. Visions were also the reward for spiritual discipline, which placed a premium on fasting and self-denial. A Sufi thus went out of his way to put himself in a position where he might have a direct experience of God[10]. Quranic verses were repeatedly recited as a form of devotion or dhikr, which sometimes left the reciter in a hypnotic state. In 1794, the young preacher received perhaps the most important of his visions in which he was presented with the 'sword of truth' by Abd al-Qadir al-Gilani, the Persian Saint who founded the Qadiriyya order of Sufism to which Dan Fodio belonged, and who had died more than 600 years before. In this vision, he was commanded to 'Unsheathe it [the sword] against the enemies of God.'[i] This marked the transition of the Son of the Jurist from peaceful persuasion to armed militancy.

The hoisting of the Islamic flag in the wilderness of Gudu was followed by the publication of a manifesto for the jihad. Titled *Wathiqat ahl al-Sudan, wa man sha Allah min al-ikhwan* ('Dispatch to the folk of the Sudan and to whomsoever Allah wills among the Brethren'), it listed 27 points, each one either obligatory or unlawful

---

i Taken from the 'The *Wird* (Litany) of Shehu Dan Fodio' - disseminated to his followers when he was around 40 years old.

'by assent.' It named five classes of people - heathens, apostates, backsliders, warmongers, and oppressors - who were clear enemies of the jihad and against whom the war was to be waged. The letter was distributed using the existing Fulani network in Hausaland and read out publicly in various places. The die was cast. A religion which had hitherto penetrated Hausaland through scholarship and personal example had now turned militant.

Uncertain Beginnings

Dan Fodio's brother, Abdullahi, led the Fulani army and was assisted by the Sheikh's second son, the brilliant Muhammad Bello. Across the Hausa country, local Islamic preachers, military and political elite, as well as the poor and oppressed masses began to harken slowly but surely to the call for the revolution at Gudu. In retrospect, this was a precarious moment for the ruling elite in each of the other Hausa states. But internal rivalry and centuries of distrust among the ruling elite did not allow for the collection of a united force against Dan Fodio's motley crew. In the case of Gobir, bad blood from recent wars against its closest neighbours meant there would most certainly not be any supporting armed forces made available for what must have seemed like a purely internal security affair, at the onset of the jihad.

The Muslims were hopelessly outnumbered and outgunned at the beginning, but what they lacked in armour they made up for with intense organisation and a fierce devotion to their cause. Abdullahi Dan Fodio was also a scholar and was familiar with Islamic military historical documents, an education which prepared him for the various surprises he was able to spring on the Gobir forces. The first decisive battle in the war occurred on June 21, 1804, at a lake known as Tabkin Kwatto. After carrying out a four-day reconnaissance mission, Abdullahi led the charge against a superior Gobir cavalry. The early armed forces for the revolution came from the military resources of a few wealthy Fulani, Tuareg, and

Hausa supporters, alongside foot soldiers from among the ordinary followers of the preacher. Such as they were, the available fighting resources included a small cavalry, supported by volunteer troops armed with their personal provisions, limited armour, swords, spears and shields.

Yet, these nascent jihadis managed to see off the well-provisioned Gobirawa forces, numbering about 100,000 foot soldiers and 10,000 cavalry across the country[11]. The Fulani army fought using the remarkably effective 'square' formation of fighting. As we will soon see, in the execution of the square formation, tactical organisation and discipline were just as important as personal bravery and troop numbers. This is not the last time we will hear about the square formation in our story, and this first appearance perhaps sowed the seeds of the defeat of the Fulani a century later. After a surprise attack by Abdullahi, the battle of Tabkin Kwatto began at dawn, and by noon the Gobirawa had taken to their heels. This early victory buoyed the spirits of movement supporters across the Hausa country, attracting more supporters from among the elite as well as the masses. The Tabin Kwatto victory also provided a substantial portion of the military resources, particularly horses and armour, which were taken from the defeated Gobirawa forces and now repurposed by the emerging armed forces of the jihad.

In December, the Fulani-led army suffered their first loss at the battle of Tsuntsuwa, a village outside Alkalawa. They had left their women and children behind while they attacked the town. But some mercenary Tuaregs who were now fighting for the Gobirawa after originally fighting for the revolutionaries launched an opportunistic attack on the defenceless families. This meant that the Alkalawa attack force had to be split, with one half going back to defend their families. Emboldened, the Gobirawa launched their counterattack against the weakened jihadis who had been attacking Alkalawa. The revolutionaries were close to annihilation when Abdullahi, who was now invested with the title of Waziri or Vizier and Dan Fodio himself arrived to help them out. It was a critical moment, attested to by the fact that the Shehu, who had not been leading any of the battles, was now involved.

For inexplicable reasons, on the arrival of this reinforcement, the Gobirawa decided to retreat behind their city walls, even though the Muslims seemed there for the taking. This respite would prove decisive as the war would be extended for at least four years. If the Fulani had been defeated at Alkalawa at this point, the jihad may well have been over. Dan Fodio's forces lost about 2,000 men in this crushing defeat, including their Chief Justice, Muhammadu Sambo and hundreds of their learned Mallams who had committed the Quran to memory[12]. These devastating losses were to have huge consequences for the way the war was waged thereafter.

Conflict and Conflagration

Much to the regret of the broader Hausa elite, jihad would soon spread abroad from Gobir. Not far south from the Gobirawa lay the country of Kebbi, which was of strategic regional relevance as it was situated in the path of the upper river. Kebbi was also historically important as it connected the ancient, wealthy, western Sahelian empires of Songhay and Mali to the rest of the Hausa country. It happened that a member of the Kebbi ruling house named Usman Masa had quarrelled with his king, and seizing the tide of the times, teamed up with Dan Fodio soon afterwards. From him, the jihadis - who did not yet control any territory of their own - got the idea that there might be profit in attacking Kebbi using Usman Masa's inside knowledge. In March 1805, Dan Fodio dispatched a force led by Abdullahi and the Fulani Amir al-Jaish or Commander of the Army, Aliyu Jaidu, to take the capital of Kebbi, a place called Birnin Kebbi.

By April, under siege, the king of Kebbi, Muhammad Hodi dan Sulemana took to his heels and fled north to a town called Argungu, located on the banks of the Sokoto river. Abdullahi installed the instigator, Usman Masa, as king but the clever traitor would later betray the Fulani as well and lose his life for it. For now, the increasingly powerful forces of Dan Fodio took home a rich haul of gold and silver as their booty. Empowered, Muhammad Bello next led another force eastward, taking towns and territories along the way, and in the bargain even had time for a raid on another important Hausa city state named Katsina. Jihad was expanding, and the war had now opened on multiple fronts across Hausa country. Another city-state named Zamfara would be drawn in next.

The Zamfarawa, for whom there was no love lost with Gobir, had been part of Dan Fodio's army and played a part in taking Kebbi. But the first signs that things were not going to plan with the jihad emerged when the Zamfarawa began to rebel against emerging Fulani tyranny. The earlier losses at Alkalawa had robbed the jihadis of a lot of focused and disciplined soldiers, leaving Dan Fodio with what might be called his second string. This B-team did not quite have the resolve of the original cohort and were happy to loot and enslave Muslims and non-Muslims indiscriminately, a direct contravention of the Sheikh's manifesto. One of the earliest direct conflicts between the newly victorious Fulani army and its leadership was over the precise allocation formula for the distribution of war booty, which Mohammed Bello attempted but failed to restructure according to strict Quranic doctrine. Bello, in his characteristic forthrightness, would later write that 'All Zamfara rose against us because our people were oppressing them'[13].

By the end of 1805, the war began to spread beyond the North-West theatre of Hausaland. Expeditions went as far as Borgu and Bauchi, at which point the revolution began to get rather messy. The further the jihadists went, the more they came up against Muslims who did not quite support their reforms, for various reasons. One such town was Yandoto (in today's Zamfara State), to the east of Gobir but then under Bornu's hegemony[14]. Mohammed Bello led an expedition to Yandoto. The town had been the centre of vibrant Islamic scholarship for at least a century before the jihad and even one of Dan Fodio's ancestors, Muhammad Sa'ad, had studied there[15]. The local Muslim scholars had thus built up a good relationship with the ruling elite, who in turn viewed them as the custodians of true Islam and granted them various privileges. For the Yandoto Muslims, submitting to these newly arrived jihadists would have meant starting all over again, so they resisted Bello's overtures. His response was to destroy the town and 'Books blowing around in the wind' became a figure of speech used by Zamfarawa scholars to describe the attack on their town and its scholarship[16]. This was in effect an attack on Muslims by Muslims, again, in direct contravention of the jihad manifesto - so early in the life of the emerging new power.

In 1806, the war was won and lost in a decisive battle near a stream called Fafara. Tuareg mercenaries, this time acting on behalf of the Gobirawa, attacked the Fulani, leading to a bloody battle. The Tuaregs had planned to pin their opponents inside the town of Zurmi and lay siege to them. But the increasingly confident Fulani instead charged out to fight them. They won this battle and it was at this point that the fickle Tuaregs decided they had had enough of fighting other people's wars. They would soon after reach a peace deal with Dan Fodio's forces, abandoning Gobir to its fate. The besieged Gobirawa were now pinned inside their capital, cut off from all their external allies. The jihadis decided to keep things that way while they dealt with Kebbi and Zamfara once and for all. After more than 18 months of blockading Alkalawa, Dan Fodio's forces finally decided it was time to make their move, in October 1808. Led by three columns of armed Fulani, under the command of Mohammed Bello - appointed by his father for this last stand - they came against Alkalawa from the east, north and west. 'God then opened Alkalawa to us,' wrote Bello[17]. King Yunfa, the former student of Dan Fodio who lit the touchpaper for the armed struggle with his attack on the Sheikh's followers four years earlier, was killed. With the successful siege on Alkalawa, the jihad was effectively over, at least in Gobir. Or so it seemed.

In the Cold Light of History

After nearly five years of fighting, Dan Fodio's war had morphed into something quite different from the original plan. Early on in the Fulani revolution, there were already complaints and outright rebellions against the conquering forces by people who were incensed at the sudden realisation that they had exchanged one form of tyranny for another. Believers watched with dismay as the Fulani raiders, hungry and in search of food, made no distinction between Muslims and unbelievers in their looting[18]. Before the end of the jihad, Abdullahi Dan Fodio got so upset by what he saw as the corruption and lack of discipline among his soldiers that in October 1807 he decided to quit the army altogether. 'I considered flight incumbent upon me,'[19] he wrote. He embarked on a pilgrimage to Mecca but stopped in Kano where he had a change of heart and spent his time there writing a book on government for the local Muslim community, which was in disarray[20]. Dan Fodio himself was aware of the corruption and tried to square the circle by redefining the terms of engagement. Taking a pragmatic stance not dissimilar from one previously assumed by the Holy Prophet himself when faced with a similar conflict of interest during the Mecca versus Medina hostilities of early Islam[ii], the Son of the Jurist wrote 'If a man intends to fight for making Allah's law supreme, he will not be harmed by what he is possessed by during the fighting [...] Allah has excused us for that'.

With the fall of Gobir, the Fulani revolution presented itself as a compelling opportunity for anyone that wanted to take territory from the ruling elite in surrounding countries and possessed the resources to attempt it. Many Fulani clan leaders thus broke off to

---

ii   Having settled in Medina with his followers after their Hijrah, the Prophet Muhammad (PBUH) was faced with a similar difficult choice on what to do about his followers who had not been integrated into Medinese society and were constantly on the receiving end of aggression from the ruling Quraysh tribe in Mecca. In the end, he received a new revelation upon which he relied to sanction raids on Mecca's trade caravans by his followers.

fight wars of conquest against surrounding kingdoms. In this way, battles raged as far as Nupe towards the Niger, the prize on offer being that the successful generals automatically became the *Emir* of the conquered territory. Other Fulani who had been engaged in long-running battles with their Hausa hosts, usually over cattle grazing rights, also took the opportunity to launch their own freelance revolutions. In this fashion, Emirates were established at Zabarma (Kebbi) by Abubakar Luduje and in Hadejia by Sambo dan Ardo[21]. Much of the ensuing kingmaking reflected the diverse coalition that Dan Fodio had cobbled together to fight the war, and in all fairness, some of the victorious combatants had been provoked into joining the jihad, even though they didn't want to. When the war began, Yunfa wrote to other Hausa kings in Daura, Kano, Katsina and Zaria warning them that he had neglected 'A small fire in his country until it had spread beyond his power to control.'[22] The Hausa rulers mainly reacted to this warning by going after the Fulani in their midst, ironically triggering solidarity with the early jihadists. In retrospect, it is easy to understand the visceral fear of radical preachers arising among the population, which now belatedly haunted the previously negligent Hausa elite. As we shall see, this same concern then became the most innate neurosis of the new Fulani rulers and is something that continues to haunt the ruling elite of northern Nigeria till this day.

The outcomes of jihad also reflected the fact that Dan Fodio was much more of an idealist than some of the people he led, who saw the war as an opportunity to lay their hands on booty. But perhaps more importantly, there had been no plan for the postbellum period per se: fighting had started as a defensive action against the Gobirawa and had morphed quickly into a war of conquest. Dan Fodio was thus faced with the tricky balancing act between letting his increasingly confident, victorious warriors fight as they knew best, or keeping them on the straight path. By 1809, he had already composed his poem *Tabat Hakika* ('*Be sure of that*') lamenting how the jihad was losing its way and promising hellfire for those who departed from its ideals. While possibly apocryphal, contemporary reports repeated in later years even indicated that Dan Fodio had predicted that the new Fulani Empire 'would not last more than one hundred years'[23].

Even more revealing of the shift in ideology was the jihadists attempts to take Bornu, about two months' travel time to the east of Gobir. Contemporaneous with the jihad, Fulani communities in Bornu led by a former student of Dan Fodio, Gwoni Muktar, along with a certain Ibrahim Zaki and the brothers Umar and Somba Abdur, rose against their Mai, accusing him of tolerating polytheism[24]. Dan Fodio gave them his support and the Mai fled to his neighbours, Kanem, where he asked for help in launching a counterattack. The Kanems didn't just send anyone; they sent their very best - Muhammad al-Amin El-Kanemi, a truly remarkable man. Born of a Kanem father and an Arab mother, El-Kanemi came onto the scene at a moment of great distress for Bornu, after their old capital Ngazaragamu had been burnt to the ground.

El-Kanemi was not just a warrior, but a thoroughbred Islamic scholar, and just the man to stand up to Dan Fodio. Between these two learned Muslims there followed a series of letters[iii], wherein El-Kanemi authoritatively laid out his case, contesting the very validity of Dan Fodio's jihad in Islamic jurisprudence. While remaining respectful, El-Kanemi asked Dan Fodio to call off his forces, stating clearly that Bornu was Muslim and as such was not a lawful target for jihad. Leaving legality aside, he went on to accurately challenge the motives of the jihadis when he wrote that 'We perceive that your true object is the power to rule over others.'[25] Dan Fodio tried to get around this unassailable logic with the dubious argument that in providing help to the Hausa states against the jihadis, Bornu had somehow forfeited its right to be Muslim. These letters continued back and forth in an often-confusing manner and if nothing else, gave the jihadis serious food for thought. In the end, El-Kanemi's

---

iii Mohammed Bello also took part in the exchange of letters with some long and detailed responses to El-Kanemi, including some which he wrote with his father.

forces defended Bornu against the invaders and the Mai was returned to the throne, albeit with the erudite scholar becoming the real power behind the throne of the country. He would construct a new capital for Bornu at Kuka, becoming the de facto ruler of the country as the Shehu of Bornu, while the titular Mai retained their positions. By right of defence and conquest, Shehu El-Kanemi's son Umar would eventually ascend the throne as sole ruler of Bornu. This ended the 800-year-old Sayfawa dynasty of the previous Mai and the descendants of El-Kanemi remain on the throne of Bornu today.

Was the jihad a success? In one clear sense, it was. The structures it put in place lasted a century, and some of them remain to this day. But judged on its terms, the revolution missed the targets it set for itself in several ways. In a thirty-year preaching career before the start of the war, Dan Fodio had a lot to say about Hausaland and the ruling elite who caused him great displeasure. The *Kitab al-farq bayn wilāyāt ahi al-islām wa bayn wilāyāt ahi al-kufr* (*Differences between the Government of Muslims and the Government of Unbelievers*), among the works attributed to him, offers perhaps the best single-volume detailing of what it was about the Hausa kingdoms that he disliked so much. But it also provides us a basis for measuring how much of its ideals his new administration lived up to. 'One of the ways of their government is their imposing on the people monies not laid by Sharia,' he complained, as he railed against the jangali and several other taxes specifically[26]. Yet, many of these same taxes remained in place several decades after he had died, happily collected by the new Fulani Emirs. He was particularly angered by corruption, polytheism, traditional practices and the forceful enlisting of Muslims to go to war. The jihad at best had only mixed success in reforming these practices, as we will see later in our story when we investigate how the Caliphate was administered in practice. His complaints about corruption will read as familiar to any Nigerian today - inaccessible rulers who could only be reached by bribing their courtiers and justice only available to those willing to pay the highest for it. Dan Fodio also complained that the ruling elite often took money instead of punishment even when the law prescribed death sentences. While some of his complaints about music and dancing may have been excessively prudish, the preacher queried very reasonably why any ruler might keep a harem of up to 1,000 women, all the while living in luxurious palaces. We will come to see later the extent to which these criticised practises were reformed in the Caliphate inherited by the preachers' successors.

A Contemporaneous Revolution

At about the same time that Yunfa was holding out against the Fulani at Alkalawa, a different kind of battle was concluding thousands of miles away in London, England. William Wilberforce, an Evangelical Anglican Member of Parliament (MP) and one of the most persistent politicians in British history finally had his victory. Wilberforce had begun his campaign to abolish the British slave trade in 1789. Since then, he had brought several motions into the House of Commons to end the trade in humans. In 1795, his motion was defeated by 3 votes. In 1796, it was defeated by 4 votes, possibly because some MPs had gone to see a new opera which opened on the same night[27]. In the years 1797, 1798 and 1799 Wilberforce's motions were defeated by 8 votes. Meanwhile, the international slave trade increased, with record numbers of humans being taken to the Americas from Africa on British ships. In the half-dozen years between 1801 and 1807, about 266,000 humans were traded in this manner. In 1802, war-hungry Napoleon revived the slave trade in the French empire, a factor that played into the hands of Wilberforce, as the abolitionists had been suspiciously viewed as French Jacobin revolutionaries before then.

In 1804, Wilbeforce tried again with a bill which passed in the House of Commons but failed in the House of Lords, due to his long-term nemesis, Henry Dundas (later, Lord Melville) who always seemed to argue to delay or deny Wilberforce. Dundas soon ran out of luck - he was impeached from the House of Lords for corruption (the last person ever to be so impeached) in 1805. The success in the House of Commons showed that the mood had changed against slavery and the government brought in some restrictions on the trade, such as introducing a register of all slaves and banning the import into some territories.

By June 1806, motions were moved in the Commons (114 to 15) and Lords (41 to 20) committing Britain to the abolition of the slave trade as soon as practically possible. Many former opponents of abolition openly stated that they had now changed their minds in favour of ending the trade. The Abolitionists took advantage of this momentum to rush through an Act that stopped the use of any new ships in slave trading. The Act was to come into effect in August 1807, giving the slavers a year to get used to the idea. The logical next step was full abolition and in January 1807 the Prime Minister, Lord Grenville, introduced such a bill in the House of Lords. It passed easily (100 to 34) and was sent to the House of Commons. On 23 February, after a very long debate, the Commons passed the Slave Trade Abolition Bill by 283 to 16[28]. The cause of abolition, thanks to the efforts of Wilberforce, could no longer be ignored. This was reflected in the increased turnout of MPs who voted on this occasion. Wilbeforce had called on Parliament to 'assert the rights of the weak against the strong, [and] to vindicate the cause of the oppressed.' Eventually, he was obliged, a testament to his patience, persistence, and conviction. Royal assent was obtained a month later and the international slave trade was made illegal in British dominions from 1 May 1807.

In America, the tide was also turning. In December 1806, President Jefferson - who had owned slaves himself - addressed the nation and condemned the slave trade, calling it a violation of the human rights of Africans[29]. By January 1807 - coinciding with Britain's efforts across the Atlantic - a bill was passed in the United States Senate, and in the House of Representatives the following month. This new law abolished the international trade in humans by subjects of the United States, making it illegal to import slaves into America (albeit retaining the legality of trading in humans within the country) from January 1808. The abominable international trade in Black human bodies was slowly being brought to an end.

In August 1444, a cargo of enslaved Africans had arrived in Portugal, marking the start of nearly four centuries of a brutal trans-Atlantic trade in human bodies from Africa to the New World. With the active participation of the African elite, the slave trade had continued for several generations, and in the process dramatically affected conditions in the countries from where these humans were taken. Among the peoples of the Niger-Benue hinterland, the trade in humans had become a fundamental driving factor, determining everything from population distribution to economic development. Nearly 400 years later, industrial, economic and political transformations in Europe and America had finally turned the tide against the accursed trade, even if not the condition of slavery itself. We will come to see how difficult this sudden change was for the local elite across present-day Nigeria, who found it hard to wean themselves off a multi-generational trade that had become interwoven with not just their economic power, but also their social identities and self-definition[iv].

The quite separate ideological causes of an Islamic reformer in Gobir and an Evangelical Anglican politician in London were the most unlikely to ever intersect. Yet these independent contemporaneous events were to have the most profound effects on the country we know as Nigeria today. Between jihad and abolition, two distinct and often countervailing forces were now acting in concert to create a new country beyond the imagination of any

---

iv There have long been debates about the brutality of domestic slavery in African countries when compared with plantation slavery in the New World. Whether or not that is the right comparison to make, it might be worth pointing out that there is evidence of upward mobility for slaves and their descendants at least in the Sokoto Caliphate, where slaves were often titled. Perhaps the most prominent example was Sir Ahmadu Bello, the Sardauna (Crown Prince) of Sokoto, great-grandson of Sultan Mohammed Bello and the outstanding politician of post-independence northern Nigeria. His mother was a slave concubine from Zinga in present day Taraba State.

contemporary protagonist. The future formation of Nigeria was being forged in Nigeria, Europe and America at almost the same time. History would never be the same again.

---

1. Martin BG. *Muslim Brotherhoods in Nineteenth-Century Africa*. Cambridge University Press; 1978.

2. Hiskett M. Kitāb Al-Farq: A Work on the Habe Kingdoms Attributed to 'Uthmān Dan Fodio. *Bulletin of the School of Oriental and African Studies*. 1960 1960;23(3):558-579.

3. Last M. *The Sokoto Caliphate*. Harlow: Longmans; 1967.

4. Hiskett M. *Tazyin al-Waraqat by Abdullah ibn Muhammad*. University Press Ibadan; 1963.

5. de St Croix FW. *The Fulani of Northern Nigeria: Some General Notes*. Gregg International Publishers Limited; 1972.

6. Hiskett M. Material Relating to the State of Learning among the Fulani before Their Jihād. *Bulletin of the School of Oriental and African Studies*. 1957 1957;19(3):550-578.

7. Spencer Trimingham J. *A History of Islam in West Africa*. vol 8. Oxford University Press; 1963.

8. Hiskett M. *The Sword of Truth: The Life and Times of the Shehu Usuman dan Fodio*. Oxford University Press; 1973.

9. Crowder M. *The Story of Nigeria*. Faber; 1973.

10. Spencer Trimingham J. *The Sufi Orders in Islam*. Oxford University Press; 1998.

11. Diouf SA. *Servants of Allah: African Muslims Enslaved in the Americas*. NYU Press; 1998.

12. Bello M. *Infakul maisuri*. Northern Nigeria Publishing Company; 1974.

13. *Ibid.*

14. Jeppie S, Diagne SB. *The Meanings of Timbuktu*. HSRC Press; 2008.

15. Philips JE. Causes of the Jihad of Usman an Fodio: A Historiographical Review. *Journal for Islamic Studies*. 2017 2017;36(1):18-58.

16. Jeppie S, Diagne SB. *The Meanings of Timbuktu*. HSRC Press; 2008.

17. Bello M. *Infakul maisuri*. Northern Nigeria Publishing Company; 1974.

18. Niven CR. *A Short History of Nigeria*. Longmans of Nigeria; 1962.

19. Hiskett M. *Tazyin al-Waraqat by Abdullah ibn Muhammad*. University Press Ibadan; 1963.

20. Sulaiman I. *A Revolution in History: The Jihad of Usman Dan Fodio*. Mansell; 1986.

21. Flint JE. *The Cambridge History of Africa*. Oxford University Press; 1978.

22. Bello M. *Infakul maisuri*. Northern Nigeria Publishing Company; 1974.

23. Last M. *The Sokoto Caliphate*. Harlow: Longmans; 1967.

24. Dusgate RH. *The Conquest of Northern Nigeria*. F. Cass; 1985.

25. Bello M. *Infakul maisuri*. Northern Nigeria Publishing Company; 1974.

26. Hiskett M. Kitāb Al-Farq: A Work on the Habe Kingdoms Attributed to 'Uthmān Dan Fodio. *Bulletin of the School of Oriental and African Studies*. 1960 1960;23(3):558-579.

27. Thomas H. *The Slave Trade*. Hachette UK; 2015.

28. Hansard - SLAVE TRADE ABOLITION BILL. 1807/2/23 1807

29. State of the Nation 1806. (Available online)

CHAPTER 3

The Caliphate in Session

A Family Feud

One of the most consequential horse rides of Nigerian history took place in April 1817. Abdullahi dan Fodio assembled some of his followers and rode the 15 miles from Bodinga to the Caliphate's new capital in Sokoto where his brother, Usman Dan Fodio, had been living. The journey was made necessary by the news Abdullahi had just received that the Sheikh, who had been ill since the previous year, had died. A frontline leader of the revolution, Abdullahi had every right to believe he held a valid claim to succeed his brother as Caliph, having served as de-facto Vizier to the now-departed Dan Fodio. His only real rival for the succession was his young nephew, Mohammed Bello, who was about 38 years old at the time of his father's death. Abdullahi was over 50. In this rivalry however, the older man was at a distinct disadvantage; and one that would prove insurmountable. For one thing, the Sheikh had already shown his preference for Bello in not so subtle ways, for example by giving his son command of the jihad army for the final assault on Alkalawa in 1808, over the older and more experienced Abdullahi.

Other factors also counted against the uncle in the eyes of the Fulani leaders who were to decide on Dan Fodio's successor. For one thing, the ruling elite had a clear preference to keep the line of succession to Dan Fodio's direct descendants only, with an eye on preventing future conflicts over succession rights between cousins. For another, unlike Abdullahi, Bello had lived with his father at the new capital. All of this meant that by the time Abdullahi arrived at the gates of the city, he found them locked against him. The election had been concluded in his absence, with Bello installed as Caliph and Commander of the Faithful. A few weeks after losing out to his nephew, the hurt Abdullahi wrote a treatise outlining his ideas on the Caliph's succession, making the claim, not so subtly, that he had as much right as anyone else to the seat. Bello countered with his own publication a few weeks later, making the case for the son to succeed as opposed to the brother. It was to the credit of these two warrior-scholars that such a historically important and contentious succession of power in a still inchoate Caliphate passed without a single shot being fired in anger.

The transition of power from Dan Fodio to his son marked a sea change in the direction of the Caliphate that would come to shape the history of Nigeria as we know it today. From a ragtag band of revolutionaries armed with bows and arrows, Dan Fodio, Bello and Abdullahi had laid the foundations for what would become the largest and most advanced, organised civil state in sub-Saharan Africa. Where Dan Fodio had supplied the vision, inspiration and philosophical basis for the Empire, Abdullahi would supply the legal and administrative rules for running an extended Caliphate. But it was Sultan Mohammed Bello[v] that was destined to become the practical doer, who began the work of forging the vision into reality.

The role of Caliph, as defined by Dan Fodio before his death, had been a withdrawn and academic one, in line with what he had espoused in his *Kitab al-Farq* treatise. The founding Caliph's vision was for a limited government where the ruler had no more than a Vizier, a Chief Justice, a Captain-General of the Army, Chief of Police, Imam and Tax Chief in his gift to appoint[1]. The Sheikh kept to this concept in practice as Caliph and went further by delegating

---

v   Strictly speaking, Dan Fodio himself was never Sultan. He went by the title of Sheikh or Shehu which would make Mohammed Bello the first Sultan. This has modern day implications with some scholars in Sokoto arguing that only descendants of Bello should be Sultan, a point held against the six Sultans who have descended from Atiku and Buhari (who was of course never Sultan himself); the most recent being Sultan Ibrahim Dasuki who was deposed (with much celebration in Sokoto) in April 1996 by General Sani Abacha, Nigeria's maximum dictator (See Murray Last's 'From Dissent to Dissidence: The Genesis & Development of Reformist Islamic Groups in Northern Nigeria' chapter in '*Sects & Social Disorder: Muslim Identities & Conflicts in Northern Nigeria*').

the actual work of running the government to his Viziers - Abdullahi and Bello - while he concentrated on proselytising, teaching and writing; acting as a spiritual leader. He carried out his role from Sifawa before moving to establish the city of Sokoto in 1815, where he eventually died.

In the cold light of distant history, it would be no exaggeration to recognise Dan Fodio - Son of the Jurist, intellectual revolutionary and worthy ruler - as one of the greatest men his country would ever see. Unmoved by worldly power or riches, almost to the point of naïveté, the Sheikh possessed bulletproof personal integrity that has stood up to the dispassionate scrutiny of multiple histories. To borrow Kipling's famous words - he met with triumph and disaster and treated both impostors the same[vi].

The Fulani Caliphate

'One of the swiftest ways of destroying a kingdom is to give preference to one tribe over another or to show favour to one group of people over another.' Those were the words of Dan Fodio in his Bayan Wujub al-Hijra treatise, written in late 1806. Yet it soon became clear that whatever else might have been the causes of the jihad or created the multi-ethnic coalition that came together to fight it, the leadership of the new Caliphate was overwhelmingly tribal in favour of one group, the Fulani. Fulani favouritism was as intrinsic to the revolution as Islam itself. As we have seen, not long after it began, the jihad spread like wildfire, and most of Hausaland was simultaneously engulfed. Once most of Katsina had been secured after much fighting by Mohammed Bello, he presented flags to two men named Umar Dallaji and Muhammadu dan Alhaji, putting them in charge of finishing the job and taking over Katsina. Both of these men were Fulani. Dan Alhaji died not too long after, leaving Dallaji to complete the mission and become installed as the

---

vi   Rudyard Kipling's 1895 poem "If".

first Fulani Emir of Katsina by Dan Fodio in 1807. Dan Alhaji's son, Mamman Dikko, had a smaller domain carved out for him in the western part of Katsina where he was installed as chief.

Kano was a bit more complicated, but the overall pattern was the same. Here, jihad was led by seven Fulani men, three of whom - Sulaymanu dan Abahama, Muhammadu Dabo and Muhammadu Bakatsine - had been students of Dan Fodio. Beginning in 1804, these disciples and their armies fought their way north until a battle at a town called Dan Yahaya, where they finally came up against Muhamman Alwali, the last Hausa king of Kano. The Hausa put up a brave fight but were no match for the determined Fulani forces, who finally took Kano in 1807 with Muhamman Alwali fleeing south. But the victorious conquerors of Kano left nothing to chance. This would not be another Kebbi, if they could help it. Alwali was pursued and killed, preventing him from regrouping and becoming a focal point for disgruntled Hausa in the region. Bello, on behalf of his father, chose Sulaymanu from among his conquering disciples as Emir. This left the other six unhappy, and the following year (in 1808) Dan Fodio himself found it necessary to reaffirm Sulaymanu as Emir. But the divisions were strong enough that none of the descendants of Sulaymanu (who hardly commanded the respect of his peers) ever succeeded him.

Over in Zazzau (ancient Zaria), the revolution was led by yet another of Dan Fodio's Fulani students, Mallam Musa dan Muhammad. In 1807, this disciple of the Sheikh eventually chased out Muhammad Makau, the last Hausa king of Zazzau, who fled south and somehow survived for the next two decades in ambulatory existence, launching opportunist attacks against the Caliphate as the de facto leader of some of the disgruntled fugitives. When this itinerant survivor eventually died, his younger brother, Abu Ja, took over from him and went on to establish what is present-day Nigeria's eponymous capital, first settled in 1825. Abuja would remain a relentless seat of bitter opposition to the rulers of the Fulani Caliphate, well into the nineteenth century and the arrival of

41

Europeans into the country.

Perhaps the most successful of the Fulani disciples of Dan Fodio was a man called Modibbo Adama bii Ardo Hassana. We have seen how most countries in the Sahel typically boasted a sizable Fulani contingent, and this was no different in a region far east from the Caliphate, then known as Fombina, now split between present-day Nigeria and Cameroon. Young Adama had left Fombina to become an Islamic scholar initially in Bornu but that journey took him to Degel where he became a student of Dan Fodio. In 1804, full of zeal and after earning the title of Modibbo, or lettered one, Adama returned to Fombina. Here, he found that his father had been killed in one of the numerous skirmishes that flared up on account of the long-running battles between the Fulani and the indigenous Bata population. Adama mobilised the disparate Fulani clans and convinced them to fight as a team. They then agreed to seek Dan Fodio's blessings and sent a delegation, which included Adama, to secure that objective. In the event, Dan Fodio handed one of his famous flags to Adama and gave him the grand title Lamido Fombina ('Ruler of the South') naming him ruler of a paper protectorate, a territory he did not yet control, displaying colonial ambitions in the same manner as more distant foreign powers soon to arrive.

Over the years Adama and his Fulani army fought numerous battles, sometimes losing, but more often winning and gaining territory. This new power in the country became dominant enough that Shehu El-Kanemi, the de-facto ruler of the nearby Bornu Kingdom and the Emir of a Mandara town in the area found utility in teaming up against the Fulani in 1823. This anti-Fulani collation was partly consummated by the Mandara Emir giving El-Kanemi his daughter in marriage. Unfortunately for the various independent, non-Muslim ethnic groups in the region, they now had to contend with organised attacks from both the Fulani and the Mandara-Bornu coalition, who raided them incessantly for land, treasure and human bodies. By late April 1823, the Mandara-Bornu coalition had come to blows with Adama's Fulani army, in a struggle for supremacy over the area South-East of the Caliphate. Major Dixon Denham - an English soldier and explorer - was a guest of the Bornu coalition forces and gave a detailed eyewitness account of the fighting that ensued. Denham's gory retelling of the war-making was recorded in his sections of the epic *Narrative of Travels and Discoveries in Northern and Central Africa in the years 1822–1824*, a book first published in 1826.

Suffice to say that the Fulani and their rain of poisoned arrows overwhelmed the Bornu coalition, with their small contingent of Arabs. Now long-established in Bornu and known as Shuwa-Arabs, these Afro-Arabs were itinerant settlers from the Mediterranean world who formed part of El-Kanemi's forces. The Bornu-Arabs proved to be the sacrificial lambs in this particular battle, and 45 of them were killed. The rest of the coalition took to their heels before it was their turn to be on the receiving end of the Fulani arrows[2]. This commenced a decades-long process of Adama expanding and consolidating his Fombina enclave, a process which continued well into the 1840s. His success in entrenching Fulani rule over the disparate indigenous peoples of the area can be measured by the fact that all the Lamidos of the country named after him (Adamawa) have been his direct descendants - four of his six sons took turns reigning as Lamido after him. The current Lamido is a direct descendant of his sixth son. Modibbo Adama's country survived later British, French and German competition to rule the area, a feat memorialised by the Fulani poet, Buba Jarida who wrote: 'The French fenced one part/The British did the same/ [...]/The Germans too claimed a certain portion'[3]. Adama and his descendants established their capital at a town called Yola situated not far from the annually flooded banks of the upper Benue, and which remains the capital of Adamawa state in modern Nigeria.

There was however one jihad leader who was not Fulani, even if most of the fighters he led were of that dominant ethnicity.

Yakubu dan Dadi was a Jarawa[vii] man who had found his way to Degel to be educated in Islamic studies under Dan Fodio. Upon receiving a flag from the Sheikh, he returned to Bauchi and first tried to raise an army among his own Hausa people without much success. His revolutionary message did however find purchase among the Fulani in Bauchi country, and before long he was in the business of conquering the local tribes and bringing them under his authority. Like Adama, the site where Yakubu chose to build his capital in 1811 (Bauchi) remains the capital of this area till this day[4]. But another more perverse legacy of the choices Yakubu made also remains with us today.

As much as he repeatedly raided the diverse, non-Muslim peoples of the hilly plateau country south of Bauchi (in present-day Plateau State in Nigeria), he never quite managed or bothered to bring them fully under his authority. The built-up animosity and tension between the Muslims and this native population continues to this day among the (now mostly Christian) descendants of the original populace, with frequent violent clashes in what remains one of the most volatile parts of Nigeria. In a sense, the violent trauma from these sporadic bloody skirmishes became wired into the inter-generational genetic sequencing of the Plateau country people. It was the same way for many of the fiercely independent non-Muslim peoples in the southern reaches of the Caliphate and the Niger-Benue valley, who would soon come to bear the brunt of the Fulani Caliphate in session.

Here Comes the Son

Sultan Mohammed Bello's 20-year reign began in difficult circumstances. The revolutionary war had not been easy on ordinary people, and there were severe economic consequences. Food was scarce and the populace in parts of the north resorted to buying lizards sold for 50 cowries and dead vultures for 500

---

vii   A predominantly Muslim tribe to be found in today's Alkaleri and Dass Local Government Areas of Bauchi state.

cowries each, a sign of how desperate the times were[5]. The new conquering elite frowned on a lot of cultural practices among the population, determining them to be incompatible with the vision of a righteous Islamic Caliphate that they were pursuing. There were also numerous excesses and violations to be expected in a time of war, as had already been seen in the period before Bello's ascension. Aliyu Jaidu, the military commander, had killed a man in Kebbi for having the effrontery to enter his house and ask for the return of his borrowed horse[6]. This incident infuriated Dan Fodio so much that he never spoke to Jaidu again. As such, even this early in its life, much of the budding empire was on a hair-trigger for revolt.

In the year that Bello became Sultan, Zamfara rose in a rebellion that took five years for Bello to put down. Gobir, where the jihad began, rose again in revolt during 1818 and was never quite pacified throughout Bello's reign, despite his best efforts. Each year Bello would lead expeditions against the Gobirawa, almost to a timetable, and every year they just about managed to live to fight another day. This culminated in the bloody battle of Gawakuke in 1836 where the Caliphate assembled quite possibly their largest-ever army for a showdown with the diehard insurgents of Gobir. Bello summoned all his Emirs and they arrived, leading their armies in person. They marched north from the Rima Valley through the desert where hunger and thirst did a number on them. In the end, they met the coalition from Gobir, Katsina and the mercenary Tuaregs for battle in March 1836. Bello, who often showed magnanimity to his enemies, did not do so on this occasion. He ordered about 1,000 prisoners of war to be executed. Nearly 70 years after this bloody ordeal, Captain Charles Foulkes, a British Army officer, was galloping past the same area and came across a large mound. Upon enquiry, the local chief told him that up to 20,000 people who fell in the Battle of Gawakuke had been buried there[7], making this disaster - if accurately remembered - a candidate for the bloodiest single day in Nigerian history.

Kebbi, on the western fringes of the Empire, was another

country that made life hard for the Caliphate. The hardy Kebbirawa rebelled and revolted continuously until 1830, when Bello was able to force a peace on them which lasted the better part of 20 years. In all, the energetic Bello led 47 expeditions and raids in his time as Sultan, an average of more than two per annum. One simple reason for the constant revolts was that the old Hausa rulers displaced by the new Fulani usurpers simply did not take their loss of status lying down. They escaped to ungoverned spaces outside the Caliphate's boundaries, and from there launched intermittent raids against Sokoto. Mohammed Hodi dan Sulemana, the king of Kebbi, who we last saw fleeing from Abdullahi's advancing forces in 1805, was one such diehard. This determined former ruler established himself at a town called Kimba, around 135 kilometres South-West from present-day Bornu and continued to call himself Sarkin Kebbi. It was not until early 1827 before he was finally defeated by Bello, with a force assembled from across the Caliphate.

The scorched-earth nature of the jihad meant that practically all major towns in Hausaland had been destroyed in the fighting. This offered Sultan Bello the opportunity to be a leader of consequence by stamping his mark, physically, on the new nation-state being formed. The opportunities for rebuilding infrastructure and re-ordering the economy and trade patterns were everywhere, and the young ruler seized them. His signature infrastructure policy was the expanded establishment of ribats - walled border towns - for the dual purpose of providing the first line of defence against the depredations of the diehards and rebel neighbours of the Caliphate, as well as ensuring that the trade show was kept on the road with minimal disruption. These defensive towns also contained mosques and schools where the ideas of the new Caliphate could be effectively disseminated. In reality, things didn't quite work as he planned. The main challenge was that even with the generous tax breaks the Caliph offered for people to relocate to the ribats, few people did so voluntarily. Bello's ribats thus ended up being populated largely by persons held in bondage; effectively slave ghettos.

This was just as well given the tide was now turning against the international slave trade. Offshore outlets for disposing of slaves were becoming constricted, with the inevitable second-order effect of increasing the local supply of these unfortunate humans. The constant raids and rebellions across the postbellum country produced large numbers of captured slaves at every turn. In describing one of the many triggers of the jihad, Bello had complained that Muslims were being captured into slavery by Yoruba from the south and then sold on to European Christians. This presents us with one of the greatest ironies in Nigerian history - the Sokoto Caliphate would go on to become one of the largest slave societies in history, with up to 50 per cent of the population being slaves by the end of the nineteenth century[8].

The ribats also served another unintended purpose; shifting the economic centre of gravity in the Caliphate by lowering the status of certain towns while raising that of others. In this way, Kano, with a sizable number of important ribats, gained pre-eminence over Katsina as an economic centre. Before the jihad, Katsina had been the more important economy, but its location on the outer reaches of the Caliphate opened it up to constant raids from Katsina diehards who simply refused to accept the Fulani as their new overlords. Kano, on the other hand, was mostly spared these problems as raids coming from the north would first encounter towns like Daura and Kazaure, while various other towns shielded the city from the eastern raiders.

The Ribats also served another important function, the sedentarisation of hitherto nomadic Fulani, creating a melting pot where local Hausa and Fulani mixed freely without the frequent clashes which had in part fuelled the jihad. In present-day Nigeria, the Hausa-Fulani are often considered as one conjoined and indistinguishable people, and it is perhaps not far-fetched to say that Bello's ribats played a key role in achieving this meld among the ordinary people. Leading by example, Bello himself lived in several ribats during his reign as Caliph and left instructions to be buried in one[9]. In another sense, Bello's martial ribats marked the commencement of nearly 200 years of almost unbroken militarised rule of the civil populace in Nigeria, a run that only ended in 1999 when the last two decades of civilian rule were ushered in.

Nana and Gidado, the Hands of the King

Fulani dominance continued when the time came for Sultan Bello to form a government and appoint his officials. Several ribats were placed under the control of Bello's sons. Even the incompetent Fodio, a son of Bello from a wife he took from King Yunfa, was awarded a ribat along with several cousins and brothers of the Sultan. Bello's first major appointment was his Vizier, Usman bin Abubakar dan Laima, better known as Gidado ('beloved' for his well-known devotion to Dan Fodio), who was Bello's best friend and brother-in-law. Gidado had fought alongside the new Sultan in the early revolutionary battles and was a scholarly and urbane man. He was also older than Bello and thus proved almost perfect for the role of a wise counsellor. Along with his wife, Nana Asma'u, who was also Bello's younger half-sister, they formed the intellectual backbone of the Caliphate during Bello's reign.

Nana served as the de facto education minister who championed the education of women and children in the ideals of the Caliphate, bridging the gap between Arabic - the language of the ruling classes - and Hausa - the language of the masses. This she did through her army of jajis (literally, caravan leaders) who dispersed across the Caliphate, educating women wherever they went. In turn, they created a new class of learned women known as Yan-taru, literally, those who congregate together. While there is some evidence that this system had existed in some vague form long before her, there is no doubt that it was Asma'u who turned it into the structured train-the-trainer programme that it remains to this day. Her jajis, in their recognisable hats tied with red turbans, helped take her message of encouragement to the wavering masses and in so doing performed a re-socialising function for the Caliphate. Her educational legacy lives on to this day in a variety of ways, not least in the Governor of Sokoto, Aminu Tambuwal, announcing in October 2019 the allocation of land for the 'Nana Asma'u University of Medical Sciences'[10].

The erudite Nana Asma'u spoke four languages and wrote in three of them. She was one of Dan Fodio's closest advisers before and after he became Caliph. In reprising this role during her brother's reign, she came to the job with experience and a deep knowledge of her father's vision for the Caliphate. Her prolific poetry was composed for women and children to memorise as part of their Islamic education. Her work covered social justice topics like the integration of Hausa women displaced by the upheaval of the jihad. In her own Fulani circles, her writings sought to disabuse people from the use of charms. She also wrote about love: for her father, her husband, her brother, and God. We owe a lot of the detail we now have of Dan Fodio's life to the painstaking work of Nana Asma'u in piecing together the Sheikh's papers and writings into a coherent collective after he died. She is also remembered in local folklore - the mention of her name in Hausaland is known to elicit the response 'Was she not the one who helped Bello?' a reference to the legendary story that she had been the one to throw the burning stick into Alkalawa during the siege of the capital in 1809, which had then razed the capital to the ground and ended Yunfa's resistance[11].

From the English explorer named Hugh Clapperton, who visited Sokoto in 1824 and whom we will meet shortly, we get a glimpse into Gidado dan Laima's personality. Clapperton arrived in Sokoto on 16 March that year and left on 4 May. The whole time he was a guest of Gidado who had the responsibility of looking after foreign visitors as part of his remit as the Waziri. 'Good Old Gidado', as Clapperton called him, spoke Arabic very well and was always courteous and polite. He took care to protect the British visitor from the internal politics of Sokoto, especially with a Sokoto prince named Abubakar Atiku who had lost out to Bello as Sultan but clearly did not consider the matter closed. During Clapperton's stay, Gidado's favourite son with Nana died from smallpox[viii]. 'I have met with a great misfortune but it is the will of God,' Gidado said with equanimity on this loss, for which he was inconsolable[12].

Still, another son of theirs succeeded Gidado as Waziri and all subsequent Waziris to this day have been direct descendants of Gidado and Asma'u. Perhaps the most famous of them has been Muhammad Junaidu, better known as Waziri Junaidu. He was the outstanding linguist and historian of the Sokoto Caliphate, without whom it would have been impossible to write the book you are reading. He remains one of the giants on whose shoulders you must stand if you want to see far into the past of Sokoto[ix]. The husband and wife team of Good Old Gidado and Nana Asma'u were Bello's eyes and ears on the ground. They expanded his influence to areas beyond his immediate reach on account of his being bogged down with the intricacies of building a major nation-state.

Sultan Bello's Big Government

In several ways, Sultan Bello abandoned his father's 'small government' principles, creating several new posts - some in direct contradiction of principles laid down by the founding Caliph. These included new positions like the *Magajin Gari* and the *Galadima*. Not only were the appointees into these positions ethnic Fulani (only one major post was occupied by a non-Fulani), they were

---

viii Perhaps unsurprisingly, given the rules around women socialising with male visitors in northern Nigeria, the meticulous Clapperton, who documented everyone he met (from royalty to slaves) and how much he spent throughout his stay in Sokoto, made no mention of meeting Nana Asma'u at all in his records.

ix Waziri Junaidu wrote 60 books - 50 in Arabic and four in Fulfulde, a language he only learned as an adult. He was a teacher all his life and while at Sokoto Middle School (1930-39) and as the pioneer principal of the Sokoto School of Sharia (established in 1939), one of his students would be Alhaji Shehu Shagari, Nigeria's first executive president, in office from 1979-83. The Waziri Junaidu Library in Sokoto contains over 400 documents from the nineteenth century.

also related to Bello (or Gidado) by blood or marriage. This led
to the ironic situation where the new Fulani elite became as keen
on grand titles as the Hausa whom they had condemned for the
very same thing[13]. Ibn Khaldun, the venerated Islamic scholar and
a pioneer of modern historiography, in his celebrated fourteenth-
century work, *Muqaddimah* (which Bello would have been familiar
with) popularised the concept of Asabiyyah (tribalism) to describe
a situation where, in the opening act of a dynasty or revolution,
the leaders fill all the offices with their close relatives and then in
the second act they widen the circle to bring in outsiders[14]. While
this undoubtedly described Bello's government and appointments,
it also sowed the seeds of discontent as Ibn Khaldun warned, which
Sultan Bello would have to contend with throughout his reign.

To fund the business of the Caliphate, Sultan Bello instituted
a fiscal system that is interesting for what it reveals about the
prevailing tax administration thinking in pre-colonial, pre-crude
oil nineteenth-century northern Nigeria. Officially, at least in
Sokoto, only one tax was levied by the new government - *zakat*, a
mandatory levy on Muslims. Crucially, the *zakat* was to be treated
and spent only as internally generated revenue, to be utilised only
in the locality from whence it was generated. Outside of Sokoto
however, all bets were off. While the hated cattle tax was abolished
in Sokoto where Bello reigned supreme, in other Emirates matters
of tax administration came down to the Emir in charge. In Katsina,
for example, Umar Dallaji drew a line between Muslim and non-
observant Fulani as far as cattle taxes were concerned, sparing the
Muslims the indignity of paying. Sokoto earned Caliphate wide
revenues in the form of voluntary tributes sent up to it from the
constituent states. In reality, wise Emirs made sure to pay early
and often. These tributes came in various forms: the ubiquitous
currency of the country - slaves (Zaria at one point sent up 100
slaves annually), cowries, horses, fine clothes, cash and food crops,
and military equipment. From the tributes, mood music could
thus be read about the current state of the relationship between the

giving Emirate and Sokoto. Where the tributes were stingy or non-existent, the relationship was strained.

Bello's 47 expeditions were a source of revenue for the Caliphate, generating both treasure and human captives from across the vast country. Under the perverse jurisprudence of the Caliphate, it was perfectly legal to enslave people from defeated territories, so long as they were not Muslims. Bello's frequent expeditions yielded a kind of steady revenue in this regard. For this reason, nearby Emirates which were surrounded by large non-Muslim populations (Zaria being the best example) sent more tribute to Sokoto as its share of expedition booty than others like Kano, which had slim pickings on account of being surrounded by Muslim towns.

The Battle of Gawakuke proved to be Sultan Bello's last major expedition. Some of the Katsina diehards who survived the fighting had done the usual business of fleeing north and finding a new location from which to reconstitute themselves as an opposing force to the Caliphate. Bello intended to finish the job by leading yet another expedition out against them but fell ill before he had set out. This illness lasted the better part of a year and led to his death in October 1837 at the still relatively young age of 56. The newly established Caliphate could hardly have hoped for a better helmsman than him in its earliest years.

Sultan Bello fought, wrote, built and in the end bequeathed an impressive achievement to his successors, all of whom would prove to be lesser men than him. Like his father, he managed to rise above personal corruption even when there was plenty of opportunity for it. It is to his credit that even though he wrote much of the accounts of the jihad long after they had taken place, they remain relatively balanced accounts because of his objectivity in looking back on his own side's activities and confessing to the mistakes they had made. Sultan Bello's death marked the demise of a remarkable triumvirate - Dan Fodio, Abdullahi, Bello - who had dreamt up and converted the idea of an Islamic Caliphate in sub-Saharan Africa into hard reality (Abdullahi died nine years earlier in 1828). 'I am bereft of the great enduring love and absolute confidence I shared with my brother,' wrote the inconsolable Nana Asma'u, in her most moving recorded words, after he died. As for Gidado Dan Laima, he to all intents and purposes retired from public life after Bello's death and delegated all his official duties to his son with Asma'u[15].

Buhari versus Atiku

The first contest between two men named Abubakar Atiku and Muhammadu Buhari for the highest office in Nigeria took place in 1837, following Sultan Bello's death. Unlike the eponymous contest nearly two centuries later[x], Atiku came out on top: succeeding his brother as the Sultan of Sokoto and *Amir al-Mu'minin*. Gidado Dan Laima convened an electoral council made up of heavy hitters like Aliyu Jaidu, still in office as army commander, and of course Gidado himself as the Vizier. The obvious choice, on merit if nothing else, ought to have been Buhari who was a poet of some renown and had earned his spurs in several battles that took the revolution into the Yoruba country, as well as the one that had dealt the final blow to Kebbi's Mohammed Hodi, ten years before. Even more in Buhari's favour was that Atiku was viewed with suspicion by many in and outside the establishment on account of what was thought to be his cruel nature and more than a whiff of corruption about him. Neither Dan Fodio nor Bello had trusted Atiku to confide any matters of great importance to him, although Atiku claimed that Dan Fodio told him 115 secrets before his death[16]. To compound matters, Bello had refused to name a successor, despite Gidado repeatedly asking him to do so. After a week of thinking about it, the electoral council announced the unimpressive Atiku as their choice. Unlike Bello who stood at 5' 10' and had a distinguished manner about

---

x   In 2019, Nigeria's incumbent president, Muhammadu Buhari, defeated his main challenger, Abubakar Atiku in the country's presidential election. Just four years before, they had been in the same party and their combined efforts helped to unseat the incumbent President, Goodluck Jonathan.

him, Atiku was nicknamed 'Mai Katuru' on account of his short stature and soft voice. The most charitable thing that could be said for Atiku over Buhari was that he was the older man and the council had gone with age as their tie-breaker.

Atiku immediately set about trying to be his own man by moving the capital away from Wurno where Bello had been based and converting his own house into the Sultan's palace. This contributed to Gidado's decision to retire since he had lived close to Bello's house as his Vizier. The change in location would have meant a longer commute for him in his advancing years. Under the pretext that Bello had not been faithful in implementing Sharia law, the new Sultan set himself up as the man to right these wrongs by cracking down on immorality, as he saw it, in the shape of singing, dancing and drumming, going as far as ordering a drummer executed in the middle of his musical performance[17]. Still, the new Sultan or not, the Caliphate's problems remained the same and one of such matters was Bello's unfinished business with the Katsina diehards in a town called *Tsibiri*. The first time he tried, the battle ended in a draw.

The revolts and rebellions across the Caliphate continued from Zamfara to Gobir to Zurmi and then in his fifth year as Sultan in 1842, Abubakar Atiku decided to try one more time to quell the Tsibiri rebels. This battle took place during the Ramadan fast and here his battle-weary army - which had been fighting non-stop for the best part of four decades - let him down, by openly defying his orders to attack the enemy. He was left with no choice but to abandon the endeavour and head back home. On that return journey, the unfortunate Atiku fell ill and died at Zamfara.

In the five short years that Atiku had reigned as Caliph, Muhammadu Buhari had also died, which meant that a new Sultan had to be found. Perhaps due to a lack of other strong contenders, the kingmakers settled on Bello's eldest son, the then 34-year-old Aliyu Babba (nicknamed Mai Ciniki, 'The Trader'). If nothing else, they appeared to have gone for the opposite of the mirthless Atiku in character, as Aliyu Babba was known to be good-natured, with a fondness for laughter. Still, the Caliphate needed more than a nice guy to deal with the myriad problems buffeting it on all sides. The new Caliph seems to have underestimated the problem of the diehards at the northern frontier. When he attempted to answer the elusive Tsibiri question, he met with failure. He then compounded the mistake by abandoning further attempts. Having faced down Aliyu Babba, his father and his uncle, the Tsibiri insurgents took this as a sign that outright victory might be feasible, changing their strategy from defence to offence. In this quest, they were aided by Sidiqu dan Umaru, the son of Umar Dallaji who had been deposed as the first Fulani Emir of Katsina by Aliyu Babba in 1844. Throughout his 17-year reign, many of Bello's hard-won victories to hold the Caliphate together were slowly lost to Aliyu's unwillingness or inability to fight as his father had done. By way of comparison, Aliyu carried out 20 expeditions in total during his reign.

Some of this might have been the result of a broader generational shift in the leadership of the Caliphate. Even though they were still alive, men like Gidado and Aliyu Jaidu had now become too old and tired for affairs of state and were handing over their duties to their sons. These younger men did not always have the experience or ability of their fathers, with clear consequences for the state of the country. Insecurity increased across the Empire and whole parts of the country became impassable for travellers and trade. The German traveller, Heinrich Barth (who we will meet in more detail later), passed through northern Nigeria during this period and reported seeing demoralised soldiers in Wurno willing to sell their weapons even for kola nuts, observing that 'Almost all the leading men seem to be imbued with the melancholy conviction that their rule in these quarters is coming to an end'[18]. Still, Aliyu Babba had not yet made the biggest mistake of his reign, a major misstep that he reserved for last. The peace of the graveyard that his father, Mohammed Bello, had obtained in Kebbi in 1830 had only held because Yakubu Nabame dan Ismaila, a son of a previous Emir of Kebbi (Karari Ismaila), had been exiled to Sokoto and kept under house arrest there, not far from the watchful eyes of the Caliphate's leadership.

As long as he was kept away from Kebbi, this inveterate schemer's mischief-making opportunities were reduced or non-existent. But in Sokoto, he wormed his way into the heart of the ruling family, and over time came to be seen as one of their own. Eventually, Nabame asked Sultan Aliyu Babba for permission to return to his native Kebbi, and the naive Aliyu granted this request in 1847. Within two years the wily Ismaila was up to his old tricks and in 1849 he renounced his allegiance to Sokoto, mobilising a local army to fight the Fulani wherever he found them. The Sultan did not manage to put down this rebellion over the next ten years until he died in 1859, at which point Dan Fodio's empire was visibly disintegrating.

The Beginning of Decline

A succession of hapless Caliphs took turns in attempting to resolve the intractable problems bequeathed to them by Aliyu Babba's unfortunate reign. First up was Ahmadu Zaruku ('Mai Cimola' on account of where he moved the capital to from Wurno), son of Abubakar Atiku. He stumbled on some good fortune when two of the leading lights among the Gobirawa diehards fell out, with one of them deciding to make peace with the Fulani as protection from reprisals. Ahmadu seized this opportunity with both hands and offered the defector the chance to build his new town, Sabon Birni, within the borders of the Caliphate, close to where the destroyed Alkalawa had been. This bought him peace in that part of the Empire and allowed trade and commerce to resume. Sultan Ahmadu died in 1866 and Aliyu Karami, a son of Mohammed Bello was elected Caliph to succeed him in November of the same year. Within a year Karami died, in October 1867 and it was at this point that the much-dreaded succession crisis of the earliest Fulani kingmakers manifested, adding to the many problems of the Caliphate.

Given the emerging succession pattern, it ought to have been straightforward to choose someone from the house of Atiku to succeed Karami. But the leading contender, Abdurahman, did not fill anyone with confidence, least of all the electoral council. Abdurahman eventually got his chance in 1891 on account of being the most senior contender. But in 1867, the Atikus were never going to take this lying down and they were spoiling for a fight. The solution that the council arrived at was to return to an actual son of Dan Fodio, maintaining some credibility over the process. Even fifty years after the Shehu's death, the crafty kingmakers were able to find one such man for the job - Ahmadu Rufai. Once in office, Rufai considered the long list of problems he had inherited and came up with the novel idea of seeking peace with the Caliphate's most implacable enemies, Kebbi. In this enterprise he was successful, and for a time, he managed to put out the raging fires across the empire by offering peace to anyone who would have it. No expeditions were carried out during his time and on the handful of occasions he travelled outside Sokoto, it was to attend a funeral or rebuild a destroyed ribat[19]. This nonviolent approach would have a telling effect on the Caliphate for it became much harder for Sokoto to raise a Caliphate-wide army for the obligatory jihads and annual fundraising expeditions.

Rufai died in 1873 and was succeeded by three rather uneventful Sultans - Abubakar Atiku na Rabih (who lost the peace that Rufai had brokered in Kebbi), Mu'azu Ahmadu dan Bello (who was elected in 1877) and Umaru dan Aliyu Babba (elected in 1881). Following Umaru's nearly ten-year reign, ending with his death during an expedition, the 62-year-old Abdurahman dan Abubakar, who had been passed over in 1867, was chosen as Sultan. The argument can be made that his selection was the biggest mistake the electoral council had yet made, even with strong competition. Lacking in character or temperament for such a job, he had earned himself the derogatory nickname Danyen Kasko (the 'Unbaked

Pot') for the chip on his shoulder which led him to execute people for even minor offences. In 1892, he managed to rouse the Emirates for one big push against the stubborn holdouts at Kebbi, with an attempt to take their capital Argungu. This ended in a fiasco when his army walked into a trap laid for them by the Sarkin Kebbi, Muhammadu Ismaila (son of Yakubu Nabame), sending the Fulani army fleeing back in the direction from where they had come. Still, this battle was notable for the rise of Muhammad Mai Turare (so-called for his love of fragrances), a son of Ahmed Zaruku, better known as Marafa. The losses would have been worse for the Fulani had Marafa not led a counterattack against the Kebbi army which gave them pause and called a halt to the fighting. The military brilliance of Marafa would allow him to usurp the title of Sarkin Yaki from the descendants of Aliyu Jaidu. He also introduced the innovation of a private army into Sokoto politics made up of Tuareg immigrants which he armed and funded[20]. As much as he knew how to fight, however, he could also be pragmatic when he needed to be, as we shall see later in our story.

The Kano Civil War

The defeat in Kebbi did not stop Abdurahman from triggering what would prove to be one of the biggest self-inflicted wounds suffered by the Caliphate. A major cause of the rout at Argungu had been a lack of enthusiasm by many of the Emirs who had sent their armies. But Prince Muhamman Tukur, representing his father Muhamman Bello, the then Emir of Kano, was not guilty of this and his commitment and enthusiasm was not lost on Abdurahman. The following year when the Kano king died, Abdurahman saw an opportunity to appoint someone he considered a loyal ally as Emir of one of the most important Emirates in the Caliphate. The Sultan thus directed his Vizier to secure the appointment of Tukur as the Emir of Kano. But the Kanawa electoral council had other ideas and told the Vizier that they had decided on Yusuf Abdullahi as Emir, politely asking him to convey their message of non-interference in Kanawa internal leadership selection to Abdurahman. Now finding himself in a tight spot (at risk of losing both an ally and his reputation), Abdurahman stuck to his guns and insisted on Tukur. By this time, much bad blood had spilled between Tukur on the one side, and other contestants to the Kano throne, who now rallied behind Yusuf, the latter being quite popular among the Kanawa. With his large following and support, Yusuf moved to a town called *Takai*, about 80 kilometres south of Kano city. While there, he did what any self-respecting rebel would do - surrounding himself with other disgruntled rebels that had an axe to grind with Sokoto, soon forming them into a powerful coalition.

With this new army in place, Yusuf marched on Kano with vengeance, triggering a brutal civil war. The city walls proved formidable however and the invaders were unable to break-in, even though they did their utmost to unleash devastation on the place. In due course, the siege triggered a famine, even as Yusuf's army detoured, waging war on smaller neighbouring towns. Three months later, Yusuf and his army mustered for another direct assault on Kano, but just as he was nearing the city, the ambitious Prince fell ill and died in his war camp. Before he died however, he chose his younger brother Aliyu Dan Abdullahi-Maje Karofi, better known as Aliyu Babba - nicknamed Mai Sango for his arsenal containing thousands of guns - to succeed him. We will see more of this Aliyu Babba of Kano later in our story. Meanwhile, Tukur remained holed up inside the city, receiving little help from Sultan Abdurahman, his supposed benefactor. By early 1894, Aliyu Babba was ready for a second attempt on Kano and this time, with Tukur a sitting duck, he found success. The walls were finally breached, and the invaders of Kano took the city, with Tukur fleeing to Katsina. The Unbaked Pot at Sokoto now belatedly showed his (weak) hand, directing the Emir of Katsina to provide the fleeing Tukur with refuge.

This wise Emir pretended not to receive the message, electing not to participate in other people's conflicts by locking his city gates.

With nowhere to hide and Aliyu Babba's forces in hot pursuit, Tukur was caught and killed by Muhammadu Abbass, brother of Aliyu Babba. With mud on his face, the embarrassed Caliph had failed to impose his choice on the Kanawa, and with both Tukur and Yusuf dead, he accepted Aliyu Babba as the new Emir. But the damage had been done. The Kano succession war exposed how weak Dan Fodio's Caliphate had now become. From Sokoto's halcyon days of naming undisputed flag-bearers of the jihad, a violent war of attrition had now become the primary means by which a succession dispute could be settled among the Fulani elite. Going further, in direct contrast to the distinctly civilised succession episode between Mohammed Bello and his uncle Abdullahi Dan Fodio which we saw at the start of the Sokoto imperial era, violence was now the blunt and destructive tool being utilised to settle matters among the ruling class.

The expanded Sokoto Caliphate was now in transition, learning to evolve from centralised rule enforced by superior military capabilities, to power-sharing among far-flung vassals, regional allies and immediate neighbours. The intellectual revolution of the Fulani had run out of steam; and the future of the Caliphate would now be determined less by the forceful leadership of its early narrow inspired elite, and more by games of violence and political survival among a larger, wider-spread and still-expanding newly melded Hausa-Fulani ruling class. In any event, with the arrival of Europeans in large numbers on the river, the Caliphate would soon collide for the first time with an outside civilisation, an even greater military power than any it had yet encountered. One English explorer who visited the country in the final decade of the century would write that 'The Fulas have never yet encountered disciplined troops with English leaders and it is impossible to say how they will fight'[21].

A Coming Reckoning

More than arms, ammunition, organisation or, propaganda, the ability to persevere, hold together and negotiate that coming encounter would soon prove to be the single most important quality required for the survival of Fulani rule in the country created by Dan Fodio. Before we arrive at the story of that coming reckoning however, we must detour to affairs unfolding in a nearby country on the lower Niger. Not least, because the entry point of the new civilisation that would shortly infiltrate and unravel the empire assembled by the Sheikh's descendants would be from within these hitherto distant neighbours. For better or worse, the coming reckoning would determine in very conclusive terms, the future of the several millions of people living in these vast lands surrounding the Niger river. In the end, the outcome of this historical encounter would prove to be one of the more spectacular transformations to occur in the history of the modern world.

1. Last M. *The Sokoto Caliphate*. Harlow: Longmans; 1967.
2. Denham D, Clapperton H, Oudney W. *Narrative of Travels and Discoveries in Northern and Central Africa: In the Years 1822, 1823, and 1824*. 1828.
3. Bashir Abubakar MM. Muslim Responses to British Colonialism in Northern Nigeria as Expressed in Fulfulde Poems. *Islamic Africa*. 2013/6/3 2013;4(1):1-14.
4. Johnston HAS. *The Fulani Empire of Sokoto*. Oxford University Press; 1967.
5. Watts MJ. *Silent Violence: Food, Famine, and Peasantry in Northern Nigeria*. University of Georgia Press; 2013.
6. Last M. *The Sokoto Caliphate*. Harlow: Longmans; 1967.
7. Sperl S. *Classical Traditions and Modern Meanings*. BRILL; 1996.
8. Lovejoy PE. *Jihād in West Africa during the Age of Revolutions*. Ohio University Press; 2016.
9. Last M. *The Sokoto Caliphate*. Harlow: Longmans; 1967.
10. Nigerian Tribune Newspapers - Tambuwal allocates land for proposed

Nana Asma'u University in Sokoto. 2019/10/15 2019; (Available online)

11. Boyd J. *The Caliph's Sister: Nana Asma'u, 1793-1865, Teacher, Poet and Islamic Leader*. Routledge; 2013.

12. Denham D, Clapperton H, Oudney W. *Narrative of Travels and Discoveries in Northern and Central Africa: In the Years 1822, 1823, and 1824*. 1828.

13. Johnston HAS. *The Fulani Empire of Sokoto*. Oxford University Press; 1967.

14. Ibn-Haldūn '-A-RI-M, Khaldūn I. *The Muqaddimah : An Introduction to History*. Princeton University Press; 1967.

15. Boyd J. *The Caliph's Sister: Nana Asma'u, 1793-1865, Teacher, Poet and Islamic Leader*. Routledge; 2013.

16. Last M. *The Sokoto Caliphate*. Harlow: Longmans; 1967.

17. Johnston HAS. *The Fulani Empire of Sokoto*. Oxford University Press; 1967.

18. Barth H. *Travels and Discoveries in North and Central Africa: Being a Journal of an Expedition Undertaken Under the Auspices of H. B. M.'s Government, in the Years 1849-1855*. 1857.

19. Last M. *The Sokoto Caliphate*. Harlow: Longmans; 1967.

20. *Ibid.*

21. Mockler-Ferryman AF. *Up the Niger: Narrative of Major Claude MacDonald's Mission to the Niger and Benue Rivers, West Africa (Classic Reprint)*. Fb&c Limited; 2018.

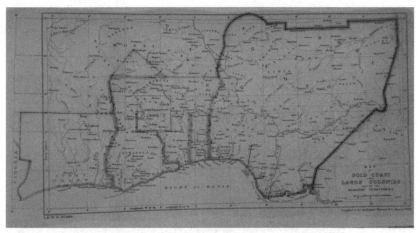

Map of West Africa 1898

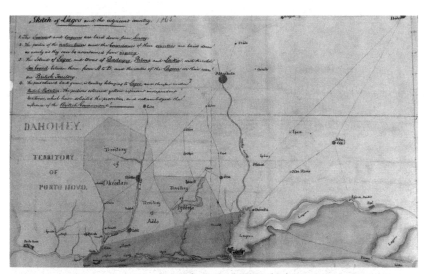

Map of Lagos 1865. UK National Archives

Obi Samuel Okosi I of Onitsha and some of his Chiefs.
Image captured at Onitsha by Walter Egerton in 1907

Gilbert Carter (centre) Governor of the Colony of
Lagos and Govt House Staff Lagos 1898

Women and children at a public water tap on
DOCEMO Street Lagos 1900 Image - Postcard by
Fourier Dakar

Mary Slessor and some of her wards c.1900 Colourised
Alto Historical Media

*Walter Egerton Governor of Protectorate of Southern
Nigeria and Nanna of Itsekiri Koko 1910 at Nanna_s
residence Walter Egerton Collection UK National
Archives*

*Railway - Train at Iddo Railway Station 1900 UK
National Archives*

Kano c.1899 Image retained within C.T Lawrence
Collection at the UK National Archives

Governor Gilbert and Mrs Carter (Governor of
Lagos) with other British officials during a visit to the
hinterland at Offa 1899

*Sultan Attahiru of Sokoto c.1902 before the invasion
of Sokoto and his deposition at Burmi*

*Carriers on Niger expedition 1897. Native carriers
bear the equipment and materials of the expedition
leading to the invasion of Benin in 1897*

*King Koko Mingi 1 of Nembe. Image captured by
Jonathan Adagogo Green c.1894 Mingo was later
to lead his people on the raid of Akassa in protest at
RNC tyranny*

*George Taubman Goldie Vice Chairman of the Royal
Niger Company c.1881. Image Source Royal Niger
Company File. UK National Archives*

CHAPTER 4

Sunrise within the Tropics

War and Blood

Dan Fodio's jihad, the seminal event in Nigeria's history up to the early nineteenth century, would trigger outsized reverberations across time and space, eventually affecting the lives of millions of people across multiple continents. The immediate consequence of the jihad south of the Niger-Benue rivers would be an armed conflagration of previously unimaginable proportions. Revolution was in the air not just locally but also abroad, with the Napoleonic wars then raging across the Mediterranean, North African and Ottoman worlds, and it was sweeping away everything in its path that was not tethered to firm ground. The Fulani jihad officially ended in 1808, when Dan Fodio established his new headquarters at Sokoto, more than 600 kilometres and at least a two-week trek from the nearest point on the Niger. But it did not take long for blood, toil, tears and sweat to find their way downriver.

Now known as Yoruba, the primary country across the banks of the river from the emerging dominions of the jihadists was ruled by another imperial nation, albeit one in decline. Once great and dominant across several hundreds of kilometres in all directions from its central capital, the Oyo Empire controlled a coastal seaport at a town called Ouidah and received homage from many tributaries including multiple sub-tribes, such as the martial Dahomey nation. At the height of its powers, Oyo's properties included the domains of several other nationalities, extending at various times up to the banks of the Niger, forming the empire's north-eastern border. Only Benin, the impregnable former imperial power on its south-eastern border came close in significance and importance to Oyo at its late eighteenth-century peak. But internal rivalry for economic and political control of this martial merchant-state had begun to weaken it substantially by the time of Dan Fodio's revolution and the rise of the Fulani Empire.

Matters came to a head in the internal politics of Oyo with the formal secession of its strongest military sub-state in early 1817, the same year as Dan Fodio's death[1]. This catastrophe was the culmination of a multi-year military, political and personality struggle between a weakened and unwise Emperor at Oyo-Ile, the metropolitan Oyo capital and an ambitious, imperious prince-general who then ruled over a town called Ilorin, a few days march south from the river. Decades before this rancorous denouement, Oyo had been reduced from its primacy by severe political disharmony among its ruling elite of constitutional chiefs, war generals and leading merchants. At the time of its secession, Ilorin was the primary entrepot for military equipment, particularly cavalry sourced from trading partners further North. The sub-province had become stronger over the years, just as the metropolitan capital was being weakened by intrigue and scheming. Afonja, the Oyo prince now infamous for his tortured and momentous decision to tear apart from an empire built and revered by his ancestors, acted to preserve his personal position and power over Ilorin, a recurring trend that we will observe across our story.

In this task, the secessionist prince was aided by a local community of Fulani elite Mallams within his domain, supported by several thousands of Hausa-speaking foreign soldiers, merchants, servants and slaves held within Ilorin as part of its armed forces. Prominent among Afonja's accomplices and enablers were several Muslim leaders of these groups, including, notably, a Fulani Mallam named Alimi and his adult sons. Afonja's spectacular secession would lead to frenzied armed conflict across Oyo, as multiple sub-groups of elite military and political leaders began to act and re-align given the dangerous new realities of the time. War and blood had arrived from across the upper river.

Dahomey Unshackled

The weakened Oyo Alaafin at the intrigue-riddled capital was unable to unify his still quite significant imperial forces to quash Afonja's rebellion. This was partly because problems were now popping up for the king all across the Empire. Around the same time, in a western country called Dahomey that was still formally acknowledging the suzerainty of Oyo, a new king ascended the throne by an armed revolution. Usurping his brother, this new power was assisted by the finances and armed forces of the largest Brazillian-Portuguese slave dealer then active at Dahomey's main seaport, a certain Francesco Felix de Souza. This new king was named Ghezo, a preening, tall and physically imposing character that was soon to become one of the most feared and entrenched rulers in West Africa. Ghezo proceeded to appoint De Souza as his 'Chacha' at Ouidah, effectively the sole commercial consul from the king to all European traders at the coast. In doing so, Ghezo strengthened his position at the coast (from his inland capital at Abomey) in the all-important exchange of human bodies for European weaponry and merchandise at this critical moment of Oyo's weakness. Soon, access to Ouidah, the strategically important seaport was lost to Oyo in all but name. Within a few years, Dahomey under Ghezo was comfortable enough to throw off the centennial shackles of Oyo entirely, defeating the diminished armed force that was sent to subdue it.

From here on out, open season was declared on political and military affairs across the formerly peaceful Yoruba country. An internecine, scorched earth civil war commenced, with changing allegiances, alliances, and partnerships, resulting in devastating consequences for human life across the former empire. Simultaneously, an increased appetite for slaves had been triggered in the Atlantic world partly by the Louisiana Purchase of 1803, which doubled the size of the continental United States and made it the globally dominant exporter of slave-hungry cotton. There was also growing demand for Black bodies in the Portuguese and Spanish colonies, even after the abolition of the trade by Britain in its empire in 1807.

These factors combined to exacerbate the Yoruba civil wars, which became as much about regional political dominance as about the kidnapping of weaker humans for export. The strong market demand for human bodies was complemented by a newly efficient coastal port, which was being ably serviced by an energetic Chacha De Souza alongside his brother and sons, in partnership with Ghezo. In this way, the Yoruba wars became as much about political survival, as slave-raiding expeditions. Lagos, the nearby coastal city-state which only really emerged as an important port city for slaves in the late eighteenth century also capitalised on this boom, under the leadership of the successor sons to the late Oba, Ologun Kutere, the first truly modern leader of this slave-state. Ironically, this resurgence in slaving activity was occurring on the back of the major recent bipartisan victories for abolitionist politicians and activists in the United States and Britain.

These reformers, standing on the shoulders of the great pioneer abolitionists from the late eighteenth century, had succeeded in achieving a lawful prohibition on the international (though not domestic) trading of humans in both countries. In the case of the British, the prohibition extended across all its overseas dominions. To put some teeth on this landmark legislation, an anti-slavery naval patrol which came to be known as the British 'Preventative Squadron' was fitted out, funded and empowered to sail strategically around the Gulf of Guinea, with powers to randomly stop and board any vessel suspected of carrying illegal human cargo, and to seize such vessels in the name of the British government. Impounded vessels were towed to the British port of Freetown (founded in 1792) where a colony made up of freed African slaves had been established.

From Oshogun to the World

Into this disturbing milieu of insecurity and constant warfare was a young boy thrown in 1821. Ajayi was born in Oshogun, a Yoruba town under the nominal control of Oyo. But in those days of open war and destruction, all but the best armed and physically protected settlements were at the mercy of armed raiders from wherever. One day, Oshogun was destroyed and all its people were killed or taken captive, including Ajayi, his mother and two sisters.

Nearby and in the same year, the so-called Owu War also commenced, between armed combatants from among the Ife and the Ijebu (both Yoruba-speaking sub-groups, the former previously subject to Oyo) on the one hand, and the Owu-Egba people, a semi-independent group formerly subject to Oyo. These Egba people had lived for centuries in a large, relatively well-protected forest settlement, paying tribute to Oyo and governed partly by emissaries or ambassadors (called Ajele) from the capital[2]. Upon sensing the weakness of the Empire, and in the general commotion and lack of authority ensuing after the secession of Ilorin, the Egba had set themselves upon their Ajele and murdered them, declaring their independence. Thus, the Owu War followed, as the remaining rump of Oyo's armed forces, other nominal Oyo tributaries and their neighbours attempted to re-subjugate the Egba to some form of external control.

Meanwhile, the young Ajayi was held in chains and traded multiple times over that tumultuous year. He was eventually separated from his mother and sisters, ending up at a slave warehouse on the coast, from where he was forcibly embarked on a vessel intended for the Americas. Lucky for its occupants, this vessel was soon intercepted by a Royal Navy steamer, *The Myrmidon* under the command of a certain Captain Henry Leeke (later, Sir), part of the Preventative Squadron. Leeke's vessel deposited Ajayi and the several hundred other inmates at Freetown, where the 15-year-old boy was taken under the protection of British missionaries from the Church Missionary Society (CMS), the leading missionary organisation in Africa.

Founded in 1799 as the Society for Missions to Africa and the East, through the agency of Anglican clergy and laymen including great abolitionist politicians like William Wilberforce who served as its first Vice President, CMS had by 1822 become the leading church and educational organisation in Sierra Leone, a colonial British settlement on the west coast of Africa. With time, CMS will come to play an incredibly pivotal role in our story, and we will return in greater detail to this in a subsequent chapter. Suffice to say that young Ajayi (renamed Samuel Crowther in his new environment) began life afresh as a Christian convert under the supervision of British missionaries, who came to appreciate early on his intelligence, devotion, talent, linguistic and leadership ability. In light of the emerging population of young Black men like Crowther, in 1827, a new college for young Africans seeking Western education was established by the CMS at Freetown, called Fourah Bay College, and Samuel Ajayi Crowther was enrolled as its very first student.

Meanwhile, back in the Yoruba country, the Egba suffered a major defeat in the Owu War, leading to the devastating destruction of all their major towns in the forest, namely Ijemo, Igbore, Igbein and Ikereku; all eliminated by the scorched earth fighting policy of the combined Oyo and Ijebu armed forces. Large numbers of captives were sold as slaves at Badagry (a smaller port down the lagoon from Ouidah) and Lagos. The inland wars continued to create brisk business for coastal slave merchants and challenging patrol work for the Preventative Squadron vessels like that of Captain Leeke, with a resulting influx of Yoruba re-captured people at Freetown. In short order, these Yoruba people (then known as the Aku), who were forced migrants from the wars in their country became the dominant ethnic nationality in that metropolis.

The Birth of Abeokuta

At Ilorin, the tables had turned on Afonja, the rebel prince, who in 1824 was overthrown in a neat palace coup by his erstwhile accomplices. Once in control of Ilorin, Alimi, the Fulani Mallam, accepted the sovereignty of Caliph Mohammed Bello at Sokoto, making Ilorin the latest Emirate to emerge from Dan Fodio's revolution. This introduced a further violent dynamic into the Yoruba wars, with the political, military, and economic goals of the broader (and still expanding) Fulani-led Caliphate becoming relevant to the calculations of all the combatants and state actors in the country. By 1827, refugees from the fighting in various locations across Yorubaland (but particularly from among the Egba) began to establish themselves at a new, more secure location around and beneath large rocky outcrops near the eastern banks of the Ogun river. This was far south from their prior homes and away from their most dedicated enemies in Yorubaland proper, with whom they had been fighting since the Owu War broke out.

This new city, which came to be named Abeokuta ('Under the Rocks') was populated in waves by many different groups from across Yoruba country. The Egba moved under the leadership of a remarkable war chief named Sodeke, who had first risen to prominence in the moment of their independence declaration, as one of the ringleaders when the Ajele were murdered in the Egba forest. The tall and fair-complexioned Sodeke proved as astute a postbellum statesman as he had been a revolutionary war captain[3] consolidating his power and authority over the diverse groups as they arrived at Abeokuta, while being careful not to attempt or appear to dominate or subjugate them under any centralised authority. Under Sodeke's leadership, Abeokuta began to prosper, away from the immediate scenes of the Yoruba wars, and several more groups of wholesale refugees arrived to settle in the broader metropolis.

By the time the area was fully colonised by the Egba, more

than 150 distinct groupings of settlements could be identified at Abeokuta, broadly corresponding to the same townships that had existed before their relocation from the Egba forest and other places[4]. This motley organisation was now loosely grouped into four major divisions: the Agbeyin or Ake, Oke Ona and Agura, each with its paramount rulers, the Alake, the Osile and the Agura respectively. Making up the quartet were the Owu, under the leadership of their Olowu. Each of these major subdivisions, and many of the smaller township groups continued to maintain their independent governance structures as before they arrived at Abeokuta, comprised of their apex legislative council, the Ogboni, their war chiefs, the Ologun, and their chambers of commerce or trade regulators, the Parakoyi. Their only concession to unity under the liberal policy of Sodeke was to a central Ogboni council, which met periodically in the Ake section of the town where Sodeke hailed from. This original tradition of meeting at Ake arose from the gatherings having been held in the General's own house. This group of chiefs were the ultimate authorities in matters of defence, foreign policy, and taxes, but not for judicial matters in each settlement, in which the local Ogboni council house claimed jurisdiction. The leadership of the various central executive organs was distributed among citizens from the various quarters of Abeokuta.

Suffice to say, this unwieldy political agglomeration had been brought together by providence, the exigencies of war and the exceptional personal leadership of Balogun (General) Sodeke. The foundational leader of his country, Sodeke transmuted easily from wartime hero to civil leader of a newly independent country and began to forge the necessary political and economic alliances to ensure the survival of this new nation. The chief strategic concerns of Sodeke and his co-leaders at Abeokuta were physical and economic security. As concerning the former, they proceeded to construct a wall around the core settlement and to establish a functional defensive organisation, which was essentially a federal army with troops and officers contributed by leading war chiefs from each quarter. As for economic security, agriculture being the primary employment of the people, the question of trade routes to export cash crops or human bodies was the next most important, because the proceeds from those exports would fund the import of weapons and other items of foreign manufacture. Being connected to the great Lagoon of Lagos by the Ogun river, and within a few days' march from Badagry, these were the obvious export channels available to be considered by Sodeke and his chiefs. The natural desire of the Egba elite to open and control these trade routes would begin to set the scene for the future of Nigeria.

Lagos, City of Slaves

By 1830, the port city-state of Lagos had become even more deeply entrenched in the slave trade, which was its raison d'etre from early in its history. Several descendants of Ologun Kutere (the pioneer merchant-king who enhanced the trading infrastructure and relationships with major Portuguese traders at Lagos) had entered the business. Kutere's son and successor, Adele had continued in his father's footsteps, until he was usurped to the throne by an ambitious brother named Osinlokun, whose relatively short reign as head of the merchant kingdom ended in 1829. At this point in its history, the natural leader of Lagos was already a young, energetic, wealthy merchant-prince named Kosoko, who was also a descendant of Kutere. But political and personal disputes between this arrogant prince and the Lagos kingmakers precluded his nomination to the throne, and so he departed the city in protest when his cousin Idewu Ojulari was selected over his claims.

In exile, Kosoko continued to grow strong and wealthy, partnering with the largest Portuguese dealers at Badagry, Ouidah and Porto Novo to deal in the slaves being traded down to the coast from the hinterland. Before long, the prince of Lagos had become a major commission broker as well as a trader of human cargo for his personal account. The deposed Adele in exile, meanwhile, had become a surly and despondent old man, still living in Badagry and scheming to get back his throne. He launched several attacks on Lagos from his new base, and when the Lander brothers (British adventurers that we will soon meet) passed through Badagry in 1830, they met with a very depressed and anxious Adele ("Adooley" in their writing) who had just lost most of his armed forces and key generals in a failed attack on Lagos. The City of Slaves was deeply divided, with two powerful claimants in exile nearby.

The situation at Lagos was a political opportunity now presenting itself to the Egba elite. The chiefs at Abeokuta saw in Adele a man they could do business with, given his de facto control of Badagry, and his clear desire and birthright to resume control at Lagos. The exiled king also deployed his forces in support of the Egba at some point during the Owu War, which brought him closer into political and economic friendship with Abeokuta. In 1833, Adele formed even firmer ties to the Egba when he married an enterprising young woman member of the Abeokuta elite named Efunroye Tinubu. This enterprising woman trader would later become the largest indigenous slave dealer on the west African coast, rivalling even Kosoko in her reach and trade volumes. More famously known as Madam Tinubu, the young Efunroye would have been about 23 years old when she married Adele. He was not her first husband and would not be the last either. However, Tinubu's marriage to Adele placed her within the emerging Egba-Lagos political and commercial elite nexus, marking the beginning of her long, extensive, and impactful commercial and political career in pre-colonial Nigeria. Efunroye Tinubu's omnipresence in matters of state and trade up and down the coast and deep into the hinterland reflects itself in innumerable important references throughout our narrative, making her easily the most important woman figure in Victorian era Nigeria.

Within a year of this portentous strategic-romantic combination, political intrigue in the court at Lagos led to a palace coup. Idewu Ojulari was compelled to commit ritual suicide by the king's council (the only such recorded case of a king forced to exit the scene in such a manner at Lagos). This hardly used constitutional remedy for unpopular Yoruba rulers had also contributed to significant constitutional crises and instability at court in antebellum metropolitan Oyo. Several kings had been compelled to commit suicide by a powerful Bashorun (Supreme General), named Gaha. This fatal device appears to have been resurrected and employed again by clever old hands at court in Lagos to ease out Ojulari and introduce Adele, who was the preferred ruler of the politically astute old chiefs at Abeokuta. Again, Kosoko, the most energetic and enterprising man in the Lagos royal lineage, was passed over for the throne, being a much less pliant figure with independent wealth and a following of his own.

The Saro-Egba Alliance

Thus, with an ally now enthroned at the port of Lagos, began an early period of peace and prosperity at Abeokuta, continuing even after the death of their old friend, Adele in 1837. At his passing, Adele was succeeded by his son, Oluwole, Kosoko being again passed over by his relentless opponents at court and in Egba. Within a few years, an interesting thing began to happen at Abeokuta. Relative prosperity, access to a flourishing seaport and internal markets in the Yoruba hinterland, and the wise leadership of Sodeke, began to attract migrants even from the diaspora to this growing city-state. Ethnic Yoruba residents of Sierra Leone (freed captives and their offspring) began to seek opportunities to trade with the old country, by way of Abeokuta. In 1839, the first set of so-called 'Saro' returnee migrants (Saro being a corrupt pronunciation of Sierra Leone by the Yoruba) began to arrive at Lagos, Badagry and Abeokuta.

These bold returnees were from a newly Western-educated class that had managed to achieve a degree of success in trade and commerce at Freetown, and had begun to purchase old, abandoned slave vessels captured by the Preventative Squadron, to use in trading back and forth with Lagos and elsewhere. This trickle of returnees, typically with European names acquired abroad, gradually grew into a flood, with Abeokuta under Sodeke being their preferred settlement destination. At Oluwole's Lagos, they were robbed and treated very poorly, the city being focused purely on slave trading as opposed to any other economic opportunities.

One of the earliest Egba returnees was a young woman, a recaptured slave named Sarah Taiwo. Taiwo, who died in 1874, returned home to the Egba country via Badagry in the early years of the re-migration process, alongside her Saro husband who would die shortly after their arrival. One of Sarah Taiwo's most famous descendants (her great grand-daughter) would be a woman named Olufunmilayo Thomas (later, Ransome-Kuti the Lioness of Lisabi). The political successor to Madam Tinubu as woman leader of the Egba, the first modern, socialist, and feminist politician from Nigeria, founder and President of the highly influential Abeokuta Women's Union (AWU), Olufunmilayo would grow up to become the most important Egba political activist of the early twentieth century. Under her leadership, the AWU would spearhead women-oriented political and social reforms in pre-independence Nigeria, including her now legendary protest action leading to the deposition of an Egba king. This pioneering Nigerian feminist's even more famous offspring, Olufela, would become popular internationally simply as Fela, the pan-Africanist musical, political and cultural icon from Nigeria.

Returning to early nineteenth-century Abeokuta, the outcome of the tragic First Niger Expedition of 1841 (which Crowther had joined as a translator, and which our story will soon come to) had further increased appetite at Freetown for trade and commercial opportunities in the Nigerian hinterland[5]. As Abeokuta was the most advanced, liberal-minded, and best governed metropolitan location behind Lagos from where to do business, greater immigration of educated diaspora seeking economic opportunities followed. With this growth came greater ambitions among the Egba elite. And so to increase its control and volume of trade at the coast, Sodeke and his chiefs at Abeokuta in 1842 organised an armed effort to occupy the town of Ado in the immediate hinterland of Badagry.

Dahomey and the Egba-British Entente

The Ado attack brought the nascent Egba power for the first time within the sphere of influence maintained by Ghezo of Dahomey, which considered Ado its tributary and sought also to control the Badagry port more directly. Perhaps just as important, Ghezo's country was a military and primarily slave-trade driven state. Like Lagos, trading humans was the only basis for Dahomey's economic existence. Even Ghezo's mother had been sold into slavery in Brazil by her stepson, who was king before Ghezo[6]. From this perspective, Abeokuta presented a lucrative opportunity to Dahomey - given the nearly 100,000 humans residing within its walls by this time. Within two years, therefore, the Egba were back at war with a new enemy. This time, the Egba were not fighting aggressors from the old country but Ghezo's forces seeking bodies for the New World. The Egba triumphed in this first encounter, properly routing Ghezo's forces at Ado, and coming close to capturing the king himself on the battlefield. This would not be the last time these two neighbouring states would come to blows, and in several ways, from this point onwards, the conflict between them became the most important defining factor for the future country to be known as Nigeria.

The leading lights of the CMS were led by an important man named Henry Venn, who was appointed honorary secretary in 1841. Venn and his co-leaders at CMS had also noticed the progress of Abeokuta from far-away London. They had heard of and seen the increasing outflow of British educated migrants away from Sierra Leone into this emerging inland mecca. Public opinion about Africa in England was particularly aroused at this time, with the publication in 1842 by James Bandinel of *Some Account of the Trade in Slaves from Africa as Connected with Europe and America*. This was a popular book about the continuing and thriving slave trade on the continent, despite the nominal prohibition of more than 30 years prior. Bandinel was a civil servant with the British Foreign Office for some 50 years, and his book became a lightning rod for a new generation of anti-slavery humanitarians in Britain. It was universally accepted in these early years of the Victorian era that trade, commerce, industrial and missionary enterprise were the only viable means by which a conclusive end could be brought to the evil trade. Most importantly, it had become clear that even the best efforts of the Preventative Squadron attempting to police huge areas of open seas would never be sufficient to end the trade. It would be necessary for interested humanitarians to proceed inland and attempt to affect the economic situation within the continent itself, creating alternative and commercially viable export value chains that the energies of the domestic elite might be attracted towards.

This inland development agenda was no longer a particularly revolutionary idea by the mid-nineteenth century. Sierra Leone was converted into a British colony in 1808 with similar lofty goals, and the founders of the American Colonisation Society in 1816 had entertained broadly similar ambitions for Liberia. The big difference with Abeokuta in the 1840s was that the post-slave trade inland development agenda was being advocated by a forward-looking indigenous nation-state under the visionary Sodeke and his political elite, rather than philanthropic Europeans and Americans[7]. The CMS under Venn and other informed groups close to the scene saw an immediate once-in-a-lifetime opportunity for missionary enterprise and moved quickly to fulfil it. In 1842, Thomas Birch Freeman (a famed missionary at the Gold Coast, in present-day Ghana) arrived at Abeokuta, the first European to visit the city. He met with Sodeke and was generally impressed at the level of development and progress in the city, as well as the growing influence and prosperity of the Saro returnees within the polity.

At about the same time, a young British CMS officer named Henry Townsend was mandated by headquarters in London to visit

Abeokuta on a reconnaissance trip, before the establishment of a permanent mission there. Born in 1815, the 27-year-old Townsend had been trained professionally as a missionary at the CMS college in Islington, London and had already learnt a great deal of Yoruba language from the local Saro community upon arriving in Sierra Leone. A committed Afrophile - albeit in the nineteenth-century sense of the word - Townsend was not yet ordained a priest but had already set his sights on a career in the church as a West Africa pioneer. Townsend arrived in Abeokuta shortly after Freeman, and the two men spent Christmas together in Badagry on their respective journeys in opposite directions. Like Freeman, Townsend was also impressed at the level of development ongoing, and the general wisdom and foresight of the principal chief, Sodeke.

At a meeting with the Egba Ogboni council, Townsend was informed of the strong support and desire of the Abeokuta elite for an English missionary party to settle in the city, establish a school and a church, and support the growth of trade and intercourse with Britain. The wily Sodeke was well informed of the naval strength and distant wealth of Britain and foresaw the value to his emerging state of partnering with such an important foreign power. Surrounded as the Egba were by enemies on all sides, a rich foreign partner whose clerical emissaries also happened to be eager to enter into relations with them would have seemed like an opportunity too good to miss. Sodeke's designs on Badagry and Lagos were already evident, and regular export trade with the Atlantic world was the prize that would guarantee the independence of Abeokuta in his mind. Thus aligned, an agreement was struck, land allocated to the CMS, and Townsend invited to return at the earliest possible date with the rest of his missionary party to settle at Abeokuta. In preparations for establishing the Abeokuta mission, Townsend and Crowther (the first Black person to be so appointed) were both ordained CMS pastors in London during 1843, and they were mandated to proceed inland with necessary resources for the work ahead. Within a year, they had departed Freetown for Badagry, along with their wives, children, and a large party of Saro carpenters, labourers, catechists, interpreters, and other workers. They were also joined by another CMS clerical officer, a German missionary named Carl Anders 'Charles' Gollmer, also trained at Islington and recently arrived in Sierra Leone.

Sodeke's Death and Kosoko's Rebirth

Unfortunately for this enterprising party, their arrival at Badagry coincided with Sodeke's death in 1845, which created a temporary leadership vacuum at Abeokuta. The war with Dahomey at Ado had only been recently waged, and much of the area between Badagry and Abeokuta was troubled and considered unsafe for a large party of travelling foreigners.

Meanwhile, intrigue had continued at the royal court in Lagos and four years earlier (in 1841), Adele's successor Oba Oluwole was spectacularly killed in a gunpowder stockpile explosion within his palace. This brought a new king, Akitoye, to the throne. Akitoye was a much younger son of the great Ologun Kutere, and thus an uncle of Kosoko. Attempting to find profit from peace, Akitoye unwisely conceded to invite his wealthy nephew Kosoko back to Lagos from exile - against the advice of many chiefs, particularly the most strident anti-Kosoko party at court. The leading opponents even departed to Badagry in protest at Kosoko's return, a group that included Eletu Odibo, Kosoko's nemesis and an important kingmaker among the chiefs. Akitoye's concession to Kosoko was intended to defuse the rivalry between them, and improve his personal position and security, while consolidating trade and prosperity in the city. But Kosoko had lost patience, sensing weakness, and finally made his move.

Aided by friends from Dahomey and deploying his superior armed following, he overpowered his mortal opponents in the city and at Badagry, particularly the leading kingmaker Eletu Odibo, and in the process deposing the ineffectual Oba Akitoye.

The deposed king was allowed to escape up the Ogun river to Abeokuta, but the kingmaker's fate was not going to be as pleasant. Eletu Odibo's quarrel with Kosoko had been legendary, defining the politics of Lagos for years. It had even extended to Opo Olu, the wealthy sister of the ambitious prince (she was reputed to have owned 1400 slaves)[8]. Opo Olu had been accused by the powerful chief Eletu of witchcraft and banished from the kingdom. With the success of his daring coup d'etat, the new king's long-time nemesis was murdered in a gruesome manner: Eletu Odibo was doused in a flammable liquid, placed in a barrel filled with stones, set alight and dropped into the lagoon. Finally, Kosoko, the man with the strongest personality, healthiest treasury and closest ties to the European commercial elite was sat on the throne at Lagos. In alliance with his business partners, the slave-state Dahomey, and nominally in control of the other port town Badagry, the rebirth of Kosoko was complete.

The situation could not be more dire for Abeokuta in the isolated hinterland: surrounded by old country enemies, its most important founding father had just passed away, and its coastal rivals were now in a powerful alliance against it. The ensuing partisan rivalry for control of the complex leadership structure at Abeokuta was framed by this reality, along the lines of foreign and economic policy. This divided the local elite into two broad groups: a pro-Akitoye (and British) party, which wanted to continue the forward-thinking policy of Sodeke, welcome the missionaries to Egba and pursue closer direct ties to the English; versus the (perhaps more practical) pro-Kosoko and traditionalist party, made up mostly of slave dealers and the Ologun, township war generals. The CMS party would be stuck at Badagry for 17 long months while this power tussle played out (during which Mrs Gollmer passed on).

Eventually, it took the re-entry into the scene of an interesting foreign character for a compromise to be achieved which opened up the roads and allowed the CMS to eventually establish their mission at Abeokuta. This deus ex machina presented itself in the unlikely form of Domingo Martinez, the successor to De Souza as Chacha at Ouidah. Previously an employee of De Souza, the Brazilian native Martinez had arrived in the Bight of Benin around 1835 as a crew member on one of De Souza's vessels that was captured by the British and set ashore at Ouidah. In 1838 he moved to Lagos with a new employer named Dos Amigos and established connections there, as strong as those at his primary base on the coast of Dahomey. In 1840, Domingo Martinez took over the business of Dos Amigos on the death of the latter and quickly established himself as the leading slave dealer (with no exceptions) on the west coast of Africa, and in the event, the last of the great slave merchants of Africa and Brazil.

Having made a fortune in a few short years, this adventure capitalist returned briefly to Brazil, but was dissatisfied with the sedentary life there and soon returned to the slave action in West Africa. He came back to settle at Ouidah, arriving with a small fleet of laden vessels and a significant amount of treasure and ammunition. With so much profit at stake for Domingo Martinez, the continuing stand-off between rival parties in the area leading to violent conflict and blocked roads in the interior was unacceptable to this coastal middleman. So, he brokered a settlement between the chiefs at Abeokuta that allowed the roads to re-open, safe passage for the missionaries away from Badagry, and the moderate Ogboni chief titled Sagbua (also known as Okukenu) alongside another Balogun, Ogubonna, to emerge as the leading new voices replacing Sodeke in Egbaland. As part of the compromise, Akitoye was expelled from Abeokuta to Badagry, to the satisfaction of the traditionalists among the Egba.

By 1845, Domingo Martinez was reaping the rewards of his diplomatic interventions, credibly reported in intelligence reports submitted by the British Consul to have traded about 45,000 humans within a mere three-month period, across various outlets at Lagos, Ouidah and Porto Novo. At the latter location he also kept a prime cattle farm and lived in the highest style comparable to elites in Europe and the Americas. Martinez was wealthy and powerful enough to even attempt an armed putsch at Lagos in 1846, seeking to overthrow his commercial rival, Kosoko who was now beginning to trade directly with Brazil. For his part, Oba Kosoko was chartering vessels of his own and bypassing the other middlemen at the coast, much to their displeasure.

Abeokuta under CMS Protection

Meanwhile, in Abeokuta, the CMS party (under Crowther, Gollmer, Townsend and several leading Saro laymen like Andrew Wilhelm and John McCormack) had fully settled and was achieving great success converting indigenous natives to Christianity. These included famously a former slave handler and leading local enforcer named Desalu, who was baptised 'John Baptist' Desalu upon his unlikely transformation experience. Desalu was so reviled and feared among the locals that his appearance and acceptance at church by Crowther created quite a stir. John Baptist Desalu would go on to become famous for his epic life story (which covered multiple continents) and that we will return to shortly. By 1846, the Reverend Crowther's wife (a Saro known as Hassana at birth but renamed Susan) had established a primary school at the newly founded St John's Church at Igbein, in Abeokuta. This important crucible would provide early childhood Western education to an entire new generation of local Egba elite, including Olufunmilayo Ransome-Kuti, who was born in 1900 and attended the school in her early childhood.

Sodeke's vision of closer ties with Britain received its biggest boost when Townsend returned to England with a letter and gifts from the Egba chiefs (the correspondence was dictated by head chief Sagbua) for Queen Victoria. The letter was well received in CMS circles and at the royal court, and Townsend was able to return in 1848 with a response from the CMS high command as well as a gift of a steel mechanical corn grinding mill, courtesy of Prince Albert. More importantly, the name of Abeokuta had begun to resonate in British political circles as an ally that must be protected by any means necessary. Specifically, Sagbua had asked in his letter for British intervention to make the Ogun river safely navigable into the lagoon (the Ossa) such that 'the evil slave trade at Lagos' might be replaced with legitimate and mutually beneficial commerce. The historic letter from the Sagbua and chiefs of Abeokuta to the Queen is worth quoting at length.

The chiefs wrote:

'May God preserve the Queen in life forever; Sodeke, who communicated with the Queen before, is no more. We have seen your servants, the missionaries, whom you have sent to us in this country. What they have done is agreeable to us. They have built a house of God. They have taught the people the Word of God, and our children beside. We begin to understand them. There is a matter of great importance that troubles us: what must we do that it must be removed away?

We do not understand the doings of the people of Lagos, and other people on the coast. They are not pleased that you should deliver our country people from slavery. They wish that the road may be closed, that we may never have any intercourse with you. What shall we do that the road may be opened, that we may navigate the River Ossa to the River Ogun? The laws that you have in your country we wish to follow in the track of the same - the slave trade, that it may be abolished.

We wish it to be so. The Lagos people will not permit; they are supporting the slave traders. We wish for lawful traders to trade with us. We want, also, those who will teach our children mechanical arts, agriculture, and how things are prepared, as tobacco, rum, and sugar. If such a teacher should come to us, do not permit it to be known, because the Lagos people, and other people on the coast, are not pleased at the friendship you are showing to us. We thank the Queen of England for the good she had done in delivering our people from slavery. Respecting the road, that it should not be closed, there remains much to speak with each other.'

The missionary efforts of the CMS *required* a different West

African narrative from the grim version offered in Bandinel's then popular book. Their work needed a counter-narrative like that which Abeokuta offered, to gain traction in Britain. At the same moment, selected members of the Abeokuta elite (local chiefs and Saro migrants) in pursuing their own foreign and economic policy, were more than happy to oblige this influential British body. The political weight of the CMS in Britain around this time was best displayed by the defeat in 1849 of a motion in Parliament to remove the Preventative Squadron from the coast of West Africa, because it was uneconomic and ineffective. It took the combined active effort of CMS grandees like Henry Venn, in deploying active mass propaganda against the motion, to convince then Foreign Secretary, Henry John Temple (better known as Lord Palmerston) to employ the whip and enforce a party line defeat of the vote.

By 1850 therefore, Abeokuta was fully under CMS protection, with Townsend as de facto foreign affairs officer, Venn as London-based mentor and cheerleader, and Samuel Ajayi Crowther as the local emblem. Crowther was invited by Venn to tour London and Cambridge in 1851, during the same period as the famous Great Exhibition of British Industrial Technology held at the Crystal Palace in Hyde Park. Crowther was so highly regarded that he gained direct audiences with Palmerston, Lord Baring (at the Admiralty), and Prince Albert, the queen's consort - with whom he held a more than 30-minute long interview. Ultimately, Reverend Samuel Ajayi Crowther would also meet with Queen Victoria herself, who quietly joined the Prince's interview midway. The remarkable life of this former slave boy captured at Oshogun turned Saro Anglican pastor, improbable enough as it was already, was about to get even more interesting.

Knocked Down by All Means

On the strength of Sodeke's vision for Egba survival, and the CMS party's efficient political propaganda in favour of Abeokuta, the future of Nigeria was increasingly being shaped in the direction of British influence. Remarkably, Prince Albert commented to Crowther in the presence of the Queen, that 'Lagos ought to be knocked down by all means,' powerful words that Crowther noted down. With that royal interview, Oba Kosoko's fate had been sealed thousands of miles away, even if he was blissfully yet unaware of it. The first step in the reduction of Lagos was a renewed intensive blockade by the Preventative Squadron, alongside an aggressive implementation of the Aberdeen Act of 1845, which gave the Royal Navy authority to stop and search any Brazilian ship suspected of carrying slaves on the high seas, and to arrest slave traders caught on these ships.

The Act stipulated that arrested slave traders could be tried in British courts. The law had been specifically designed to suppress the Brazilian slave trade, and to make effective Brazilian laws and international treaties to end the Atlantic slave trade, which that country had signed since the 1820s, but never enforced. Palmerston later said that the achievement which he looked back on with the 'purest and greatest pleasure' was forcing the Brazilians to give up the slave trade[9]. In 1851, British warships began entering Brazilian territorial waters and even its harbours to attack slave vessels. These combined actions served to dislocate the slave markets at the coast of West Africa, with Domingo Martinez entirely halting purchases of human cargo, and Kosoko even beginning to welcome palm oil traders at Lagos for the first time. A severe economic recession followed, with a near-total collapse in credit supply to internal markets, credit being broadly based on the so-called 'Trust System' which entailed advancement of goods to middlemen at the coast for an extended period, while slaves or other commodities were collected by wholesalers in the interior. Similarly, the sudden dramatic increase in the unwanted supply of slaves - the MP, William Hutt (later, Sir) told Parliament the year before that there were reports of 8,000 slaves in Brazil with no buyers and some of them had been used to pay freight[10] - created essentially a major devaluation in the effective currency of exchange that was humans in bondage.

Amazons at the Egba Gate

Meanwhile, war and blood were continuing to spread across the country. On 1 March 1851, Dahomey armed forces led by several battalions of the all-female Agoji or Mino ('Our Mothers') regiment finally set out for the destruction of Abeokuta. These women were the ones about whom the celebrated American former slave, Cudjo Lewis, said 'No man can be strong like the women soldiers from Dahomey'[11]. By the mid-nineteenth century, the ferocious Mino were already famous for their awesome prowess in warfighting, as well as their frightful ruthlessness. According to one contemporary observer: 'One of their favourite amusements was to see which of them could first get through a high circle of thorns and kill a helpless prisoner tied to a stake. Though their limbs were shockingly torn by the spikes, they thought it was an excellent sport.'[12] It was also said of the Mino that when one of them sneeringly said to another: 'You are nothing but a man,' only the death of one or the other could settle such a heavy insult.

The Egba expedition led by these fierce feminists had been at least a year in planning, and Ghezo had made no secret of his desire to reduce Abeokuta in revenge for his earlier defeat at Ado, and to secure further supplies of slaves. During Dahomey's spectacular annual royal celebration of tributes in 1850, the first British Consul for the Bight of Biafra, John Beecroft was invited to visit Ghezo's capital, Abomey for six weeks, alongside a naval officer of the Preventative Squadron, Commander Frederick Forbes. Ambitiously hoping to find a diplomatic approach to end trading in slaves by Ghezo, it was on this trip that the young slave girl who would come to be known as Sarah Forbes Bonnetta (partly raised as an English lady in the care of Queen Victoria), was handed to the British visitors as a gift to their sovereign. The anti-slavery diplomatic outreach was derided and barely even acknowledged. Firstly, King Ghezo was at the height of his powers, testified to by his recent military victories over nearby Atapahm, and Okeadan (in present-day Togo and Nigeria respectively) and also by this extensive, lavish, elaborate and morbidly violent 1850 bacchanal. Secondly, slaving and slavery were fundamentally the sources of Ghezo's immense military and political powers over such a large country; and there was no chance of him willingly giving this up. At the Abomey celebrations, Beecroft had observed the following dramatic scene during the ceremonial parade of Ghezo's forces:

Standing before Ghezo, one Agoji chief cried out on behalf of the terrible sisterhood: 'As the blacksmith takes an iron bar and by fire changes its fashion, so we have changed our nature. We are no longer women, we are men!' The Mino began clamouring to be sent forth on an errand of conquest, and one word was upon their lips. Louder and louder that cry arose as one division after another pressed to the throne, a fierce, vengeful cry, one word, and that word was 'Abeokuta!'. With countenances becoming more and more hard and cruel every moment, the women waved their weapons and bowed before their king. 'We have conquered the people of Mahi,' they cried. 'Now give us Abeokuta! Have we not destroyed Attahpahm? Let us go to Abeokuta! We will conquer or die! If we do not conquer, our heads are at your disposal.' 'As sure as Abeokuta now stands, we will destroy it!' cried another officer as she knelt before the royal stool. 'Give us Abeokuta!' yelled her division in chorus. And as the standard bearers came forward with their skull-decorated ensigns, yet another regiment saluted and there came an even more sinister note; one officer reminded the king that, two years before, the Abeokutans had defeated an Amazon regiment; and at that reference, a loud cry for vengeance rent the air. And again, there was the cry: 'Give us Abeokuta'[13]!

Upon Ghezo being informed by his transfixed European visitors that British subjects now resided in Abeokuta and that they should be left alone, Ghezo retorted that the White men should remove themselves ahead of his coming. On his return to Lagos, Beecroft passed this intelligence onto willing ears at Abeokuta (the city walls were hurriedly reinforced in response), and Commander Forbes sent arms and ammunition in support of the imminent defensive effort. When about 16,000 Dahomey troops (including 6,000 warriors of the fearsome sisterhood) arrived at the banks of the Ogun river in March, they camped near a village called Ishaga, the chief (Baale) of which engaged in some clever double-dealing aimed at keeping his people alive and free. He pledged support to the Dahomeans, but also secretly sent intelligence to the Egba as to their plan of attack. For his coup de grâce, the heroic Baale of Ishaga deliberately misinformed the attackers as to the least secure positions in the city walls, and the shallowest point to ford the river. This combination of subterfuge and deceit very likely saved the Egba, who were thus better equipped to fight. With recent British supplies of arms and ammunition, tactical and moral support from Townsend and Crowther respectively who were both present during the fighting, the Egba managed a crushing victory and mounted a counterattack to protect Ishaga. Hundreds of Mino were killed and captured. Crowther alone counted 80 dead just outside the walls, out of an estimated 3,000 Dahomeans slain and 1,000 captured. But even defeat and capture failed to subdue these fierce Amazons, as two of them managed to murder the servants who tried to feed them while in captivity.

On the other side, among the Egba captured in the fighting was the former slaver John Baptist Desalu, who at the time was thought dead, but was soon after discovered by Crowther to be a captive at Abomey. The intervention of Gollmer with Madam Tinubu (who maintained connections at Ghezo's court) led to the temporary release of Desalu from Abomey, but he was soon recaptured at Ouidah while waiting for the agreed transport to return him to Badagry. It was only by a miraculous twist of fate that Townsend many years later discovered at Plymouth, while serving as a translator for some freed Cuban slaves, that John Baptist

Desalu was still alive and working in Havana, having secured his freedom from slavery. Crowther wrote to the British Consul in that city, offering the full costs of transporting this resilient survivor back to Lagos, from where he returned to his long-suffering wife, Martha (also a convert), and family at Abeokuta. Poor Martha had been kicked out of the family compound by his relatives after his disappearance. It was from John Baptist Desalu that the CMS was able to obtain one of the few eye-witness descriptions of the middle passage across the Atlantic aboard slave ships (Olaudah Equiano's was another), and his remarkable life story became much retold in church circles. It would not be appropriate to conclude Desalu's head spinning story without adding the coda that many years after his return from Cuba, he was excommunicated from the church for taking a second wife at Abeokuta.

The Lagos Civil War

But back to our main story: similar to Ghezo, Kosoko was spoiling for war at Lagos. Now aware that a noose was being tightened around his neck, he pre-emptively attacked Badagry, the base of his rival for the throne, Akitoye. When fighting between armed supporters of both pretenders to the throne broke out, reinforcements were sent down river by the Egba to aid the former Oba, who was now fully conniving with the British-Egba alliance to re-emerge at Lagos. Amidst the fighting, the once and future king Akitoye met aboard a gunboat with Beecroft and agreed a treaty to end the slave trade in Lagos, once he was able to resume his rule. Kosoko, for his part, eschewed any diplomacy, snidely informing Beecroft (when he offered protectorate status at a palava, or summit, to discuss peaceful terms) that his suzerain was Benin, and he could not sign any agreements without the approval of that king. This was of course disingenuous in the extreme as in reality, Lagos had by this time long operated independently of any Benin supervision, despite the clear cultural and historical linkages. Kosoko was simply not prepared to countenance giving up the kingdom that he spent his life working for, nor did he see what right any European had to force him out of the bonafide trade in less fortunate humans that his grandfathers before him had founded the kingdom upon.

Talks having failed as expected, under the political command of Beecroft, the British mounted an initial attack on Lagos. Their first foray was successfully repulsed by the Lagosians, when a British gunboat ran aground in the lagoon, allowing Kosoko's sharpshooters to inflict several casualties on the British side. Among the injured British seamen was one interesting individual named Lieutenant James Pinson Labulo Davies, a Saro naval seaman trained in Britain under a scholarship program founded by Henry Venn. The future husband of a grown Sarah Bonetta Forbes, he was also an important pioneering cocoa farmer in Nigeria. We will return to the story of their remarkable lives soon.

Meanwhile, on New Year's Day 1852, a second attack was attempted, during which a rocket was (perhaps inadvertently, but nonetheless successfully) fired into the arms depot at Kosoko's palace, setting the building and much of the city alight. In a few hours, the battle was over, and Lagos had been 'knocked down,' to frame it in the immortal words of Prince Albert to Samuel Ajayi Crowther. Kosoko escaped back into exile again at Badagry, while Akitoye marked his signature on the treaty accepting British 'protection' over his regained kingdom. Upon his death, Akitoye would be succeeded by his son, Dosunmu, also selected by the British to rule under the same terms as his foreign-installed father.

By sunset on New Year's Day, 1852 the deed was done; the upstart state, Abeokuta, against existential threats to its prosperity, had secured the frontispiece property of Sodeke's expansive vision. In the process, Britain had assumed nominal responsibility for a strip of land on the coast of a giant country, about which it knew infinitesimally little and for which it had even less of an inclination or ability to rule in any shape or form. The CMS party in Britain was elated. Their precious inland mecca, the beam of *Sunrise within the Tropics* (the title of a popular book on Abeokuta at the time) was safe, at least for now. The mighty Ghezo licked his wounds at Abomey, biding his time until he would attack again - there being no other path that he recognised outside of the trade in humans. The valiant buffer town of Ishaga would be destroyed in a subsequent Dahomean expedition, but the walls of Abeokuta would never be successfully breached by Ghezo and his ruthless Mino.

Domingo Martinez may not yet have seen the handwriting on the wall, but 1851 was the peak of his powers, as he was neither equipped nor inclined to compete either with the new breed of palm oil and produce traders now on the ascendancy at the coast, or the recalcitrant international black market slave dealers, who would increasingly aim to deal directly (and clandestinely), rather than through local middlemen that could be easily arrested. He died at home in West Africa early in 1864, significantly diminished in influence and wealth after the Brazilian government, now very much opposed to the slave trade, refused his request to retire to Bahia[14].

In the meantime, the relationship between Brazil and Lagos was also changing. Starting with the so-called 'Revolta dos Males' or Male Revolt of Muslim Afro-Brazillians at a city in Brazil called Salvador da Bahia during Ramadan of 1835, a reverse migration of these former slaves to West Africa had begun. Like the Saro before them, the trickle of these Afro-Brazillian returnees who later came to be known as the Aguda (for the Popo Aguda area of Lagos where they settled) quickly grew into a flood. The Aguda came back with money, Western education, tradecraft, industrial expertise, foreign language skills and international connections, which they quickly deployed into building a prosperous community based in their historically important Brazilian Quarter of downtown Lagos Island. This area is still a significant architectural highlight of the city's landscape, with so many landmark buildings evocative of the nineteenth-century Brazilian style of construction. Among the Aguda were both Muslims and Catholics, many of whom would go on to form a core constituency among the educated and wealthy commercial and political elite of colonial Lagos as well as the future country, Nigeria. A famous example of these Aguda returnees was a man named Joao Esan Da Rocha. Joao became a wealthy local trader and was the father of Candido Da Rocha, who was born in 1860 on the eve of Lagos' annexation and would become one of the most prominent Lagosians of his generation. The Afro-Brazillian returnees would also leave their mark on the architectural landscape at Abeokuta, where many of them settled. One such legacy is the Central Mosque at *Kobiti,* in Abeokuta, which is still standing and was built by Afro-Brazilians in 1925 using their signature Baroque style, on the same plot of land originally provided by Balogun Sodeke in the 1830s, for one of the earliest mosques ever built in the city.

Capitalists and Educationists

For their part, two adaptive entrepreneurs were also quick to adjust to the new realities. By as early as 1854, the now 44-year-old Efunroye Tinubu (lately strategic romantic partner of Oba Adele) was putting her strong influence and personality to work at the court of the British puppet, Dosunmu - manoeuvring herself into becoming the leading middle-man between coastal slave dealers and Egba suppliers still engaged in the contraband trade. A few years later, another impressive woman entrepreneur was also making a different set of moves. In her case, this 40-year-old already successful Abeokuta trader emigrated from her home to settle at a new Yoruba settlement called Ibadan (a city we will learn more about later in our narrative).

Like other emigrants and new arrivals in the Yoruba country around this time, Efunsetan Aniwura - a hardy Egba survivor whose father was born in the old country - was gambling on the ascendancy of this new settlement in the geopolitical affairs of the hinterland. It was a gamble that would pay off in spades, with this remarkable woman going on to become probably the wealthiest person in her country. In addition to other commodities, Efunsetan Aniwura was (of course) also a major dealer in human bodies, with an expansive business that boasted branches and connections in every major market in the country. Her wholesale relocation from British-allied Egba to Ibadan around 1860 must therefore be viewed in the context of the emerging power of this latter city in the business of slave dealing (through alternative export routes), giving the changing dynamics of the Egba-Lagos export corridor. We will encounter Aniwura again later in our story, as her rise to wealth and power was inextricably linked to the regional politics of her country.

Also in 1854, the former slave-boy Samuel Crowther embarked on a diametrically opposite mission to Madam Tinubu, joining yet another historic mission led by Macgregor Laird (a Liverpool businessman whom we will come to meet) up the Niger and Benue rivers, seeking to expand non-slave trade and Western education in the interior of the country[15]. Another European entrepreneur (a missionary not a capitalist) would also proceed into the inner country behind Abeokuta in 1851. His name was David Hinderer, a German Anglophile (after Gollmer, the second of several we will encounter in our story) who was ordained by the CMS in 1847 when he was 28 years old. Hinderer followed Freeman, Townsend, Crowther and Gollmer as one of the pioneers of Christian missionary enterprise in the Nigerian hinterland when he made the brave journey north-east from Abeokuta to settle at Ibadan, even before the reduction of Lagos by the British. Along with his wife Anna, who followed him soon after, David Hinderer was responsible for expanding Western education and literacy into the broader Yoruba country beyond Abeokuta and Lagos.

The Hinderers' remarkable joint legacy of educational and political enlightenment is most notably represented in the future careers of four prominent Saro brothers: Nathaniel, Henry, Samuel and Obadiah Johnson. The father of these boys, Henry (Senior) was one of Hinderer's earliest recruits from Sierra Leone to serve at Ibadan; and the Johnson brothers grew up under the tutelage of David and Anna Hinderer. As we will see, one of these brothers would utilise his critical position in this time of great turmoil, and his unique privilege of early dual literacy in both English and Yoruba to become an advocate for peace, as well as the foremost and most important chronicler of the latter people's written history (in the English language). As we will also see, the youngest Johnson brother (born 1849) would become one of the two pioneer Western-educated medical doctors in the country, while the two older brothers would become important Anglican pastors across the Yoruba country.

Dan Fodio's jihad accelerated the independence and secession of the mighty Ilorin (heralding the collapse of Oyo), triggering internecine warfare among the Yoruba with the unintended consequence of seeding a liberal traditional elite at Abeokuta and a diaspora community at Sierra Leone. Out of this chaos emerged the intrepid Egba nation, requiring an alliance with the British for her very survival among such determined enemies. None of the actors and combatants in this saga could imagine what was to come, and none of them got out of it the outcomes they would have desired. For the ordinary person in the Yoruba country - the simple individual unconnected to royalty, the merchant elite or traditional institutions - much had already begun to change, however imperceptibly. Alliances had shifted, White men now ruled Lagos, Abeokuta was an enclave of peace and security (away from the Yoruba wars, which continued), and the likelihood of being kidnapped and sold far away into foreign slavery had reduced, even if the institution of domestic slavery remained firmly in place.

We will return to Abeokuta shortly, to better understand the aftermath of these momentous events, and how the dynamic interactions between British government officials (locally and at home in London), the missionaries and the local elite changed dramatically once the political and economic objectives shifted from being simply about humanitarian goals to the cold, hard reality of regional economic and political hegemony.

1. Law R. *The Oyo Empire, C.1600-c.1836: A West African Imperialism in the Era of the Atlantic Slave Trade.* Clarendon Press; 1977.

2. Biobaku SO. *The Egba and Their Neighbours, 1842-1872.* Clarendon Press; 1957.

3. Harunah HB. SODEKE: Hero and Statesman of the Egba. *Journal of the Historical Society of Nigeria.* 1983 1983;12(1/2):109-131.

4. Biobaku SO. *The Egba and Their Neighbours, 1842-1872.* Clarendon Press; 1957.

5. Walker FD. *The Romance of the Black River: The Story of the C.M.S. Nigeria Mission.* Church Missionary Society; 1938.

6. Thomas H. *The Slave Trade.* Hachette UK; 2015.

7. Ade Ajayi JF. *Christian Missions in Nigeria, 1841-1891; The Making of a New Elite.* Longmans; 1965.

8. Mann K. *Slavery and the Birth of an African City: Lagos, 1760--1900.* Indiana University Press; 2007.

9. Bulwer HL. *The Life of Henry John Temple, Viscount Palmerston: With Selections from His Speeches and Correspondence.* Adegi Graphics LLC; 1871.

10. Hansard - Slave Trade. 1850/3/19 1850.

11. Hurston ZN. *Barracoon: The Story of the Last "Black Cargo".* HarperCollins; 2018.

12. Stone RH, Stone RH. *In Africa's Forest and Jungle: Six Years Among the Yorubas.* University of Alabama Press; 2010.

13. Forbes FE. *Dahomey and the Dahomans: Being the Journals of Two Missions to the King of Dahomey, and Residence at His Capital, in the Years 1849 and 1850.* Longman; 1851.

14. Ross DA. The Career of Domingo Martinez in the Bight of Benin 1833–64. *J Afr Hist.* 1965 1965;6(1):79-90.

15. Crowther S, Taylor JC. *The Gospel on the Banks of the Niger: Journals and Notices of the Native Missionaries Accompanying the Niger Expedition of 1857-1859.* Cambridge University Press; 2010.

CHAPTER 5

Mad Men and Missionaries

Mad Man on the River

A curious apparition manifested upon a large lake on the Niger sometime in 1805. It was late in the year and the annual Harmattan dust storms had dried up the air. The river would have shrunk in many parts, flooded banks receding to reveal marshland and swamp in various sections. The river's characteristic mobile islands, sandbanks and rocky outcrops would be observable in the middle of its path, a treacherous time for any long-distance travel on this massive waterway. Two large canoes had been hitched together to form a large (40-feet long and six-feet wide) schooner of some sorts, within which sat a most unusual party, armed to the teeth. The group was led by a tall, skinny, bearded, and scraggly looking mad White captain, but also included his very Black but foreign lieutenants. This astounding spectre would have been alarming to the local armed forces from Bussa that were at the shore waiting for them, if they were not already forewarned and prepared.

The news had come through initially as a rumour and then later as confirmed intelligence from overland scouts and travellers. There was a mad White man on the river, armed with more than a dozen muskets, and waging war on any force that would dare to stop him from proceeding. This was ridiculous information just by itself. Everyone knew that a party did not simply embark on a long-distance trip down the river without elaborate preparations, approval in advance, tolls paid, preferably in the company of a large group, and with clear objectives known to parties at its intended destination (typically, attending a market). But it was true, there was a mad White man - six-foot-tall - on the river, and he was intending to pass by Bussa, just as he had done dozens of settlements and camps all along the banks. What the Bussans might not have been aware of was the following incredible datapoint: this approaching party had already travelled nearly two thousand kilometres on the river before arriving here. Their now decimated group had embarked at *Segou* (in present-day Mali) as a much larger party several months before, and they were aiming to fight their way through to the terminal point of this river, wherever that might be, come hell or high water.

That mad White man was Mungo Park, the Scottish son of a farmer. A medical doctor turned African explorer; Park had received a commission as a Captain in the Royal Navy to undertake this disruptive journey. The stated objective of Park's mission (which the Bussans neither knew of nor would have cared much for) was to follow the 'River of Rivers' wherever it led. This was not Captain Park's first trip to West Africa. Surviving his original visit, hazardous and life-threatening as it had been, must have convinced him that this hare-brained idea was worth pursuing again. On his first visit to West Africa nearly ten years before his inauspicious arrival at Bussa, the then 24-year-old Mungo Park had escaped death by the skin of his teeth. More than a thousand kilometres deep into the interior (from the Gambia River where he had commenced his journey), the White man had been summarily arrested and kept imprisoned for nearly four months (left alive only by the kindness shown him by the Queen of his Moorish captors, named Fatima). Escaping, he managed to find the Niger at Segou and began a tortuous journey northward, attempting the foolhardy task of navigating this immense water body and the vast land areas which it drains.

It was a remarkable thing that he did not die there and then and be lost forever to history. Park fell ill and lived in the area for seven months, saved only by the generosity and care of native women who found him a pitiful curiosity, before returning to the coast and on to Scotland. However, his bestselling account of this epic adventure (titled *Travels in the Interior of Africa*) made him into something of a celebrity in British scientific and geographical circles because it was the first African travel book written by a European in the English language.

From Pall Mall to the Heart of Africa

Park had been sent out the first time not by the British government, but by the 'Association for Promoting the Discovery of the Inland Parts of that Quarter of the World' (more commonly known at the time as the African Association). Originating from a Saturday eating club which met at St. Albans Tavern in the Pall Mall area of London, this impressively named collective had been founded in early June 1788, as an exclusive club dedicated to the exploration of Africa by a dozen fancy denizens of London, led by a certain Sir (also Baronet) Joseph Banks. Sir Joseph Banks was as blue-blooded a British aristocrat as they come, having attended both Harrow *and* Eton before dropping out of Oxford, where he had been training as a Botanist.

Banks had become famous for exploring virgin Canada and participating in Captain Cook's first voyage into the New World. Cook was the famous explorer who best captured the spirit of this 'Age of Discovery' with his exploration of the islands of the Pacific Ocean. Entitled men like Sir Joseph - who was also part of a 'Literary Club' started by Samuel Johnson along with other luminaries like Charles James Fox and Edmund Burke[1] - decided in the late eighteenth-century that too little was known about Africa, that this was unacceptable, and that it was their business to change things. Hence the formation of the Africa Association. These hobbyists knew, as did most educated people since the time of Herodotus, that several great rivers defined the unknown mass of land known as Africa. They also 'knew' that one of these - called the Niger - was speculated to rise northwards on the west coast, drain thousands of kilometres of land, passing by an ancient city called Timbuktu, and empty itself into another great river, the Congo, right in the middle of the continent. This was as much that these curious aristocrats knew, and the stated objective of their ambitious scientific association was to put together a funding and governance framework for the exploration work that would expand the unacceptably flimsy knowledge base.

For exploring the interior using the natural means of transportation that was the Niger, one logical starting point for British adventurers in the 1790s was the west African coastal settlement of Senegambia, which was well known (the Gambia River having been fairly well navigated already). As it turned out, the Africa Association was propositioned for sponsorship in 1794 by this Scottish doctor with an apparent death wish. Park was not the first man sent on an exploratory journey into Africa by the Association. Interest free loans totalling £453 (about £65,000 in present-day money) had already been made to three men named Lucas, Ledyard and Houghton for similar expeditions prior to the Scotsman. All three of his predecessors had died in their attempts to penetrate the interior of Africa from different directions. With the support of Sir Joseph (the young doctor was also a botany enthusiast and a protege of the older man), Park was commissioned as the fourth African Association sponsored man to undertake the journey, and he departed for Gambia in May 1795.

Following his first trip and the celebrity arising from his writings (he hid his notes in his hat), Park and the Africa Association were able to secure the support of the British government for the next mission. Remarkably, Sir Joseph had argued for official support in a speech at a public conference of the Association in 1799, which might credibly count as the first public call for British imperialism in Africa. For this second, much better armed and provisioned expedition, a few dozen European and African expeditioners were engaged. This brash party under the command of Park was determined to sweep through every obstacle before them onto and down the river. They were sadly mistaken. By the time they embarked on the Niger itself after a horrific march through the country, most of the Europeans were sick or dead. Apart from illness and general travel fatigue, the party was meeting opposition from native communities along its route. Mungo Park had made the mistake of announcing early in the journey (to the chief at Segou where he re-embarked on the river) that he intended to follow the Niger '...to the place where it mixes with the salt water, and if I find no rocks or danger in the way, the white man's small vessels will come up to trade....'[2] Telegraphing his intentions in this manner had the dual effect of spooking all the middlemen traders and merchants who now learnt via the rumour mill of this ambitious gambit to displace them, and also informing hostile communities (like the Bussans) of his direction of travel.

Ambush at the Bussa Rapids

By the time this rude party reached Bussa, Park appears to have been the sole remaining White man alive (some accounts indicate there was at least one other), supported by the same Africans who had accompanied him from the start, also as foreign and new to the area as he was. Their party had been shooting its way through the river, avoiding the shore, stopping only on sandbanks and islands within the waterways itself and firing upon any groups that attempted to halt their progress. This alarming news had spread fast through the countryside, and the Bussans were aware of what was coming. Thus prepared, they carefully picked the right position on the river to mount their defence of this unknown threat. Bussa, which was the port of the Borgu Empire, sits on the shore of the largest lake in the path of the river - which was convenient for easy navigation at most times of the year. But for those who knew something about it, this lake also contained upon it some rocky and narrow rapids, because of the uneven sub-surface.

This was the point at which the Bussans elected to wait for the mad White man on the river. The various accounts of Park's demise at this location are based on second-hand and possibly distorted reports (a local named Ahmadi Fatouma was a primary source). This was so because the chiefs of Borgu who sanctioned the attack were careful not to speak of it much to subsequent European visitors. What we *do* know - consistent across both African and European sources - is that at the Bussa rapids, the ramshackle *Joliba* (Park had named his hardy schooner after one of the river's names) came aground on rocky outcrops and could not be shaken free. This was exactly as the Bussans would have expected with their superior knowledge of the waterway. Upon the shore nearby were the armed natives, out of reach of gunfire, but dead-ready with spears, swords, bows and arrows. There were not many options now open to the desperate travellers: it was either death by drowning or surrender to capture. The mad White man chose to die in the river and dived in, perishing in the waterfall.

The specific details of Captain Park's demise would not become widely known outside of the immediate area for many years. Until the Lander brothers reached the exact spot in 1830, various theories remained popular. Park's son attempted a 'rescue' in 1827 but died of fever before he had travelled much inland from the coast. Ahmadi Fatouma's account had suggested that before the fatal rendezvous at the rapids, Park had stopped at *Yauri* to visit with the king of that town, but had offered unsatisfactory gifts and departed hurriedly, displeasing the king. This is quite unlikely given what we know of Park's militant approach on the river since Segou, and of the distance between Yauri and the Bussa rapids. In relation to the latter point, the Bussa troops must have been deployed well in advance of the *Joliba* arriving in the area. Whatever the case, we know that an armed force was dispatched to stop him at the Bussa rapids and that for decades after his demise, European visitors to the area met with experienced natives who still spoke with great distaste of the mad man that appeared on the river.

With the disappearance of the celebrated Park, inland African exploration (particularly via the Niger route) became unpopular and was not attempted again for 25 years. During that time, the African Association was absorbed into the Royal Geographical

Society, in 1831. In the intervening period, Dan Fodio's jihad began to radically transform the interior areas of present-day Nigeria drained by the river. As we have already seen, this seminal event triggered violent conflict across the country on both sides of the upper river, as well as into the vast areas north of the Benue, all the way down to Abeokuta near the coast. In 1822 (nearly two decades after Park disappeared), another young naval surgeon (this time an actual soldier who had served in the Napoleonic Wars) would successfully move the needle a little further in terms of European knowledge about the West and Central African interior.

Expeditioners from the Mediterranean

Early in 1822, a British naval surgeon named Hugh Clapperton departed Tripoli with another of his countrymen named Walter Oudney. Oudney had just been appointed by the Colonial Office as consul to Bornu, a place that no European had yet visited. These expeditioners followed the centuries-old caravan route from the Mediterranean coast (more than 2,000 kilometres as the crow flies) to the great inland sea, Lake Chad. They were joined by another military explorer, a Napoleonic War veteran and brash adventurer named Dixon Denham. A commissioned Major, Denham had attended Sandhurst and considered himself the cream of the crop, and a cut above his lowly co-travellers. The various accounts and letters of these men, which include a lot of personal drama and salacious rumour mongering between themselves but also colourful narratives of local conditions and characters, provide us with the clearest picture (in the English language) of the state of affairs above the Niger and Benue in the early nineteenth century.

Thanks to other contemporary sources, indigenous writings and oral evidence, a more complete picture has since been painted, the main highlights of which are that revolution was in the air, and everywhere there was fighting, slave-raiding and war. Oudney died early in the trip and in all the turmoil, neither Clapperton nor Denham managed to travel as far as the river. The former did give us a colourful and evocative description of human and animal life on and around the great Lake Chad, in those halcyon days before desert encroachment and climate change swallowed up most of this incredible natural resource. As for Denham, one of his most important contributions was obtained from having joined a slave-raiding expedition as an observer. His reporting provides one of the most gripping independent eye-witness accounts of the bloody and devastating manner in which local armed forces (in this case, El Kanemi's fighters from Bornu, in partnership with the Emir of Mandara and some Arab raiders) undertook to harvest slaves from the native populations[3]. Things did not quite go to plan and it was by sheer dumb luck that Denham managed to escape with his life, losing even the shirt off his back as he fled the Fulani forces. Clapperton for his part met with both Sultan Muhammed Bello and Shehu El-Kanemi, the only known reporter to have met *both* of these mortal enemies and historical figures. It is from him we learn how well-informed Muhammed Bello was about very recent affairs in Europe and how widely read he was on matters of philosophy, literature and Islamic education with all its underlying pedagogy of Greek philosophy and logic. We also learn about El-Kanemi's wisdom and quiet but astute leadership. Dixon Denham was so enamoured with the Bornu ruler that he wrote about him: 'Nature has bestowed on him all the qualifications for a great commander; an enterprising genius, sound judgment, features engaging, with a demeanour gentle and conciliating: and so little of vanity was there mixed with his ambition....'[4]

The 'second' Sultan and the first Shehu were of course locked in ideological and military warfare (revolution and counter-revolution) at this very moment, and so both expressed the desire for trade (especially in firearms) and commercial intercourse with Britain. Sultan Bello even offered a local British consulate near the river (which he did not yet control), revealing the scale and scope of his territorial ambitions even this early in the jihad. 'God has given me all the land of the infidels,' Sultan Bello confidently told

Clapperton[5]. Notably, Clapperton was blithely informed by an ordinary citizen at Sokoto that the river flowed southwards into the Gulf of Guinea. But he doubted this information because it was refuted directly and deliberately by Sultan Bello. The careful ruler more than likely judged that it would not be wise to reveal intelligence about the river to the emissary of a powerful maritime nation, especially one which professed such a strong interest in ending the slave trade. Bello's subterfuge was completed when a map was painstakingly drawn and handed to Clapperton by the Sultan's official cartographer, which specifically contradicted the Gulf of Guinea theory.

Clapperton and Denham returned to England again via Tripoli in 1825, and just like their celebrated precursor, Park, the plucky adventurers became literary celebrities on the back of their writing. Their *Narrative of Travels and Discoveries in Northern and Central Africa in the Years 1822–1823 and 1824* was published in 1826 and is still in print as an important historical document. On his return, Clapperton was promoted to Commander and sent right back on a follow-on expedition, this time via Badagry. For some reason, Sultan Bello appeared to have promised Clapperton that he would have an escort waiting for him at that port, to bring him up to Sokoto. We know of course that the Sultan of Sokoto had no such capacity or influence at Badagry in December 1825 (the Owu War was ongoing, and Yorubaland itself was in disarray).

Much to his surprise, there was nobody waiting for Commander Clapperton when he arrived at Badagry, but he proceeded inland by himself, accompanied by a young British servant named Richard Lander and his local porters and translators. They managed to travel safely through Yorubaland, Borgu, and Nupe - encountering many adventures, including a marriage proposal from a jolly, obese, wealthy widow somewhere in Borgu. Eventually, Clapperton's happy party ran out of luck, arriving at Sokoto in the heat of war between the Fulani and Bornu. The Europeans were thus unable to proceed any further, and here Clapperton fell ill and died of fever (likely of malaria), having been stuck there for several months. Separately, Major Denham was also promoted and eventually appointed Lieutenant Governor (effectively chief executive) of Sierra Leone but died only five weeks into the job in 1828 (probably of malaria, too).

Two Plucky Cornish Boys

The mantle of Niger exploration then fell to the young, impressionable, and barely educated Richard Lander. He had managed to return safely via Badagry to England and considered it his solemn duty to continue the emerging tradition of British exploration in central Africa. Hardly anyone would have expected that this young man (he was 23 when his master Clapperton died) would be the one to achieve the long-desired objective of the British government and the Africa Association, with all their illustrious members and officers. Back in London, Lander managed after much effort to convince the responsible British government senior officer to sponsor a bare-bones 'expedition' staffed by just his younger brother and himself. With the benefit of hindsight, a more ill-equipped pair is hard to imagine, to chart the course and termination point of the Niger. Richard's brother, John Lander was not even offered a salary for the job (and was never paid for it). These two young men from Cornwall proceeded to Badagry in 1830, into the eye of Yoruba wars - the same year Abeokuta began to be settled by the war-weary Egba.

The Lander's journey into the interior is one of the most fascinating tales in the history of pre-European Nigeria, partly because of the sheer extent of the area in present-day Nigeria that they covered, but also because their unsophisticated (and often ignorant) narrative reveals a quite de-politicised view of events at that time. Riddled with historical inaccuracies, misunderstood cultural and political references, and poor spelling (neither of them spoke any local languages), the narrative is complicated by being essentially the understanding of two unsophisticated travellers, related through the distorted prism of multiple language translators. Nevertheless, Richard Lander's *Journal of a Second Expedition into the Interior of Africa, from the Bight of Benin to Soccatoo,* and the Lander brothers' combined *Journal of an Expedition to Explore the Course and Termination of the Niger* are important works of history.

The gutsy British boys landed at Badagry, where the exiled Adele and his wife detained them for their entertainment as long as they could, taking as many gifts off them as they could lay their hands on. Eventually, the Landers found a way to leave Badagry and managed to get an escort up into the interior. They followed well-worn and mostly safe travel paths but still managed to see the aftermath of war and devastation at several towns and villages. They wisely avoided the main hot spots in Yorubaland, arriving at the new Oyo capital after several weeks. The much-reduced Alaafin was now living here, without any of the trappings of this once great metropolis (Oyo-Ile). Much of the surrounding areas had been taken over by the Fulani, whose strong presence in the region was evident. The nearly blind old Alaafin offered the young White men his blessings and allowed them to continue their journey. The boys had been wisely advised by servants to the Alaafin's colourful and influential chief eunuch not to mention anything about their desire to reach the Niger, as they would be detained for it. Presumably, this was because it was not in the interest of the king for these foreign travellers to access his regional competitors and enemies.

Continuing into Borgu, the Landers then came into the influence of the chiefs of Kaiama and Bussa. At the latter place, they encountered a local man still in possession of Mungo Park's navy almanac and managed to purchase a colourful robe that was found in the wreckage of the *Joliba*. Kaiama and Bussa were friendly but rival sister-states, well-protected by the broad river's width and great nearby forests from the still ongoing Fulani revolution. Here, internal politics - and no real desire by the ruling elite to allow these White men to embark upon and discover the secrets of the great river - kept them detained for many months, essentially prisoners of their hosts. Now shorn of all their belongings, save for the clothes on their backs, the young travellers had to rely on bluster, trickery and luck to eventually secure transportation upon the Niger, in the form of a rickety, leaky canoe. The boys had been promised a grand boat by several members of the royal courts in Borgu, including by the solicitous Queen Kitara at Kaiama and her duplicitous brother at Bussa. But the clever local elite never delivered (perhaps hoping that the boys would give up), and it was only by the utmost deception and fraud that they were eventually able to escape unto the river in their leaking canoe, sneaking away from their friendly captors.

Perhaps their most important asset in this scheming was their interpreter and travel guide, a wily, diminutive native Hausa man named Pasko. Pasko had also worked for Clapperton. Born near Sokoto (Gobir), he had been kidnapped and sold early in life as a slave to the coast, then liberated at sea by the Preventative Squadron, following which he signed up as a ship hand, travelling widely in the Gulf of Guinea and elsewhere (in the process, learning to speak English). Employed originally as a Hausa interpreter, Pasko had successfully escorted the pair of Clapperton and Lander up to Sokoto, and the latter back down in 1826. Remarkably, this intrepid traveller then went back to England with Lander, where he lived for a while (acquiring a reputation as quite the ladies' man) before returning and joining the Landers for this mission.

Between the scheming of Pasko, their bravado and bare good fortune, the Lander boys managed to secure sufficient resources and intelligence from several communities along the shore, to sail safely down the Niger. The Landers sailed past the Niger-Benue confluence, which they were the first Europeans to see - going as far as present-day Onitsha, where their luck ran out. Around present-day Asaba, the armed men in the first major travelling party of canoes that they encountered promptly arrested them, seized their canoe and all its valuable contents and dumped the boys unceremoniously into the river. The boys were stripped near-naked and major parts of their journal had to be rewritten from memory because they lost it here during their dramatic kidnap ordeal. Now proper captives of hostile locals, the young men were taken down to Aboh near the river's delta. Here, the Obi of Aboh, an able and business-like young man saw no reason why the Landers should not have to pay him a ransom for their freedom. A solution soon presented itself in the form of a young merchant from Brass (Nembe), who was at Aboh attending the major slave market there. This eager entrepreneur saw an opportunity to farm-in the ransom for a quick profit. He paid off the Obi for the boys, intending to recoup his capital and return on investment from the captain of a British vessel that was currently lying in the Nun river, loading produce. The trade paid off for him eventually (when Lander returned to Akassa the following year and repaid the debt), but not at this time, because the unruly captain of the British ship flatly refused to pay. With a great deal of trickery and bluster, the clever risk-taker from Nembe was temporarily defrauded of his capital outlay by the hurriedly departing British party.

This was how the Landers became the first foreigners to travel nearly the entire length of the Niger within present-day Nigeria. In the process, the plucky Cornish boys made the startling connection that had eluded all outsiders up till that moment. The streams and creeks at the coast represented merely the delta of the same great river which drained thousands of kilometres from the Futa Jallon mountains in Guinea. More important than this addition to the global scientific knowledge base was the commercial intelligence now revealed by these amateur explorers about the significant profit potential of trading directly with the interior (using the Niger as a transport corridor), rather than merely with middlemen on the coast. This 'discovery' would shortly become the next most important event in the history of Nigeria, since Dan Fodio's revolution, because it laid out an alternative navigable route into the formerly insular heart of the country, by which foreign influence might be exerted if desired.

Within a year of his triumphant return to England, Richard Lander was back on the river equipped with two grand steam vessels, furnished by a Liverpool businessman named Macgregor Laird. Laird had come in it for the money, seeking to be the first trader to profit from dealing directly with primary produce sellers in the interior - ivory, palm oil, spices, leather and rare minerals being the desired items for purchase. This forgettable expedition was most notable for the design and deployment by Laird of the Alburkah, an iron-hulled steamship on an ocean-going voyage for the first time in maritime history.[6] The expedition also ended in tragedy for Richard Lander. On his way back from a resupply run to Fernando Po (the steamers were left on the upper river trading all the way to Nupe and also up the Benue), a carefully assembled canoe armada of combined armed forces from Brass, Bonny and Benin were lying in wait for Landers canoe in the river, near Angiama in present-day Bayelsa State. This unusual collaboration between fierce local rival forces was aimed at dealing a death blow to the European traders, who had historically never sailed up the river to trade directly. The remarkable Richard Lander was shot near the buttocks while escaping and died at Fernando Po on February 4 1834.

The Earnest Victorians

Stepping briefly away from these historic happenings on the river, the wider world in the 1830s was also changing rapidly. Queen Victoria ascended the throne on 20 June 1837, a symbolic ushering in of the eponymous era most notable for rapid global industrial, economic, political, and technological change, with Great Britain at the helm of affairs. Chief among the fundamental beliefs that took root among the Victorians was that positive change was not only inevitable but also necessary and worth striving towards. Political change was also afoot. In 1832 the Great Reform Act passed Parliament, expanding the size of the British electorate dramatically from about 400,000 to 650,000 people, a small sign of liberal democracy on the ascendancy.

In 1830, Lord Palmerston took over at the Foreign Office for the first time, a man who would come to dominate British foreign and economic policy for decades, in the direction of imperialism and international activism. At the heart of these changes was a more active and free press, and a populace increasingly motivated as much by the bread and butter issues of domestic relevance, as by international affairs and the use of British power abroad. Their American empire having been lost by the previous generation, the present one had redeemed itself by victory in the Napoleonic Wars, and now fully intended to consolidate by straddling the globe economically. Over the next few decades, British technological and industrial supremacy in global affairs would become established. The 'Great Cable' was laid across the English Channel by 1851, linking London to the European mainland at telegraphic speed and heralding an era of unrestrained growth: railways, steamships, factories; in turn driving imperial commerce and global conquest.

More importantly, global dominance and the industrial revolution were also seen as a means to an end: the eradication of widespread domestic poverty and deprivation, which was still a problem in Britain itself, however wealthy and powerful the empire was becoming. Charles Dickens' *Oliver Twist*, the defining novel of the era (which was serialised in the press starting from 1837 and sold 150,000 copies in three weeks) was a dramatic depiction of severe poverty, moral decadence, and inequality in contemporary Britain. So, the Victorian elite cared about political and economic dominance, but as we have already begun to see, they *also* cared about the ideology of scientific progress and social development along the lines of the 'British tradition,' both at home and abroad. Key to this progress and development in the minds of the Victorian leading lights was the global export of their culture, values, language, technology, manufactured goods, and their religion. Conversely, the import of produce and raw materials from around the world was essential to sustaining this system of economic development. It was an impressive fusion of faith in science, technology, military power, and imperial capitalism, but also social reforms and Christian missionary enterprise. As we will see, particularly in Africa, missionary enterprise was an important means of culture export in the minds of the British Victorians, and the CMS was founded at the turn of the century with this objective in mind. One illustrative group of the eighteenth-century British elite who best reflected the later Victorian mindset were the so-called 'Clapham Sect,' a collection of prominent and wealthy individuals who were also social reformers and revivalist Anglicans with shared views about politics and social justice. The members of this group (in their individual and collective actions) would come to be historically important for the future of Nigeria. Famous amongst these individuals were men like Thomas Fowell Buxton (a leading abolitionist thinker), Granville Sharp (a social justice campaigner), William Wilberforce (the most important British abolitionist politician) and Henry Venn (an evangelical minister).

Henry Venn, Humanitarian Cheerleader

All these men except the last-named are now household names with extensive history books devoted to them. But it is Henry Venn that is particularly critical to our story, not just for his contributions, but for those of his perhaps *third* best-known descendant. Among the prominent members of his later family, there was his great-grandson John Venn (who invented the eponymous mathematical diagram) and Virginia Woolf, (the famous writer, whose father was a grandson of John Venn). But most important for our narrative was his grandson and namesake, Henry Venn. Born in 1796, the younger Venn was a leading light of the CMS for decades, and its honorary secretary from 1841 until he died in 1873. The ideas, initiatives and passionate schemes of this little-known Victorian clergyman were to have an outsized impact on the future of Nigeria, especially considering that he never set foot in the country. It would not be an exaggeration to list Henry Venn among the most important non-

Nigerians ever to influence the future of Nigeria.

After graduating from and lecturing at Cambridge, Venn began to serve the CMS full-time from 1846, taking a leading role in coordinating all the affairs of the active missionaries in the field, as well as the political lobbying of government officers in London. In this regard, Venn was following in the traditions of his grandfather's Clapham Sect, who were dedicated to engaging in political activism to influence government actions in favour of abolishing slavery. One powerful tool of the CMS in influencing public opinion was the reports and journals of their field missionaries, extracts of which were circulated in church magazines, notices, and records, which provided the bulk of the reading material for the ordinary Victorians. As an honorary secretary, Venn wielded administrative, executive, and editorial influence, which was duly utilised during his 32-year career in the interest of missionary enterprise in places like West Africa. Venn's CMS career was in keeping with the ideology of T.F. Buxton, author of *The African Slave Trade and its Remedy,* a radical pro-commerce, anti-slave-trade manifesto published in 1838, and other leading thinkers on abolition. The CMS believed that nothing short of a radical socio-economic revolution to create a modern, private capital led middle class in the interior of Africa could truly eradicate slavery from the face of the earth. It was a bold hypothesis that would come to form the basis for much of the early British engagement in Nigeria.

Having come to understand the fundamental political economy behind the slave trade (international demand allied with the contest for profits and power accruing from the domestic supply), these early humanitarians set about dismantling it *also* using political and economic tools. Venn led the inland charge in this respect, starting with the conscious development of a Western-educated and empowered local elite. This was the thinking behind his passionate support and promotion of native pastors like Crowther (ordained in 1843), and later Reverends King and Macaulay (1854). It was also Venn who formed what he called the

'Native Agency Committee' in 1845. This aptly named organisation granted scholarships and placed promising young Africans at appropriate professional training institutions in Britain, educating Saro notables such as James Pinson Labulo Davies (pioneer naval officer and cocoa farmer), Henry Robbin, T.B. Macaulay (pastor, school teacher and father of the more famous Herbert), Africanus Horton (medical doctor), Samuel Crowther Jr. (pharmacist) just to name a few beneficiaries.

It was also Venn who recommended cotton cultivation at Abeokuta to Henry Townsend in 1850. The same energetic Venn travelled to Manchester in 1856 to convince Thomas Clegg, a leading industrialist, churchman, and member of the chamber of commerce to supply cotton saws and presses on credit to the Egba and accept payment in delivered produce. His objective in this enterprise was the creation of an alternative to the Trust System of import-export finance at the coast, which the slave trade was based upon. The Trust System relied on credit advanced to local wholesale traders by way of import goods, which they repaid by the gathering of human bodies and other commodities from hinterland originators, for export sales to European traders waiting at the coast. Clegg started the cotton business as encouraged by Venn, but it failed - as did many of the clergyman's enterprising schemes. Again, it was Venn who approved the establishment of CMS Grammar School (the first formal educational institution at Lagos) in 1860, a project that commenced on the initiative of T.B. Macaulay, and with financing from the now wealthy J.P.L. Davies. A virtuous cycle was forming, in line with the hypothesis of Venn and his collaborators.

The same Venn in 1861 appointed a European medical doctor named A.A. Harrison as political agent of CMS in Abeokuta, with the specific hope that Dr Harrison would establish a medical training school in Egba. This he did, and it led to the first two Nigerian medical doctors, Nathaniel King and Obadiah Johnson. But for his most ambitious economic development trick yet, in 1863 Henry Venn convinced Thomas Clegg to establish the West

Africa Company (WAC), which began to trade on the Niger, with Samuel Crowther and his son Josiah as shareholders and leading representatives. Clegg in turn employed a well-known Lagos trader named William McCoskry to join the WAC. This company (which chartered vessels and owned storage depots up and down the river) became one of the most important trading concerns on the Niger, until it was subsumed by the Royal Niger Company of George Taubman Goldie, a corporate financier that we will meet later in our story. McCoskry, an old hand on the coast, (he first arrived in 1847 as an agent for a firm called W.B. Hutton and Sons) would later earn his place in history by being appointed British vice consul for Lagos[xi]. McCoskry was the political officer on the spot in 1861 and hence his signature adorns the treaty signed in August of that year when Oba Dosunmu - the successor to the British puppet Akitoye - ceded Lagos in perpetuity to the British, under pressure from gunboats and regional rivalry.

While the WAC was never profitable, its mere existence was indispensable to empowering the missionary work led by Samuel Crowther on the river. The company provided a basis for legitimate commercial interaction with chiefs and communities at key towns. WAC also helped to transport mission officers, stores, and provisions to various locations during the travelling season when the Niger was flooded and navigable. All of these initiatives were aimed (most of them successfully) at creating nothing short of a socio-economic revolution among the indigenous people, without which - it was understood - Christian missionary enterprise could not be sustainable. But perhaps the most important contribution of Venn to Nigeria was his unceasing support for the career of Samuel Ajayi Crowther. It is probably safe to speculate that without Mr. Venn, Bishop Crowther would not have existed. Against the opposition

xi The ginger haired McCoskry, with a long beard of the same colour parted in two on either side of his chin, was so popular with the locals that they nicknamed him 'A l'ag-bon pipon' (The Red Bearded One). This was eventually shortened to Apongbon and is where a small part of Lagos Island - so named till this day - derived its name from.

of many within CMS, including overt and vicious disagreement by Henry Townsend - who harboured racist ideas about the capacity of Black men, Venn promoted, supported, and nurtured Crowther. It was he who organised the 1851 publicity tour that included an interview with the royal couple, and also, he who recommended the appointment of the first Black bishop in Anglican history, leading to the consecration of Bishop Samuel Ajayi Crowther by Queen's license on June 29, 1864.

In the letters and correspondence between the men, it is not difficult to view the genuine love, support, and encouragement of Crowther by Venn throughout the Black bishop's career. It is not altogether surprising therefore that not too long after Venn's death, a crisis of confidence began to develop between European and African missionaries within CMS. This culminated in a viciously partisan report written against Crowther's leadership and the African clergy more broadly, by a visiting White CMS officer in 1878. Multiple infractions were alleged in this ugly report, from adultery and idolatry to financial impropriety. This marked the beginning of what we might call the post-Clapham Sect period, during which deliberate steps were taken to remove Africans from the positions of political or administrative authority they had held in previous years. The 'Scramble for Africa' had begun.

The First Niger Expedition

In tracing the origins of this post-Clapham Sect period, we can now return to the earlier mentioned commercial expedition of Macgregor Laird on the Niger in 1834, in which the historic Richard Lander was shot and killed by a native armed force. This was a commercial expedition, not sanctioned by the British government. It did not achieve spectacular profits, and so there was little to follow it for a while. Most traders reverted to using the Trust System for gathering produce at the coast, rather than venturing inland and incurring the wrath of the natives. Seven years later, in 1841, thanks to the relentless publicity and lobbying by the indefatigable T.F. Buxton (and with the support of Prince Albert), the British government eventually approved the expenditure of £100,000 (£3,000,000 in today's money) on the official 'First' Niger Expedition.

The organisation of this expedition had been kicked off the previous year at what might be termed the first-ever Africa Conference in London, a tradition that continues till this day. This event (which came to be known as Exeter Hall) was held on 1 June 1840 and was attended by Prince Albert in one of his first public appearances after his marriage to Queen Victoria[7]. However, not everyone was happy about this new evangelical zeal for Africa gripping London, though. In his novel, *Bleak House*, Charles Dickens created the character, Mrs. Jellyby to parody those he called 'telescopic philanthropists' who cared about faraway problems while ignoring problems at home. 'Whatever Exeter Hall champions is the thing by no means to be done' Dickens deadpanned[8]. Nevertheless, the show got on the road.

As it turned out, the greatest Victorian era writer was not too far off the mark with his caustic scepticism. In purely human terms, the First Expedition turned out to be a disastrous escapade. At a time before Malaria Fever was properly understood, the death toll was hideous. It was not until 1897 that Europeans discovered the transmission of malaria by mosquitoes, and an effective prophylactic or cure was not yet in production. Warburg's Tincture was not yet in widespread use, and the curative value of quinine not widely known. Of the 162 Europeans that entered the river, 54 did not return, while their 158 African co-travellers returned safely. Still, the medical report of the expedition concluded, presciently, that its many pages will prove 'very interesting to naval surgeons and naval officers whose destiny may lead them to the pestiferous shores of Africa - and especially into that fatal river, the Niger'[9].

From the perspective of intelligence gathering and dissemination of information however, the First Expedition was a great success. Still a young Sierra Leone teacher at the time, Samuel Crowther was one of 25 Saros that went up the river, travelling from Freetown back into the interior for the first time since he was kidnapped and sold as a slave. The favourable reports of this Saro Expedition party about the opportunities for trade and commerce in the interior contributed in no small measure to the flood of Sierra Leone emigrants to Abeokuta, many of whom were seeking to profit from that trading potential. An attempt was made to establish a farm settlement at present-day Lokoja, and land was allocated for it by the Attah (literally, 'father' but used to mean 'king') at Igala, the dominant kingdom near the confluence of the rivers. But not much came out of it, given the terrible death toll. Not many further official attempts were made to significantly open-up non-slave trade on the Niger for the next decade, with all the attention of CMS and the British government focused on the Egba-Lagos nexus. Crowther himself resettled with his family at Abeokuta shortly after returning from the First Niger Expedition.

Heinrich Barth and the Second Expedition

It is at this point that one of the most important nineteenth-century European travellers to visit the interior of Nigeria enters our story. Born near Hamburg, Germany in 1821, Heinrich Barth was a scholar, widely travelled in the Mediterranean, who held a doctorate in trade relations and was a fluent Arabic speaker. Barth departed from Tripoli in early 1850 and thanks to his prior education arrived in Africa with the benefit of historical context and insight into the ideas, words, and thoughts of his hosts. Barth was also a patient traveller and would live in the country for five years, returning to Europe in late 1855. On his extensive visit, he managed to pick up elements of the Hausa, Kanuri, and Fulfulde languages prior to his return. Writing in words accessible to European language speakers for the first time, he succeeded in publishing some important historical and cultural information about the countries north of the river.

Barth travelled as far south as Adamawa, crossing first into present-day Cameroon and then going across the Benue into southern Nigeria. His *Travels and Discoveries in North and Central Africa* published in both English and German was the most important scientific work about Africa of the period. In 1854, exactly 14 years after the first attempt, and in part to find and relieve Barth, a Second Niger Expedition was organised. This Second Expedition was again financed by the British government, but this time via a concession to Macgregor Laird, who had been lobbying for it. The year before, Laird was awarded a contract to carry monthly mail packets from Sierra Leone to Lagos on a subsidised basis. Now he was charged with an ambitious second attempt to open the river to trade and missionary enterprise. Again, the omnipresent Samuel Crowther joined the Expedition, publishing his *Journal of an Expedition up the Niger and Tshadda Rivers in 1854*. Crowther's travel journal provides (along with Heinrich Barth's scrupulously scientific records of his travels around the same time) the most authoritative eye-witness reports of the continuing conditions around the country during this period following the major slave trade suppression efforts at the coast.

Led by yet another Scottish medical doctor turned naval officer named William Balfour Baikie, the Second Expedition was a spectacular success, with no loss of lives recorded over the several months long voyage. 65 people sailed this time, comprising 12 Europeans and 53 Africans and importantly, quinine wine was served daily. The enterprising Macgregor Laird had struck a deal with the British government under which he was to build a special purpose transport vessel for the Expedition. Hence, a 260-ton iron schooner named the *Pleiad* was built at Birkenhead, Ireland for the purpose. The boat soon entered a long, well-provisioned, and momentous transport service on the river.

Crowther and Barth's work, together with Baikie's book *Narrative of an Exploring Voyage up the Rivers Kwóra and Bínue (commonly known as the Niger and Tsádda) in 1854* combine to provide us with comprehensive, nuanced and educated insights into the situation at key locations in the country. Their crisp writing bore witness to the significant potential that existed for commercial enterprise, and the genuine desire among nearly all the ruling elite for Western 'book' knowledge. The energetic Reverend Crowther offered a school on the spot to every chief he met, an offer that was always eagerly accepted, as many of the native elite in the interior appeared to view written words as potent charms. On account of this, Baikie handed out many autographs to eager recipients. This reverence for the written word was in part a legacy of the Mallams who had first brought literacy to the area and had been renowned for their 'charms'. These charms were mostly based on the written word, a popular manifestation of which was the writing down of verses from the Quran on a slate, washing it off and offering the mixture as a drink for healing or protection. Fulani raids were still a common occurrence around the country at this time, and the travelling party encountered towns, villages and reports of settlements recently sacked by the armed forces of the relentless jihadists. In many places, people were living in abject fear of being attacked again. Dan Fodio's war was continuing southwards decades later, but now largely as a general scheme for usurping power and establishing a new hegemony, rather than for any social revolutionary or ideological purposes.

Third Expedition and the Clapham Sect Era

In 1857, Baikie, Crowther and others returned to the river on the Third Niger Expedition, which led to the establishment of Christian missions by the Black bishop at several points on the river. At Onitsha, a Saro pastor of Igbo parentage named John Taylor was left behind by Crowther with the charge of founding the local church, which slowly expanded inland over the years, providing Western education to numerous indigenous peoples. One of the beneficiaries of this missionary expansion was a man named Chukwuemeka Azikiwe. Born in 1879, Azikiwe grew up to become a British senior colonial clerk at Lagos and Zungeru and is now better known as the father of

Niger Coast Protectorate Officials at Calabar, 1897
Front row R.F Locke and Major Copland-Crawford.
(Image_ Hulton) Colourised

Marina Lagos 1911. Image by Henry Sanya Freeman.
Government Photographer COLOURISED

Shehu of Borno 1901 C.T Lawrence Collection
captured during tour of duty in Northern Protectorate.
UK National Archives

Kano City Wall c.1905 colourised Royal Geographical Society

*Kano Gate 1899 From CT Lawrence Collection UK
National Archives*

*Lord Lugard, at work at the Government House,
Lagos 1914. Image from the C.T Lawrence Collection
UK National Archives COLOURISED*

*Oba Ovonramwen and wives during his exile at Cala-
bar image by Jonathan A Green 1897 COLOURISED*

*Market day Old Calabar 1905.Image by Jonathan
Adagogo Green COLOURISED UK National Archives*

Shehu of Borno 1901. Image by Major C.T Lawrence
during tour of duty in Northern territories

Ralph Moor High Commissioner of the Niger Coast Protectorate and later the Southern Nigeria Protectorate.Image UK National Archives COLOURISED

Dr. Nnamdi Azikiwe, the first President of independent Nigeria. In preparation for the trip, Crowther and Taylor had worked together to produce the first book written in the Igbo language, using Karl Richard Lepsius' Latin-script Standard Alphabet. They called the 17-page primer *Isoama-Ibo*, and it quickly became one of the most important contributors to the development of Western education and literacy in the broader Igbo country. Taylor started a girl's school within a week of setting up his church at Onitsha, with the Isoama-Ibo primer forming the major pedagogical tool. In 1882, Bishop Crowther would eventually publish the first comprehensive dictionary in Igbo, called *Vocabulary of the Igbo Language*.

Taken together, the Third Expedition and Barth's travels further enhanced the understanding of present-day Nigeria's interior, and established the use of the Niger as a regular communication and transportation artery for commercial and missionary enterprise, along the lines espoused by T.F. Buxton and the descendants of the Clapham Sect in Britain. Naturally, Western-educated Saro (and to a lesser extent Aguda) returnees were conveniently in the driving seat of these transformational happenings. This was on account of their hardier constitutions, which meant they did not die of malaria as frequently, and their unique acceptability to both the inland traditional elite and the European (mostly British) commercial interests in the country.

Formation and Transformation

Thus, began a nearly thirty-year period between 1860 and 1890 during which rapid economic expansion and Western education began transforming the interior of the Niger-Benue country. This work was led by the untiring Bishop Crowther, in partnership with the CMS and other recently arrived missionary organisations and European trading concerns, and with limited involvement of the British Government. The Victorian exchequer was unwilling to devote significant resources to developing and administering the area, unlike their energetic French and German colleagues in the same period. It was not all plain sailing, however. At the coast as well as on and around the river, the contest for commercial dominance often resulted in armed conflict. Fighting regularly broke out between rival British traders, between the foreigners and the indigenous communities, among the competing Europeans, particularly the French and English, and even between Saros, Agudas and indigenes.

Criminal syndicates, gratuitous violence, grand and petty fraud, murder, kidnapping and punitive expeditions; all the ills that might be expected in any fast-growing, rapidly transforming economy, lacking any common legal foundation or political administration, were present. The more historically prominent of these occurred at the coast, where most of the trade continued to happen. As we will see later, the Bonny civil war in 1869, which pre-empted King Jaja's reign at Opobo during this period was the culmination of this sort of multi-party trade and political rivalry. But there were other notable incidents up and down both rivers, where entire settlements were razed to the ground on account of trade disputes - at Onitsha and Aboh, among the Tiv on the Benue, at Akassa which was the leading depot, and even among the Yoruba whose wars now became about preferential access to the ports at Lagos and Badagry.

There was even an extended period of belligerency and armed conflict in late 1877. This was the same period during which Goldie Taubman visited the river and formed his ideas for its future exploitation and governance. This bloody conflict later came to be known as the Niger War, because of the near-total breakdown of relations between foreign and local trading parties on the river. Messy as it was, economic progress was occurring. And native agency at all levels, among the traditional elite, ordinary natives and the emerging middle class was pivotal to its sustenance. Domestic slavery remained firmly intact, and even the international slave trade across the Sahara was yet to be eliminated. But the coastal trade in other cash commodities, particularly palm oil, shea butter, ivory and precious minerals like silver was thriving. In the process, the areas behind the rivers were becoming rapidly integrated into international, modern, commercial export value chains.

This is the period that might be rightly christened the 'Clapham Sect Era' in the history of pre-colonial Nigeria. This era was bookmarked at its commencement by key events like the remarkable decision of Dr Baikie to settle down locally in 1858. It was a decision with cultural ramifications for the future, as Baikie would become a hugely influential political and economic actor on the river. To this day, one of the more common Igbo words for a White person or Englishman is *Onye Bekee,* a derivation from 'Baikie.' Similarly, a large and storied Hausa Christian family continues to bear the Baikie name, which they adopted from one of the first of many Europeans to 'go native' in the interior of Nigeria[10]. The doctor's steamship was wrecked badly near Jebba, and instead of returning overland, he elected to remain and focus on economic development work at Lokoja near the confluence of the rivers. Another key bookmark of the Clapham Sect Era's commencement was the establishment in 1860 of the CMS Grammar School at Lagos by Venn beneficiaries and Crowther mentees J.P.L. Davies and T.B. Macaulay. The latter member of the Saro elite further distinguished himself by marrying the saintly Bishop's daughter, Abigail Crowther, and together raising several children, including the most famous Macaulay of them all, Herbert. We would be remiss not to highlight here a more ominous early event during this period: in 1858, a baby boy grandly named Frederick John Dealtry Lugard was born at Fort St George in Madras (present-day Chennai), India to a chaplain father then working for the British East India Company. We will return later to the story of this new-born's remarkable long life, and short career in Nigeria.

By contrast, the tail end of the Clapham Sect Period, (as we will observe later in our story), can be landmarked by key events like the resignation of the then more than 80-year-old Bishop Crowther from chairing the board of the local CMS governing committee. The Black bishop's departure was in protest at challenges to his authority by newly arrived 'young Turk' European CMS officers. One of these men, a passionate missionary named Thomas John Dennis who arrived in 1894 would make a herculean and misguided attempt to create from whole cloth a so-called 'Union' (later also known as 'Standard') written Igbo language. This preposterous amalgamation of multiple dialects by Dennis was an audacious attempt at re-doing much of the original work done by Crowther, Taylor, Jonas, and many others to commit various dialects of that language properly into writing. These younger men like T.J. Dennis, who were mostly born after Venn had died, were described by the good Bishop Crowther using a wonderfully polite epithet, 'The Anthropological Type' for their belief in the then popular ideas of European natural superiority to Africans. These were the men who would bring the Clapham Sect Era of native agency in Nigeria to an end in the late nineteenth century.

Other events heralding the end of the Clapham Sect Era in Nigeria would include the arrival of the most important capitalist in the history of Nigeria, George Taubman Goldie, on the river. Goldie's merger of all the main trading concerns into one single conglomerate called the United African Company (UAC) was another important milestone. Other notable bookmarks were the Berlin Conference of 1885, carefully engineered as it was to satisfy the commercial lust of the murderous King Leopold, and the death of Bishop Crowther in 1891. We have already seen some of the political events locally, in Britain and globally that made possible (nay, necessary) those three golden decades of African-led human development in pre-colonial Nigeria, assisted and directed by well-meaning international philanthropists and scientists. Our story will in subsequent chapters follow the unstoppable global forces that collided with the immovable local powers and made this human development approach unsustainable for a longer period, setting the stage for the ensuing loss of local independence and the emergence of British colonial rule in newly formed Nigeria.

The Mad Men adventurers of our story forced open the Niger to the world in their quest for celebrity. The ambitious missionaries and their ideological Victorian backers hustled behind them into the interior of the country, promoting the fortuitously educated Saros. Led by their hero Samuel Ajayi Crowther, the indigenous people rose to the challenge of lifting their country from its state of violent chaos and human degradation. Modern education, trade, and economic progress followed, replacing the abominable use of human bodies as the primary means of international exchange. In the process, a new domestic elite of educated professionals and responsible administrators was being created. Our formation story will soon come to follow the descendants of this Clapham Sect Era generation of the newly educated indigenous elite, who would much later come to form the core of a radically transformed future country. These descendants of Venn and Crowther would become notable as much for contributing to the social and economic prosperity of their people, as in the contest for political control of their homeland.

But the remarkable progress made during the Clapham Sect Era was still not fast enough, and as we will see shortly, the biggest obstacle to more rapid improvement in the conditions of the people turned out to be the local, long-standing traditional elite. In the event, outside events and extraneous forces would soon combine to overrun both the traditional and newly emergent educated elite and in the process, contorting the countries around the river into shape and design unprecedented in their various histories.

---

1.   Tombs R. *The English and their History: The First Thirteen Centuries.* Penguin UK; 2014.

2.   Park M. *Travels in the interior districts of Africa: performed in the Years 1795,*

1796, and 1797 by Mungo Park ..., with an Account of his Subsequent Mission to that Country in 1805. vol 2. Murray; 1815.

3. Denham D, Clapperton H, Oudney W. *Narrative of Travels and Discoveries in Northern and Central Africa: In the Years 1822, 1823, and 1824.* 1828.

4. *Ibid.*

5. *Ibid.*

6. Baker GL. *Trade Winds On the Niger: The Saga of the Royal Niger Company 1830-1971.* Tauris Academic Studies; 1996.

7. Buxton C. *Memoirs of Sir Thomas Fowell Buxton, Baronet: With Selections from His Correspondence.* H. Longstreth; 1849.

8. Storey G, Dickens C. *Dickens: Bleak House.* Cambridge University Press; 1987.

9. Medical History of the Expedition to the Niger during the Years 1841-2, Comprising an Account of the Fever Which Led to Its Abrupt Termination. *Edinburgh Medical and Surgical Journal.* 1845/4/1 1845;63(163):415-454.

10. Daily Trust Newspapers, Nigeria - The Baikies: Hausa Christians with European background. 2018/2/17 2018 (Available online).

CHAPTER 6

Exit the Bible, Enter the Gun

From Adversity to the Stars

The Clapham Sect Era ended with much weeping and mourning at Opobo and Abeokuta in 1891, when in July and December, the much-loved former King and Bishop, Jaja and Crowther respectively, died of natural causes. Two of the most famous Victorian era Nigerians, with curiously parallel but radically different careers had passed away, within months of each other. Jaja was born in the same year that young Crowther was kidnapped at Oshogun, both men rose from slavery and captivity to prominence and royalty in their respective fields, eventually reaching the highest positions possible in their chosen areas. Per ardua ad astra, literally: 'from adversity to the stars,' is probably the most appropriate label for the lives of these great men, and the period of Nigerian history in which they lived. We have already followed the life and career of Bishop Crowther in some detail, and it is useful to now turn to the rise and fall of King Jaja, as a means of beginning to understand the end of the Clapham Sect Era, and the path to British colonial rule in Nigeria.

Born Jubo Jugboha sometime in 1821 near the present-day town of Orlu (his actual village of Umuduruoha-Amaigbo still exists), Jaja was also sold away like Crowther as a slave, when he was still a young boy[1]. In his case, Jaja ended up the property of a chief named Iganipughuma Allison at the coastal merchant-kingdom of Bonny, only about three-days march or 170 kilometres away from his hometown. Arriving at Bonny, little Jaja was following a path that had already been taken by generations of Igbo emigrants and slaves-turned-merchants, to this centuries-old trading kingdom. Bonny was a major coastal depot for the export of slaves from and import of commodities into the greater Igbo hinterland. The merchant city-state was a multi-ethnic melting pot, where hinterland Igbos combined with indigenous Ijaws and other nationalities to form a metropolitan trading society, in close intercourse with the European traders settled at the coast.

These settled White men lived in and traded from so-called 'hulks' (converted sailing vessels) which were anchored at the coast and in the numerous creeks, streams, and rivers around Bonny Island. Using these floating warehouses, trade goods and produce were transhipped from and into calling vessels from Europe. From these hulks, the expatriate Europeans traded in arms, ammunition, gin, textiles, and other assorted items of foreign manufacture. Originally, this centuries-old trade was in exchange for human cargo, but then later in the Victorian period demand grew for palm oil, which was pressed out from the fruit of trees growing in abundance within the Igbo hinterland. An important lubricant for industrialisation in Europe, it was palm oil that would also grease the rise and fall of Jaja Jugboha.

Slave Boy Turns Strong Man

Jaja would have arrived at Bonny not very long after the Lander brothers had miraculously re-appeared at the coast having circumnavigated the Niger in the interior, and about the same time as Macgregor Laird's original expedition, during which Richard Lander was killed by armed forces - including those of Bonny. Up and down the river, this was a time of rapid change, particularly from an economy based on the international trade in humans to the new Clapham Sect Era trade in agricultural commodities. Mid-nineteenth century Bonny was a hard-core slave economy in transition[xii] and Jaja the slave boy would have been one of the

xii   A British businessman named J. A. Clegg told a select committee of the House of Lords that not up to ten people were free in Bonny, implying that servitude was widespread there. He added that there was not a chief in the kingdom who did not trade in slaves (See Hugh Thomas' *The Slave Trade*, page 562).

first young men to learn the trading business at Bonny in these new circumstances. Young Jaja learned under the tutelage of Chief Allison but fortuitously for him, he fell out with this master and was gifted to a more prominent chief named Madu. Madu was a very important man in the complicated politics and economics of Bonny which we must explain briefly before our story can continue.

The Bonny political and administrative structure was based on the 'Trading House' system; each trading house being a semi-autonomous group of anything between a few hundred to several thousand free men, together with their families, servants and slaves, under the jurisdiction of a chief, typically the leading trader within the House. The chiefs in turn served and traded under the authority of the revered, traditional king of Bonny, who was typically not an autocrat, because his position depended on the loyalty of the various House chiefs. Nonetheless, the monarch was a powerful and influential institution for dispute resolution and maintenance of law and order. So-called 'supercargoes' - essentially the lead European trader resident on each of the several dozen hulks anchored around the island at any point in time - also formed an important economic and political pressure group within Bonny. The slaves within each House formed a critical component of the trading infrastructure and depending on their ability typically went on to become important members of the House themselves, in turn owning property including other humans who in that way further enlarged the House.

So it was that in this milieu, the young Jaja grew up under the most prominent of the Houses, the Anna Pepple, which in 1830 was ruled by the successful chief named Madu whom Jaja had been gifted to. Chief Madu was so prominent among the House principals that he was named regent of Bonny, upon the death of the universally revered King Opubu Pepple earlier that same year. Opubu's heir, Dappa Pepple came of age a few years later, ascending the throne after the death of Madu, whose own son, named Alali had followed him as regent of Bonny. It was ill-fated for the future of Bonny that the transfer of leadership happened to occur in this inopportune fashion, with insufficient institutional memory and power retained in the process. The ensuing crisis from this unfortunate transition would result in a civil war, the emergence of Jaja as a leader of his people, and the loss of Bonny independence to the British. For the young Jaja, diligence and trustworthiness as a domestic servant of Madu led to his promotion to an apprenticeship aboard a hulk, working directly with a supercargo and deepening his understanding of the commodities trade.

Palm Oil and the Ruffians

By the middle of the 1800s, trade in palm oil originating from the so-called 'Oil Rivers' had come to be of enough global importance to warrant the emergence of several profitable European trading firms at Bonny. When Baikie visited Calabar before embarking on the Second Niger Expedition in 1854, he estimated the total value of palm oil in a single fully laden 2,500 tons vessel he found lying in the river at nearly £100,000, a princely sum even at that time[2]. The Oil Rivers was a general European term for the other rivers (apart from the Niger) linking the palm oil-rich Igbo interior with the coastal trading cities of the delta city-states, including Bonny, Brass and Old Calabar, of which Bonny was now the most prominent. Several significant British trading firms had become established all around the Oil Rivers, with hundreds of European residents in the area at any point in time. These so-called 'Palm Oil Ruffians' acquired quite a reputation both locally and in Europe for 'going native' and essentially transmuting into vicious, armed and politically important competitors in active community and intercourse with the local merchant elite.

One colourful albeit late vintage palm oil ruffian would achieve perhaps more local and international fame than all the ones who came before him. Born into poverty in 1881 at Ardwick, Manchester, he arrived on the river in 1905 from elsewhere in West

Africa, Conakry the modern-day capital of Guinea. Originally known as John Young, this Englishman wrote himself into both native folklore and metropolitan controversy in London with his outlandish and extravagantly homoerotic literary productions and lifestyle. Later gentrifying his name as John Moray Stuart-Young, the tall, effeminate, and gay Englishman settled down at Onitsha and became one of the wealthiest 'palm oil ruffians' ever to work on the river. Apart from oil, Stuart-Young also traded in European imports, timber, ivory, rubber, and animal skins. He was also a prominent philanthropist, partial to young local men whom he showered his financial favours and physical affections on. So popular did he become in Onitsha, that Stuart-Young was lionised locally for his great wealth with the grand-sounding Igbo nickname Odeziaku, meaning 'Keeper of Wealth'.

His bachelor status and lack of children would lead the locals to conclude that this palm oil ruffian was married to the Water Spirit Goddess or *Mami Wata*, who had made him wealthy in exchange for whatever children he would have had. But most astonishingly, this wealthy trader was also an avid and imaginative writer whose forte was the fake memoir genre. Among other false claims in his published works, Odeziaku would insinuate himself into relationships with no less famous men than Oscar Wilde, Walter Egerton, Roger Casement and Rudyard Kipling. Living with a succession of male servants in his 'Little House of No Regrets' on New Market Road in Onitsha, Stuart-Young would become a local hero of some sorts for his generosity and racial openness; eventually dying in Nigeria where his passing generated a tremendous outpouring of grief. According to a contemporary newspaper report at the time of his death in 1939, 'A mourning party of two hundred aged women visited all his buildings singing dirges and eulogising his name. The young men of the town sounded the ogene in his honour as if for a free Prince of the land, and all the while Onitsha main market remained practically deserted'[3]. At all events, the life of Odeziaku provides us with a well-recorded picture of the kind of influence and power that individual European traders shorn of any major corporate or sovereign backing were already personally able to acquire as settled residents of major towns along the river during the nineteenth century.

Returning from Odeziaku's time to the early nineteenth century, these European trader-settlers were all attracted by the booming demand for palm oil, the reddish vegetable oil that was then becoming a critically important lubricant for machinery and feedstock for soap manufacture in the still rapidly industrialising and modernising global economy. To meet this demand, a well-organised local supply chain was quick to evolve in and around the Oil Rivers, with a complex new political economy forming quickly around the labour-intensive production, transportation and export of palm oil and associated produce. As we will see later in our story, the political and economic consequences of palm oil prosperity would come to eclipse all other considerations as the most important factor driving both domestic external relations and British foreign policy in the Oil Rivers well into the twentieth century. As with every instance of a valuable natural resource with substantial export demand fulfilled by a thriving community of increasingly important foreign trading concerns, competing European traders in the Oil Rivers began very early in the nineteenth century to jostle and exert political influence on the domestic affairs of the area.

Oil and Politics in the Niger Delta

British naval forces in the Bight of Bonny were constantly called upon to intervene when necessary in enforcing the settlement of trade and political disputes. By as early as 1837, a growing conflict between Alali and young King Dappa had already led to an intervention (at the instance no doubt of the supercargoes) by a West African Naval Squadron vessel in favour of reinforcing the latter's authority. The power tussle and violent quarrels between parties loyal to the king and his leading House chief, and between rival supercargoes protecting their trading interests, continued for nearly 20 years until the first of several mutual associations of trading chiefs and supercargoes had to be formed in 1853, which was called a 'Court of Equity.' These courts were intended to act as a neutral venue for conflict resolution and enforcing law and order among the trading community, where severely violent clashes were liable to break-out regularly on account of commercial disagreements and outright fraud. Sure enough, the Bonny Court of Equity soon became powerful enough to attempt a deposition of King Dappa the very next year, following some of the king's more outrageous and disruptive edicts. For example, Dappa declared war on the neighbouring city-state of New Calabar, which most of his House chiefs refused to support, and then introduced a new law directing all trade to go through his own House.

This was a step too far and King Dappa was removed in January 1854 by the Court, to be replaced by his nephew. This young nephew (confusingly for us, named Dappo) was unable to exercise influence over old chiefs like Alali during his short reign, and when he died mysteriously the following year, a civil war broke out in Bonny. On one side of this conflict were arrayed partisans of the royal house, backed by another large House known as the Manilla Pepple; on the other side were the Anna Pepple, Jaja's house, led by Alali. Several years of fighting, local uncertainty and disturbance followed, during which Chief Alali tried (and failed) to replace the traditional institution of Bonny King with a council of native chiefs. Alali's attempt failed most likely because the neutral and stabilising influence of the royal office was a key criterion for its past success, never mind the reverence and traditional belief in the spiritual rights of the royal. Dappa (who had been exiled with his son, 'George', to England) was therefore invited back to Bonny as King, where he died in 1866, to be succeeded by his European-educated heir, the young Prince George. Chief Alali himself died soon after, removing the two dominant rivals of the last 30 years from the scene at Bonny and ending one of the more disastrous transitions of royal power in Nigerian history. All through this period, young Jaja remained unknown politically but was focused on extending his trade, rising to the rank of a first-line chief at Bonny by 1861.

With a weak and foreign educated new king on the throne, hostilities resumed in earnest between the two most powerful Houses in Bonny, Anna Pepple and Manila Pepple. Jaja had assumed the leadership (by unanimous acclamation) of Anna Pepple House around 1867 when none of the other major contenders was interested in the heavy inheritance. Alali left behind huge debts of between £10,000 to £15,000 to supercargoes, quite substantial amounts in those days, which had to be settled by the new House chief. Stout and frail-looking but clever and capable, all contemporary acquaintances who wrote about Jaja remarked upon his great leadership and business acumen. No lesser a character witness than a British Consul, Sir Richard Burton, wrote in one of his dispatches during 1864 that 'Jaja, son of an unknown bushman, is young, healthy, and powerful, and not less ambitious, energetic and decided. He is the most influential man and greatest trader in the River, and £50,000 it is said may annually pass through his hands. In a short time, he will either be shot, or he will beat down all his rivals'[4]. As though determined to live up to this resounding prophecy, Jaja traded his way out of the Alali debt overhang and quietly determined very early in his career as Anna Pepple House chief that he would secede from the chaos at Bonny, and establish an independent trading kingdom - where he was less likely to be shot.

Eastern Secession and the Rise of Opobo

In this enterprise, the young secessionist was aided and abetted by a French supercargo with close ties to Anna Pepple house named Charles de Cardi, and an ambitious British trading firm called Alexander Miller, Brother and Company Limited (locally known as Miller Brothers). Miller Brothers had recently arrived in the area, were seeking to gain market share and saw in the enterprising

Jaja their path to success. Towards this joint future objective, Jaja selected and empowered about 20 young former Alali lieutenants of proven ability, assisting them to become independent traders. Jaja continued his empowerment efforts by purchasing canoes for these young men and connecting them to European supercargoes who gave them goods on credit, with the beneficent Jaja standing as guarantor.

Meanwhile, the enmity and jealousy of the royal party towards Anna Pepple house and its rising star merchant-chief continued, with a certain Chief Oko Jumbo who was also a former slave and leader of Manilla Pepple house being the primary unifying factor in the opposition to Jaja. By September 1869, matters had come to a head, and Oko Jumbo made his move: advising the supercargoes to move their hulks out to sea because a civil war was imminent. The aim was to crush Jaja before he became the most economically powerful trader at Bonny. At stake was the lion's share of palm oil trade valued at £1,000,000 annually. Surprising everyone, Jaja feigned surrender, stooping to conquer. He wrote to the Court of Equity and the British Consul, 'placing himself under the protection of Her Majesty the Queen of England.' It was a clever feint, for Jaja had absolutely no such intentions, and was only playing for time to complete the logistics of his spectacular coming coup. Meanwhile, multiple palavas with much fanfare were convened with the king, between both houses and the supercargoes. The royal party was overjoyed at the apparent turn of events and clever insiders were already speculating at the magnitude of fines Jaja would have to pay.

Cometh the hour, cometh the man. In October 1869, after more than two years of planning, Jaja gave the order for all the leading chiefs of his House to relocate their trading and military infrastructure to a strategically selected settlement east of Bonny island, situated at an important chokepoint near the mouth of the critical Imo river, which opened up the trade routes into much of the interior Igbo palm oil country. To secure the House chief's support, he entered into a new economic compact with them (the *Minima*

Agreement), under which Jaja would withhold only 25 per cent of the export duties levied on outgoing produce, with the balance of 75 per cent shared among the chiefs of the new kingdom. By contrast, in Bonny, the king retained 100 per cent of this commission, known locally as the 'Comey'[5]. Going further, the ever-strategically minded Jaja entered into an important military alliance with the leadership of an itinerant Igbo martial confederation of communities from deep within Igboland, known as the Aro.

Opobo and Arochukwu in Alliance

The Aro, whom we will discuss in more detail later had been responsible for a substantial amount of the trade in humans from the interior. They were the dedicated followers and enforcers of a feared native oracle known as the Arochukwu, after which their hometown was named. This oracle was notorious for accepting copious gifts of humans from its supplicants, which were 'eaten' through the mouth of the oracle, only to be expelled from the rear and escorted to the coast for sale[6]. The Arochukwu oracle was historically the most important and supreme adjudication venue for disputes in all of Igboland and remained so until its forced demise by British armed forces early in the twentieth century. The Aro were settled in multiple communities across the hinterland and also maintained a regular mercenary force at their headquarters, which was franchised out to intervene in armed conflicts across the Igbo country, the major source for their inventory of humans for export[7].

Entry into the Aro alliance allowed Jaja to secure his rear connection with the Igbo hinterland, as well as to dominate the Qua Iboe communities eastwards from him across the channel. Simultaneously, the Anna Pepple naval force was deployed to police the opening channel into the Imo river itself and prevent any unsanctioned trade with the interior. Jaja was strategic in naming his start-up coastal kingdom. He called it 'Opobo,' evoking nostalgia with its favourable remembrance of the palmy days under the great former Bonny king. 14 of the 18 largest Houses ultimately followed Jaja to Opobo. Sure enough, with their excellent strategic positioning, Jaja and his chiefs at Opobo were able to establish a stranglehold on palm oil trade from the interior. This new monopoly was at the expense of a stunned minority of Bonny chiefs and all the stupefied supercargoes remaining at Bonny. For his coup de grâce, Jaja offered exclusive offtake deals to Charles de Cardi and the newly arrived Miller Brothers, who were struggling to win market share in the crowded and rowdy atmosphere at Bonny. Their vessels anchored off Opobo and provided Jaja with a ready market for all the output from his new settlement, as well as international trading connections, particularly direct communication with Europe.

In 1870, the new sovereign of Opobo very quickly established direct relations with the British consul at Fernando Po, writing to declare his openness to enter into friendly relations with Britain. For his communications, Jaja employed a Western-educated Saro secretary named D.C. Wileiams, another instance of Saros in influential positions across the country. Meanwhile, King Jaja's spectacular coup completely disrupted the economy of the Oil Rivers, leading several of the smaller British trading firms to go bankrupt. As we saw with Efunroye Tinubu at Lagos, the Trust System of trade, with its intimate credit linkages exacerbated any radical break-off in commercial relations such as this one. Worse for them, some of the British trading firms had permanent fixtures like warehouses and cargo handling facilities on the beach at Bonny and could not easily relocate to Opobo even if they were allowed to.

The supercargoes of these firms were spoiling for a war to crush Jaja, providing arms and ammunition to the Bonny party, while lobbying the British consul for a gunboat blockade of Opobo. One Bonny supercargo (a certain Mr Cheetham) was known to have gone as far as to purchase a gunboat in England for private use in fighting Jaja but was discouraged from proceeding when informed by Consul Livingstone that the vessel and its crew would be treated by the British navy as pirates. The situation was bad enough for the

British government to intervene, which it did by sending a senior naval officer named Commodore Commerell with five warships to Bonny in 1873. Commerell's mandate was to enforce a peace agreement and reopen Opobo to trade with all comers. Peace was duly made, and the 'Livingstone' Treaty between Opobo and Britain was signed. A carefully orchestrated fait accompli had been attained by this remarkable leader; and Opobo's independence from Bonny was recognised, an unrivalled masterclass in secession execution. The ever strategic Jaja showed further diplomatic wisdom by sending 50 of his fighters to support British efforts in the Ashanti War of 1873.

Thus, began the best years of this impressive new king's career. Jaja's heyday at Opobo coincided with the finest years of Bishop Crowther's reign on the Niger. Consecrated in 1864, the bishop also served via the West Africa Company as the effective British Consul on the Niger until 1876. As with Abeokuta earlier in the nineteenth century, educated Africans elsewhere on the western coast soon learnt of Jaja's ambitious kingdom and were attracted to it. A British-style school was established in 1873, under the leadership of a Saro teacher named Gooding, offering a high standard of education for the children of Jaja and his leading chiefs, according to a contemporary observer. Soon after, a Liberian woman named Emma White, the daughter of former slaves who emigrated to Monrovia, joined Jaja at Opobo, employed originally as a kind of governess and personal teacher to his children, but ultimately also writing correspondence and becoming influential in his business and political affairs. Sadly, as we have seen already with Crowther, by the 1880s, the end was approaching for this period of unrestrained native agency in Nigerian commerce, missionary enterprise, administration and even governance.

The Non-African Association

In September 1887, Jaja's short career as king at Opobo was ended by one of the same kinds of arrogant young British arrivistes that forced Crowther's retirement in 1890. The instrument of Jaja's demise would be one forgettable British vice consul to the Oil Rivers, a certain Harry Johnston. Johnston was much under the combined influence of his boss Consul Hewett (who fiercely opposed Opobo independence but was then on leave in Britain) and a newly formed trade group of supercargoes ridiculously self-labelled as the African Association. This decidedly Non-African Association was resisting Jaja's monopoly, and attempting to reassert dominance over the coastal trade, in a similar manner as had recently been accomplished on the river by the Royal Niger Company (a story we will come to shortly). Jaja for his part was strategically countering the threat through direct diplomacy with London and had already sent four of his senior chiefs to the British capital earlier in 1887. Their mission was to meet with the Foreign Office and present his case for an independent jurisdiction at Opobo. This was entirely legal and appropriate as recorded in the 1873 Livingstone Treaty between Britain and Opobo, which was still in force.

Those meetings were already about to commence when Johnston (supported by the so-called African Association at Bonny) determined that the time was right to make his move. These actions were against the direct instructions of the Prime Minister, Robert Arthur James Gascoyne-Cecil, the 5th Marquess of Salisbury or more simply, Lord Salisbury. The British Prime Minister was yet to be convinced that King Jaja posed any threat more malign than that of a 'local ruler asserting his trading prerogatives'. Yet, Johnston took advantage of a mix up in cable communication with the Foreign Office to summon the British gunboat HMS Goshawk and its marines quickly to the scene at Opobo.

After much correspondence back and forth, with the vice consul attempting to set up a palava aboard the Goshawk without providing the customary European hostage onshore, Johnston sent the following note to Jaja on September 18, 1887: 'I have summoned you to attend in a friendly spirit. I hereby assure you that whether you accept or reject my proposal, no restraint whatever will be put on you. You will be free to go as soon as you have heard the message.' Accepting this written commitment of safe conduct from a responsible officer of a leading European government, King Jaja boarded the gunboat. Here, he was summarily informed that the simple message from the British government was that he must surrender immediately and leave Opobo into exile, or have his town razed to the ground within the next hour. With a gunboat already training its deadly sights on his hometown, exile (and the chance to continue fighting by peaceful means) must have seemed the more attractive option to the founder of the prosperous settlement. Hence, he departed Opobo peacefully as a political prisoner, never to return. Deported to Accra, Jaja was convicted in a sham trial of made-up charges, and sentenced to exile in the Caribbean, with an annual pension supposedly equivalent to his estimated share of the export duties, or comey, at Bonny as determined by the British government.

The commercial interests of rival British palm oil traders at Bonny and later Opobo had both created the opportunity and ultimately the trigger for the rise and fall of a self-made indigenous merchant prince in the Oil Rivers. In the same way, the philanthropic vision of the Clapham Sect descendants led by Henry Venn had created the conditions for Bishop Crowther's rise on the Niger, only to be replaced several decades later by a different kind of vision and mindset towards the end of the nineteenth century. The rise from adversity to the stars and fall from grace of the merchant prince and sainted bishop were now complete, in both cases the result of a change in thinking and strategy about the future of their country.

Arrival of a British Golden Boy

Perhaps the most important member of the *dramatis personae* leading that change in thinking about the future of Nigeria was a corporate financier named George Taubman Goldie. Born in 1846 to a wealthy family in the Isle of Man (the tiny piece of land off the coast of the island of Great Britain), Goldie was a rebellious fourth son who joined the army (Royal Engineers), dropped out unceremoniously, and travelled to Egypt (around the time the Suez Canal was being built) to live for three years in the desert with an Arab lover. It would not be the last time he would elope or otherwise enter into an inappropriate (in Victorian era terms) love-match. In Egypt, Goldie became acquainted with the rigorous work of Heinrich Barth, exposing him for the first time to scientific knowledge of Africa's interior. Upon the death of his Arab mistress, this young Lothario returned to England, and soon eloped with his family governess to Paris. The lovebirds were trapped in the French capital during the 1870 Franco-Prussian War which led to the unification of Germany the following year. Luckily for the restless Goldie, not only did he survive the siege of Paris, he also had relatives looking out for his best interests back in England.

Upon his return, he was introduced through a family connection to another family with Niger interests. Goldie's eldest half-brother had married into this latter family. From this profitable connection arose an opportunity to participate in trade and commercial enterprise on the Niger. In 1876, aged 30, George Taubman Goldie formed the Central African Trading Company and proceeded on a visit to the Niger the following year. For his travel up the river, the ambitious young man arranged for a 90-foot steam launch named the *Binue* to be built and sent in a knocked-down form to Akassa for assembly. Described contemporaneously as a 'fair, thin, young man with piercing blue eyes looking [like] something between a vulture and a mummy,'[8] George was accompanied on the trip by his brother, Alexander. The grandiose ambition of the young men was to sail up the Niger to the Benue, following originally in Barth's footsteps, but then going further to travel overland across the Sahara Desert to the Nile.

In the event, the golden brothers had travelled no further than Nupe before Alexander fell quite ill, and so they aborted the trip and returned to the coast. But Goldie had seen enough on this trip to support a business case in his mind for the consolidation of British interests on the river into a single state-backed company. Specifically, Goldie had observed high trade volumes amidst chaotic trading arrangements, tight competition, frequent disputes, violent conflict and civil disturbance, among other problematic business conditions during this era. This young man with no prior business experience was convinced that the solution lay in a scheme of mergers and acquisition, and that he could bring such a consolidation into being, at the expense of the hard-headed veterans trading in the area. There were four major companies trading on the river at this point , the West African Company (as we know already, owned by Clegg, inspired by Venn, run by the bishop's son, Josiah Crowther), and three other British enterprises (including the Miller Brothers, who we have already met at Opobo).

In 1879, after two years of negotiations and discussions, Goldie was able to secure an agreement with the promoters of all four existing companies on the Niger to merge all of their assets and equipment on the river into a newly registered company he called the United African Company (UAC), capitalised with the impressive sum of £250,000 (nearly £30 million in present-day money). This rich new company would trade exclusively on the Niger, allowing the selling shareholders to continue with their business interests elsewhere in the neighbourhood (particularly on the Oil Rivers as we have seen with Miller Brothers). However, a fifth entrant into the river (a new French company named Compagnie Française de l'Afrique Equatoriale or CFAO) was founded around the same time as UAC, with the strong support of the French government, denying Goldie the monopoly that he sought. CFAO quickly became a thorn in the flesh of the aspiring young British businessman, especially as its shareholders with their strong government backing saw no reason to sell their interests to a seemingly harmless private-sector competitor.

In its dealings with the local chiefs and Emirs on the Niger (particularly with Emir Masaba of Nupe, the most dominant of the river chiefs), CFAO made clear that it was seeking to dominate trade and politics in the area. Goldie had already come to realise that he too would need very strong government support to strengthen his hand in the competition with the French and achieve his original goal of dominating all the trade up and down the river. As Goldie said to a Reuters correspondent in one of the only interviews he ever gave, he had to play out his plans on the river 'like a game of chess' to obtain the much-desired monopoly. To this end, he set his mind to obtaining a royal charter, like the one secured in November 1881 by the British North Borneo Company in present-day Malaysia. Studying the Borneo charter, Goldie was able to identify the key terms and conditions he would need to fulfil, to obtain similar official support on the Niger, essentially: a large capital base, a dominant commercial position on the river, and a highly influential board of directors.

Corporate Financial Shenanigans

Utilising his strong family connections and friendships in the city of London, Goldie was able to overcome the key obstacles to his desired charter, beginning with the biggest one. In 1882, Goldie convinced an extremely well-connected Liberal politician named Henry Bruce to become the chairman of a newly established successor company to the UAC. Bruce was previously Home Secretary under Gladstone, and later, Lord President of the Council and invested by the Queen as the first Baron Aberdare. Lord Aberdare, who was strongly connected to Gladstone, Foreign Secretary Lord Granville, and all the key political figures in late Victorian era London was exactly the kind of influential personality that could deliver a royal charter for a young man's new enterprise in West Africa.

Goldie also brought an influential investment banker named C.W. Mills, and a major cotton trader named J.F. Hutton onto his board of directors. Hutton was also a Liberal MP and president of the Manchester Chamber of Commerce. With Baron Aberdare and the rest of this blue-chip gang now on board, Goldie proceeded to undertake a stock market issue of new shares, increasing the company's working capital to more than £300,000 in 1882 (about £34 million in present-day money). Flush with cash and support, Goldie and his bankers proceeded to Paris in mid-1882 to enter into negotiations with CFAO in relation to a buy-out of the French company from the river. His offer was rebuffed, and the team returned across the channel empty-handed. They would meet on the river. The newly renamed National African Company then began to hire experienced senior trading professionals on the Niger, including men like William Wallace (later, Sir, and Agent General of the Royal Niger Company), opening up new trading stations and 'factories' at multiple towns and settlements on the river.

Duplicitous Capitalists in Berlin

In 1882, the 'Scramble for Africa' entered high gear. The British surprise occupation of Egypt after some riots and violence targeted at Europeans caused a great deal of resentment in France, whose leaders did not mind having Egypt for themselves. The persistent but cunning efforts of King Leopold of Belgium, who was using his duplicitously named International African Association to carve out a lucrative personal empire for himself in the middle of Africa, were not going unnoticed. These factors led to the convening of the now-infamous 'Berlin Conference' by the first Chancellor of the newly united German Republic, Otto von Bismarck. Each of the great European powers (14 countries, including the United States of America) agreed to send delegates to this meeting, which was organised to create a framework for recognising the various 'spheres of influence' and interests of different nations in Africa.

The murderous Leopold had stage-managed this opportunity to have his designs for the gigantic area drained by the great Congo river 'legally' recognised by the larger European powers.

George Goldie represented Britain's Niger interests at the Berlin Conference. He was joined by a Liverpool trader with a great deal of experience in the Oil Rivers named John Holt. Holt had been trading in the area since 1862, when he was 21 years old, and had started his own business in 1867 by buying out Juliana, the African widow of his former employer, James Lyslager. The Nigeria triumvirate was completed by Alfred Jones, an executive officer of the Elder Dempster Line. Elder Dempster was the dominant shipping company in the area, founded by Jones and two other former employees of Macgregor Laird's family business in Liverpool. Together, this trio represented British shipping interests on the Niger and in the Oil Rivers. For most reporters and history recorders, the major outcome of the conference was the Berlin Act, which laid out the terms and conditions of the 'Scramble for Africa.' For Goldie however, the most important result from Berlin was an agreement he finally struck on the sidelines of the conference with CFAO, to buy-out its Niger interests, in exchange for newly issued shares in the NAC. The stage was increasingly being set for the British colonial takeover of Nigeria.

In advance of this summit, a great effort had begun to be exerted in on-the-ground treaty making and flag raising across West and Central Africa, with each party attempting to justify its claims to any given area as a 'sphere of influence.' French and German field officers began to make efforts to enter into treaties with chiefs and emirs in the vicinity of the Niger. These efforts were cleverly played up by Goldie and Lord Aberdare to the British Foreign Office, as evidence of potential threats to British trade and commerce in the area. In June 1884, the NAC formally applied to the British government for a royal charter, which would license it to administer the areas around the Niger in the name of the Queen, warding off competition from other foreign countries, and securing the area for British trade.

Dubious Charters and 'Illegal' Trade

The application process was long and drawn out, with strong opposition from both the Treasury and the Foreign Office, neither of which was keen on exposure to the potential financial and administrative expenditure that might accrue to the government as a result of the agreement. After much pressure and intrigue, including subtle threats by the company to accept a charter from another European power, the final draft of a charter was issued and formally accepted by the newly renamed Royal Niger Company in March 1886. The royal blessing was secured nearly two years after the application, and more than seven years since Goldie began merging the British interests on the river, with this goal in mind. The Clapham Sect Era was now officially over, replaced by the Imperial Era, which would be led by ambitious British traders and capitalists, rather than missionaries and local agents. The unstoppable force of global capitalism had arrived on the Niger to meet with the seemingly immovable object of local traditional rule. The latter would inevitably yield after a hard-fought battle, but only because it lacked the unifying and single-minded determination of the former.

During the late rainy season of 1887, the practical realities of Goldie's wheeling and dealing in London were beginning to be felt by ordinary traders up and down the river. In one typical example, a local man from Brass was travelling up one of the many creeks in the river's delta with a canoe load of goods for sale. He was spotted by an RNC-owned boat called the *Vigilant*, which had been placed in the Niger to (among other things) police 'illegal' trade, that is trading not sanctioned by the 'chartered and limited' Company. According to a contemporary witness, 'A long chase ensued, with the Brass man ultimately running his canoe ashore at (a nearby village of the Patani tribe), whose inhabitants turned out and opened heavy fire on the Vigilant, which eventually had to retire'[9].

Early the following year, a strong force of RNC constabulary was dispatched to the Patani village, destroying it completely. Not too far away on a large, placid water body adjacent to the river called the Oguta lake, a similar scene played out about the same time at a town called Idu on the left bank of the lake. Idu was a long-standing major sourcing market for palm oil to be traded with Europeans at the coast. Middlemen from the New Calabar depots of Buguma, Abonema and Degema travelled up to purchase oil at Idu, which they sold at European factories back home. Now it happened that sometime in 1885, the chiefs of Idu agreed to a 'treaty' of some sorts with the representatives of Goldie on the river, much to the chagrin of the New Calabar middlemen. Under the so-called treaty, the RNC, which was an organisation that the irate New Calabar traders had never heard of, purported to have the rights to charge import and export duties on produce brought to or taken away from Idu.

The middlemen naturally ignored this intrusion into their domestic affairs and refused to pay anything at the Idu 'customs station' designated by the Company. For two years, nothing happened, until September 1887 after the RNC had come into possession of that dubious legal instrument issued via the proclamation of 'Victoria, by the Grace of God, of the United Kingdom of Great Britain and Ireland, Queen, Defender of the Faith.' In short order, the Company instituted a blockade of the Oguta lake, placing a heavily armed grand old hulk in the water, manned by two Europeans and 21 men of its constabulary. Their mission was simple: no trade was to be allowed in the area without a duty being paid to the Company, and any attempt to evade the duty resulted in the seizure of such canoes and the confiscation of its contents. It would take a while for enforcement to be total, but the direction was set: Exit the Bible, Enter the Gun; the Clapham Sect Era was over on the River Niger.

Davies, Bonetta and the Victorian Lagos Elite

Elsewhere, there would be other local commercial victims from the arrival of Goldie and the end of the Clapham Sect Era in Nigeria.

One of the more prominent examples among the established local merchant-financial elite may serve as a case study for this change in fortunes. We have already met Captain James Pinson Labulo Davies, one of the young beneficiaries of Henry Venn's philanthropic endeavours in West Africa, who would rise during the era of the native agency to be a vanguard among the indigenous elite at Lagos. Captain Davies was born of Yoruba recaptive parents (they were both from villages in the old Oyo empire) at Bathurst village in Sierra Leone. The intelligent young Saro was privileged to attend the CMS Grammar School at Freetown, coming under the influence of the missionaries and later of Venn directly through his Native Agency Committee (NAC), which granted scholarships to promising young African men to study professional courses in England.

Founded sometime in the 1840s, through the lobbying of Venn, the NAC was supported by the British Foreign Secretary Lord Palmerston and other important cabinet members, notably Secretary of War Baron Panmure and First Lord of the Admiralty Sir Francis Baring. Venn's actions were designed to deliberately foster the emergence of an African indigenous elite, and the specific proposal which was to change the life of the young Davies provided for training young African men for service in the army and navy as military surgeons and naval officers. James Davies and two other young beneficiaries were placed as trainee naval seamen with a British Preventative Squadron vessel (named *HMS Volcano*), patrolling the west coast of Africa. The NAC furnished the young recruits (selected by a competitive examination) with financing and personal training instruments for their course of study. Joining in 1849, we have already seen how Lieutenant Davies was one of the native officers involved and wounded in the bombardment of Lagos (aboard *HMS Bloodhound*) in December 1851, leading to the removal of Oba Kosoko and the installation of Akitoye by the British the following month.

Davies completed his service and retired from the British

Navy in 1852, embarking on a private career as a contract captain or master of merchant vessels owned by African merchants at Sierra Leone. After a sailing disaster at Lagos in 1855, Captain Davies exited the contractual vessel master business to establish a trading concern of his own, originally in partnership with a West Indian firm based in London. His business model was simple: import goods were delivered to him, which he sold and in return shipped palm oil, ivory, and other produce to Europe. Success followed quickly, with the young merchant acquiring several small vessels and boats, primarily carrying palm oil and cotton down the river for export, as well as spirits and manufactured goods for import. Davies' financial success from trading was parlayed into the real estate and money lending businesses. This progression was typical for the most successful Saro merchants of Victorian Lagos, most notably in the life of the carpenter turned financier, Isaac Benjamin Williams. Born in 1846 at Freetown, Williams would become the leading merchant banker at Lagos by the 1880s. As it turns out, one of J.P.L. Davies' (and Isaac Williams') most prominent customers in the real estate-backed financing business was the ever-present Madam Efunroye Tinubu. Together, however, their joint obligor list would have read like a *Who's Who* of Victorian Lagos. The lawyers, Joseph Egerton Shyngle[xiii] and (later, Sir) Kitoye Ajasa, who was also a pioneer newspaper publisher; prominent merchants and professionals J.K. Coker, B.C. Dawodu, and Z.A Williams were all clients of I.B. Williams, who was more notable than Davies in this line of business.

Madam Tinubu secured a mortgage of £500 (about £63,000 in present-day terms) from Davies in 1864, secured by land and

---

xiii The economic magnet status of Victorian Lagos turned it into a cosmopolitan city that attracted people like Egerton Shyngle, a Gambian who had studied law in London and married a White woman named Annie. They moved to Lagos in 1890 where they had two children and set up a law firm but their union ended in a bitter divorce case - Shyngle v. Shyngle - when she returned from a trip to England and found him living with another woman (See Kristin Mann's *Marrying Well: Marriage Status and Social Change among the Educated Elite in Colonial Lagos*).

buildings she owned in Lagos, during a period in which the Iyalode (literally meaning 'Mother in the City') of Egba women was quite deeply involved in domestic politics and the defence of Abeokuta from the second major Dahomey invasion[10]. Tinubu (previously married to the old Oba Adele as we have seen) had become dominant in the court of Dosunmu, particularly in the illegal slave trade. Yet, she was still expelled from Lagos in 1856 with the assistance of British gunboats, after leading a failed uprising against the Saro immigrants (like Davies) who were growing in influence around Dosunmu. Her expulsion convulsed the import-export market for some time as she was owing more than £5,000 to coastal traders, advanced to her based on the Trust System. But by 1861, this resilient and towering entrepreneur of the Victorian era had bounced back from her temporary political setbacks and was the leading exporter of cotton from Abeokuta (more than 1,300 bales were shipped to Britain that year). Differences in politics aside, J.P.L Davies had no problems entering into large financial dealings with the most important trader in the country during the period, an indication of the increasing sophistication of the Lagos economy during this transformational era.

A protégé of Henry Venn (in a not dissimilar manner to the much older Bishop Crowther), Davies continued to expand his business and social ambitions in the country using multiple avenues. His choice of spouse was also strategic, and in 1860 Davies proposed (by letter) to marry Sarah Bonetta Forbes, the 19-year-old ward of Queen Victoria. This Sarah Forbes, originally named Aina, was the same 8-year-old girl whom we saw delivered from King Ghezo's claws at Dahomey in 1849, in the name of the Queen, and at the request of the visiting Commander Frederick Forbes. The young lady was subsequently adopted by and raised around the household of the diminutive Empress, who was noted for her interests in faraway countries, liberal causes and social experiments. Sarah had been educated in Sierra Leone (alongside Abigail Crowther, the Bishop's daughter) and England. Here she lived as a ward of the Queen in the remarkable home of the Afrophiles James and Elizabeth Schoen, which included two boys brought back from northern Nigeria by Heinrich Barth. The young and romantic Sarah Bonetta Forbes declined the proposal from the much older and practical J.P.L Davies, even though it had been sanctioned by the Queen's representatives and had the blessing of Henry Venn.

This was not an acceptable response to Queen Victoria, who expressed her displeasure in a characteristically royal passive-aggressive manner. Sarah Forbes was removed from the comfortable home of the Schoens, to live with new guardians (two unmarried old ladies) near Brighton. 16 months later, the distraught young lady assented to the match, and her grand celebrity wedding to J.P.L Davies was held at St. Nicholas Church, Brighton, Sussex on 14 August 1862, with a cast of characters in attendance that included all the fanciest Saro denizens of Victorian Lagos. The ambitious 32-year-old businessman had secured the most favourable possible connection, his bride being a direct protégée of Queen Victoria. Returning to Lagos, the couple became the leading lights of the local social scene which revolved around the Anglican St. Paul's Church, at Breadfruit Street, of which Captain Davies was the leading benefactor. This colossus of Victorian Lagos was soon named one of the first native members of the largely ceremonial Legislative Council convened by the British government to administer the colony of Lagos, thus becoming *The Honorable* J.P.L. Davies.

Much prosperity followed, with Davies expanding his charmed career to include interests in commercial agriculture, becoming the first mainland West African grower and exporter of cocoa, from his large farm at Ijon (a place still called Camp Davies today) near the present-day boundary between Lagos and Ogun States of Nigeria. Nearly a century later, the cash crop would grow to become the most important export commodity in western Nigeria, and the basis for government revenues that financed an ambitious social development programme of education, healthcare, and infrastructure. This would be in direct fulfilment of the deepest

long-term ambitions held by Henry Venn and his Clapham Sect
Era co-conspirators in England, when they established the Native
Agency Committee. We have already seen how the Venn acolytes
Davies and T.B. Macaulay combined financial and intellectual
resources respectively to establish the CMS Grammar School at
Lagos in 1860, the first secondary school in the Niger area. The
school would go on to provide the educational background for
an entire generation of leading Nigerian professionals (doctors,
lawyers, engineers, and politicians), including a list of names too
long and widely known to be repeated here.

Ironically, J.P.L Davies, the same man who served on one
of the vessels that reduced Lagos to a British dependency, would
also become one of the most vocal opponents to the full British
colonisation of Lagos in 1861. Along with the CMS and the rest
of the missionary party at Lagos, Davies became the earliest
leader of the opposition to British rule. As an ally to the hapless
Oba Dosunmu, Davies was responsible for writing much of the
opposition correspondence from the Oba to the Foreign Office
(routed via Henry Venn in London) when British officers on the
scene (particularly William McCrosky) elected to formally annex
Lagos ten years after the island was invaded. This opposition party
would continue to antagonise British officials in Lagos, under the
new Governor John Hawley Glover (known locally as Oba Globa),
who sought to use all the power and authority at his disposal to
establish the British Colony government at Lagos as the primary
controlling and taxing authority for all produce emanating from all
trading routes in the hinterland. This led to political and border
disputes, as well as armed conflict between Lagos and its hitherto
allies, Abeokuta. This was a disagreement that would be further
complicated by the intermittent Yoruba wars over the next two
decades.

In this political battle, Davies, at the vanguard of the educated
Saro community at Lagos, would be a key supporter of the Egba;
while (ironically) the erstwhile slave dealers recently expelled from

power by the British would form the bulwark of local support for Glover and his successors as Governor at Lagos. This pro-British party included Kosoko and his leading chiefs, Oshodi Tapa and Taiwo Olowo, who were now focused on promoting and maintaining control over their trading routes into the hinterland. Lagos politics was changing very quickly with the increasing sophistication of economic affairs in the former slave city. Unfortunately for Davies, tragedy would soon follow in this new political environment. The expansive entrepreneur would suffer from over-extension in his financial affairs amidst a global palm oil supply glut, as well as becoming a primary victim of the intense competition which foreshadowed Goldie's arrival and amalgamation of trading interests on the Niger. On 9 August 1876 (aged 48), the highflying Venn disciple and Lagos leading light was judged bankrupt by the London Bankruptcy Court. It is not clear if this change in financial circumstances had an impact on his marriage, but a curious power of attorney document dated December 1878 refers to a prior *Marriage Settlement* Agreement between the couple, which might have been a post-bankruptcy antenuptial protection arrangement, or an actual divorce settlement[11].

In any event, Mrs. Sarah Davies (who had always been sickly) died early of tuberculosis in 1880, leaving behind two daughters, both of whom would go on to achieve some prominence in Lagos and England. One of their daughters (Victoria) was the first of many African girls to attend Cheltenham Ladies School and would become the matriarch of the popular Randle family of Lagos, while the other was Mrs. Stella Coker who founded the Bonetta Davies Memorial School at Lagos. Mrs Coker would also be later well-known as the live-in lover of Herbert Macaulay, son of T.B. Macaulay and grandson of Bishop Crowther.

Imperial Nigeria in Formation: Enter the Maxim Gun

As we have seen already, by the start of the Imperial Era, much had already changed across the country later to be known as Nigeria, particularly in relation to economic conditions. In political terms, most of the area north of the river was firmly in the control of Dan Fodio's successors. The jihadists had spread towards the Benue, and most of the areas above that river were also firmly within their control, except for Bornu, which remained independent, albeit greatly reduced in importance. Fulani rule (as we have seen) had failed to improve the conditions of living for the average citizen of the Caliphate, from the antebellum era situation in the Hausa states which created the conditions for jihad in the first place. Even worse, the less powerful non-Muslim towns and villages in areas now within the control of Sokoto were being devastated by violent slave raids, with no recourse to any outside powers for protection. Ilorin was now firmly in Fulani control, their bridgehead into Yoruba country. The rest of that country remained still in turmoil and continued armed conflict, apart from Abeokuta, the ray of sunrise within the tropics.

Lagos (following its colonisation in 1861) had been declared a Protectorate in 1886, alongside the Oil Rivers, both areas now firmly within the control of the British government, in furtherance of its trade and commercial ambitions. But even the long-standing British administrators at Lagos Colony, who had now spent more than 25 years attempting to facilitate trade with and govern the Yoruba interior had not managed to achieve great political success. British political influence in Yoruba had declined in the years immediately after the capture of Lagos, most dramatically illustrated by the 'Ifole' or 'Housebreaking' episode at Egba in 1867, during which all European merchants, missionaries and even Christian converts had been expelled from Abeokuta. This was the fall-out of a border dispute between the Egba and Lagos, as well as armed action by British raised troops against Egba forces at Ikorodu. Political conditions would later improve under successive British governors of Lagos, but the beginnings were inauspicious.

Glover had been forced to depart, amidst political intrigue at

Lagos, and shortly afterwards, a new Yoruba civil war had broken out in 1877, which would last for 16 years. This war had rapidly expanded into a conflagration involving all major states in the Yoruba country. At some point during this conflict, the Ibadan armed forces were busy fighting on *five* separate fronts. Meanwhile, an attempt at political modernisation had been tried and failed among the Egba, led by a forward-thinking Saro tailor turned politician named G.W. Johnson. Born in Sierra Leone around 1820, Johnson was a latecomer to Abeokuta having arrived only in 1863, after the missionaries were already well established. Undaunted, he proceeded to ingratiate his way into the innermost circles of the leading Ogboni chiefs, establishing an Egba United Board of Management (EUBM) in 1865. EUBM was intended to be a formal, central, and Westernised civil government body for the Egba, as a response to the encroachment of British administration.

However, ever since the death of Sodeke, the divisions and differences between the various parties and interests in Abeokuta were just too deep, and the EUBM did not succeed in becoming much more than a letter-writing organisation on behalf of the leading Ogboni chiefs. Johnson, who himself acted as Secretary of EUBM, eventually left Abeokuta in disappointment. Lampooned by the traditional and educated elite alike, he was nicknamed 'Reversible Johnson' for his political flexibility and the ineffectiveness of his ideas. However, his pioneering efforts would later yield fruit in terms of Egba governance reform, as we will see later in our story. We have also seen through the affairs of Bonny, what conditions were like in the Oil Rivers, our vantage point for viewing the situation in the insular and closed-off Igbo hinterland, which alongside ancient Benin would remain impregnable to foreign political interference until very late in the nineteenth century.

This was the environment in which the Royal Niger Company arrived. For all of its commercial savvy, London stock market capital, international trading connections, freedom from the competition with other Europeans, depots and factories alongside the river and the coast, and even British political support - the company was still in a very tenuous position politically. Strictly speaking, Goldie's wonderfully avaricious creation, while representative of the incoming, unstoppable force of global capitalism, was as yet no match for the difficult local political terrain. There was one piece of newly invented technology however, which the British Royal Niger Company would have at its disposal as it came into the river to commence the Imperial Era, and this would prove to be the gamechanger for the future of Nigeria. This piece of equipment was patented in 1884 by an American born British serial-inventor named Hiram Stephens Maxim, who was born in 1840 and learnt his trade as an instrument maker in the United States.

Into a world that was already in great turmoil - the United States civil war only ended in 1865 and the Franco-Prussian war would follow in 1870 - the revolutionary Maxim machine gun was introduced in 1884. Where early nineteenth-century musket rifles took a whole minute to load, had a range of only 80 meters and misfired nearly a third of the time, this mass-murder device could expel 600 rounds of ammunition in a single minute, utilising energy from the recoil acting on the breech block to eject each spent cartridge and insert the next one, instead of a hand-operated mechanism. This devastating killing machine was vastly more competent than anything ever created in human history up to that point, even if it typically required a team of several operators to deploy it in the field given its weight and awkward shape. Hiram's weapon industrialised the business of human destruction, commencing in the late 1800s.

In Africa, this weapon of mass destruction would be entered into service at the exact moment European imperial and colonial ambitions were reaching their zenith. In battlefields from the Cape to Cairo, Maxim's machine gun would prove to be as decisive a decision-maker in matters of politics and economics as the continent had ever witnessed. The Maxim was as much a killing machine as a tool of psychological warfare, given how dramatically its entry into one side of a contest was known to change the balance of power between combatants. Fortuitously for the ambitious men of the post-Clapham Sect era in Nigeria, this fearsome tool of destruction arrived exactly at the same time as their imperial ambitions were becoming most urgent. In the event, it would be deployed with chilling consequences to usurp the ruling traditional elite in Nigeria. They could not have imagined anything like what was coming.

1. Cookey SJS. *King Jaja of the Niger Delta: His Life and Times, 1821-1891.* UGR publishing; 2005.

2. Baikie WB. *Narrative of an exploring voyage up the rivers Kwóra and Bínue (commonly known as the Niger and Tsádda) in 1854. With a map and appendices. Pub. with the sanction of Her Majesty's Government.* J. Murray; 1856.

3. Newell S. Remembering J. M. Stuart-Young of Onitsha, Colonial Nigeria: Memoirs, Obituaries and Names. *Africa: Journal of the International African Institute.* 2003 2003;73(4):505-530.

4. Dike KO. *Trade and Politics in the Niger Delta, 1803-1885: An Introduction to the Economic and Political History of Nigeria.* Oxford University Press; 1956.

5. Baker GL. *Trade Winds on the Niger: The Saga of the Royal Niger Company 1830-1971.* Tauris Academic Studies; 1996.

6. Falola T, Heaton MM. *A History of Nigeria.* Cambridge University Press; 2008.

7. Dike KO. *Trade and Politics in the Niger Delta, 1803-1885: An Introduction to the Economic and Political History of Nigeria.* Oxford University Press; 1956.

8. Leith-Ross S. *Stepping-stones: Memoirs of Colonial Nigeria, 1907-1960.* P. Owen; 1983.

9. Baker GL. *Trade Winds on the Niger: The Saga of the Royal Niger Company 1830-1971.* Tauris Academic Studies; 1996.

10. Elebute A. *The Life of James Pinson Labulo Davies: A Colossus of Victorian Lagos.* Kachifo; 2013.

11. *Ibid.*

CHAPTER 7

The Glorious Incompetents

The Invasion of Biafra

Early in December 1901, nearly 100 years after the Mad White Man first appeared on the Niger, the first invasion of Biafra began. More than 80 heavily armed Europeans, organised into four separate columns supported by 2,100 Black equipment carriers and 1,550 soldiers, commenced an 'expedition' into the heart of the densely forested enclave hinterland adjacent to the eastern banks of the Niger. The armed White men arrived in large boats from different parts of the British world. Their local troops were supplied from further up the river in a place now called the 'Protectorate of Northern Nigeria'. Together, they set themselves up at four forward operating bases situated in friendly towns alongside convenient water transportation routes: at Unwana and Itu on the Cross River, at Akwette on the Imo River, and at Oguta, the inland lake situated only 15 kilometres from the Niger. This alarming party carried with them eight heavy artillery weapons, namely, four 75-millimetre guns and four 7-pounders, all supplied by the armoury of the so-called 'Niger Coast Protectorate,' another recently fabricated political entity.

The local leader responsible for sending this fearsome party into the unknown country, more than 100 kilometres from the southern tip of the Bight of Biafra (where, as we have seen, Europeans had lived and worked already for centuries) was a doomed imperialist who killed himself eight years later. Named Ralph Denham Rayment Moor, this imperialist was born in 1860 and by the time he joins our story, the 41-year-old was already a member of the Most Distinguished Order of Saint Michael and Saint George (a British order of chivalry founded in 1818). Moor had been knighted four years previously for his services to the British Empire at the Niger coast. He had first arrived there in 1891, travelling at his own expense to set up the police force of the new 'Oil Rivers Protectorate,' as it was then known. Previously an Irish policeman - he joined the Royal Irish Constabulary as a cadet and rose to district inspector - Moor was the archetype of the zealous, post-Clapham Sect Era young British imperialists who had arrived in Nigeria in the late 1880s and early 1890s to achieve, by force of arms if necessary, what Venn, Crowther and the CMS had laboured for more than half a century to accomplish by way of Western education, the force of argument and personal example.

Early Imperialists

For his part in our story, Moor had been brought to Nigeria by Major (later, Sir) Claude Macdonald, whom we will soon come to be familiar with. Macdonald, famous for his exploits in Hong Kong more than Nigeria, was the highly regarded Sandhurst-trained officer who had served as a military attaché in Egypt. He was sent by the British Government in 1889 to investigate complaints into the Royal Niger Company's activities. Macdonald's travels across Nigeria during 1889 were quite extensive and involved, including stopovers and conferences with all the major political and commercial actors on the river and its immediate hinterland, with the notable exception of the Adamawa Emir at Bida, who flatly refused to meet him. We will still come to discuss the extensive reporting of Macdonald's primary aide, a certain Captain Mockler-Ferryman, which provides a very graphic picture of the situation in the country at the time. Macdonald's thorough investigation report - never officially released - was so pleasing to his seniors at the Foreign Office in London, that they sent him back out as Consul General and Commissioner for the Oil Rivers in 1890.

When Macdonald eventually left for China, the much less esteemed Ralph Moor was his replacement, with responsibility for the newly renamed British administration in the Oil Rivers area, which now became known as the Niger Coast Protectorate. As we have already seen, the primary objective of British policy in this area had long been to promote the trading interests of its various merchants and trading firms - the former supercargoes - who had now established themselves as the dominant parties in the booming palm oil export trade from all the coastal areas in the Oil Rivers.

Legalising Colonialism

This policy objective was changing, however, particularly following the Brussels Conference of European powers in 1890, and the arrival of a certain 'Right Honourable' Mr Joseph Chamberlain into power as British Colonial Secretary in 1895. The Brussels Conference had resulted in the promulgation of its eponymous Act, more correctly titled: *The Convention Relative to the Slave Trade and Importation into Africa of Firearms, Ammunition and Spiritous Liquors*. The Brussels Act might be regarded as the political covering legislation for the Imperial Era, empowering and encouraging men like Chamberlain to finally apply the full force of British might to its imperial project. This ostensibly humanitarian legislation recommended seven measures in its very first article, establishing its raison d'etre: a total and complete adoption of the principles espoused for more than 100 years by the Clapham Sect. The Act accepted that economic development was the only means of eliminating slavery, but now also provided for the practical reality that force of arms would be needed to achieve it. More importantly, the Act established a legal framework for achieving an imbalance in the availability of arms between proponents and opponents of the ideology.

Specifically, therefore, the Act prohibited the importation of firearms and ammunition into Africa by 'non-state' European actors, eliminating the possibility for the local traditional elite to simply source their own Maxim guns for defensive purposes in the open market. This was an important new provision because exports of guns from Birmingham to Africa in the 1860s were as high as 150,000 a year, with up to 17 percent of all British gun exports making their way to the continent by the eve of the conference in 1889[1]. While the declared reason for the conference and the Brussels Act was the elimination of domestic slavery and whatever remained of the international slave trade in Africa, the presence of the (later) much-reviled Congo Free State at the proceedings completely undermined this rationale. Ruled personally and 'owned' by the murderous, rapacious and genocidal Belgian King Leopold II, the economy of the so-called Congo Free State - as was later revealed by the Elder Dempster Shipping Line employee and amateur journalist Edmund Dene Morel - was based entirely on the importation of fire-arms and ammunition by a 'non-state' actor to perpetuate domestic slavery.

While Leopold's unmatched greed and seeming lack of humanity might be considered an extreme outlier among the European ruling elite in the Imperial Era, the fact that this monstrous autocrat was able to exist at all (and for so long) is the best evidence for the prevailing *zeitgeist* in the post-Clapham Sect Era. It was a time of great global commercial and nationalistic ambition on the part of all the existing, declining, and emerging powers in Europe, which would lead shortly to the Great War. It was within this milieu of aggressive international competition, however carefully reframed in Africa by co-opting the long-standing language and legacy of humanitarian European movement on the continent, that Joseph Chamberlain emerged into power at the Colonial Office.

Joseph Africanus Arrives the Scene

A remarkable politician who managed to successfully split both major British political parties during his career, Chamberlain was the total opposite of a British blueblood - he rose from Birmingham of all places, never held any fancy titles, attended no University or military academy, and had worked in manufacturing. Born in 1836, the rise of Chamberlain can only be understood in the context of the political reforms and changes that occurred before and during the Victorian era, some of which we have discussed earlier. To repeat and expand briefly, Britain had evolved over the century since the Mad White Man embarked on the Niger River. This evolution first became manifest in the Great Reform Act of 1832 slightly expanding the British electorate. This was followed by the Second Reform Act of 1867 which enfranchised parts of the urban, male working class for the first time. The reforms culminated in the Third Reform Act of 1884, which *still* did not establish universal suffrage, as all women and 40 percent of adult men were still without a vote, but greatly expanded the electorate nationally to more than five million people.

Hence, by 1874 when Chamberlain first contested for office, he had become a leading grassroots politician and advocate for reforms ranging from education to living conditions and of course voting rights. Popular politics was now the order of the day and in many ways, Chamberlain was the first British politician to bring the ruling elite in touch with the working class. His ideas continue to influence British politics even today. In her first major policy speech when campaigning to become the leader of the Conservative party in 2016, Theresa May named Chamberlain alongside Margaret Thatcher and Winston Churchill as Conservative champions of the working people[2]. In the evolved era during which Chamberlain entered politics, British domestic economic and international foreign policy began to focus on addressing the bread-and-butter issues of the ordinary voter, rather than just the principled ideas, petty contrivances or high-minded values of the nobility and landed elite.

In terms of the imperial project outside of India and Canada, Chamberlain, or *Joseph Africanus* as he came to be derisively known by the media, became the leading voice and actor for British interests in Africa. This won him both corporate support among the trading, merchant and manufacturing classes, and grassroots fervour among the nationalistic and working population. Ironically, having refused both the Exchequer and Home Secretary roles in 1895, Chamberlain rose to prominence locally and internationally on the back of his successful exploits at the Colonial Office. In direct contrast to the parsimony and tentativeness of the Clapham Era British civil servants and noblemen responsible for international affairs and colonial policy, Joseph Africanus' working principles were simple, clear and popular to multiple political categories and constituencies. In this new global environment, he declared that: 'I believe the British race is the greatest of the governing races that the world has ever seen, and it is not enough to occupy the great spaces of the world's surface unless you can make the best of them. It is the duty of a landlord to develop his estate.'[3]

The coming into office of this energetic imperialist was the first time anyone would make the case for holding - and developing - African colonies even if they were not profit-making. Chamberlain introduced the phrase 'colonial development' into the British political lexicon, at a time when the political class were not interested in any such thing. Hence, another one of his nicknames was 'Radical Joe'. Less than two months after taking office as Colonial Secretary, Chamberlain declared to Parliament amid cheers that 'I regard many of our colonies as being in the condition of undeveloped estates, and estates which can never be developed without imperial assistance.'[4] Keeping the same energy, the very next day, a deputation from the West African Railways visited him and he was unequivocal in telling them about Britain's West African colonies that 'If the people of this country are not willing to invest some of their superfluous wealth in the development of their great estate, then I see no future for these countries and it would have been better not to have gone there.'[5] By late 1895, Chamberlain had authorised the commencement of work on inland railways in West Africa, which had been on the drawing board since 1883, going as far as spending money which had not been budgeted for. This eventually got him in trouble with Parliament and weakened him politically. Thus, the Nigerian railway system still in existence 120 years later was birthed.

Chamberlain's colleagues in the cabinet did not find his newfound love for spending money on African colonies funny. Now Prime Minister, Lord Salisbury's preference at the time was to use the West African colonies as a bargaining tool with France in their separate dispute over Egypt and this inevitably put him on a collision course with Chamberlain. Kicking him out of the cabinet was a non-starter as he would have brought down the government, as the way he had split the Liberal Party in 1885 was still fresh in everyone's mind. Thus, it was that his ideas and policies, which would have a profound effect on shaping Nigeria as we know it today were reluctantly, perhaps unwittingly, enforced by Britain. With this political and international background in place, it becomes easier to understand the basis for the change in attitude and direction by men like Ralph Moor and Egerton (who succeeded him), as well as several others who arrived in the Niger area from the early 1890s. In comparison to Macdonald, Goldie, and the others who preceded them, the men of the empire arrived with official sanction. By 1901, the political support now finally existed for expanding the influence of the British Government and British economic agents along the river and the Niger coast, well into the interior, with the objective of removing 'obstacles' to the free flowing of trade goods in either direction. So it was that the chief obstacle in the South-Eastern Igbo country to this all-important objective (in the mind of Ralph Moor) was a shadowy, poorly understood, impenetrable but supposedly vicious and powerful martial pseudo-state organisation known to the British as the Aro Confederation.

Economic Dictators of the Hinterland

The Aro (whom we have met earlier in their dealings with the astute King Jaja at Bonny and Opobo) were by 1901 a centuries-old loose but powerful confederation of communities spread out across the Igbo country in the South-Eastern hinterland of the Niger.

Described by the great historian of Nigeria, Kenneth Onwuka Dike as 'the economic dictators of the hinterland,'[6] the Aro were likely formed in the mid-seventeenth century and were already prominent in the eighteenth century, when the Biafra-Atlantic trade in slaves became significant. Along with a few other important factors, the emergence of the Aro behind the banks of the Niger and the Bight of Biafra coast was responsible for the area becoming prominent in the slave trade. The other factors responsible were the expansion of the coastal city-states themselves, the role of the Ekpe, another similar regional group as the Aro in providing credit guarantees, and the settlement of the coast by European supercargoes dealing with the city-states. More than just economic dictators, the Aro also provided the most important traditional, judicial, cultural, and military institutions of governance for the Igbo hinterland East of the Niger, up till the arrival of Moor's armed party in the harmattan of 1901.

The mode of Aro government in the Igbo country was incomprehensible to outsiders. This was deliberately so on the part of the Aro elite themselves, for nearly all of their power depended on the ignorance of the uninitiated for its maintenance. Much of the information about this highly secretive group during the nineteenth century was obtained from second-hand sources at the coast, often whispered in awe of their alleged supernatural capabilities. The other rich source of information came from observing the Aro in their economic and political interactions with the coastal city-states of the Niger Delta. Nearly all of the intelligible reporting on the Aro that we now have is due to the incredibly painstaking oral historical sourcing work of post-colonial Nigerian historians (Dike, Nwokeji, Ekejiuba, and several others), as well as a few intelligent contemporary eye-witnesses such as a British Major Arthur Leonard's account of an Aro market at Bende sometime in 1896. The complex Aro organisation might be understood in the simplest terms as a regional franchise within the Igbo country. From headquarters at Arochukwu, an Aro Eze - this originally being the given name of a long-ago powerful Aro personality among the politically acephalous Igbo - provided the central authority figure for a large number of distributed Aro communities and settlements spread among the hundreds of nominally autonomous Igbo towns and villages in the South-Eastern enclave.

The Igbo enclave was hemmed in on all sides, with forests and rivers forming the western and eastern borders, coastal city-states, and the ocean to the south, as well as hills and valleys bordering the north. Within this hemmed country, the Aro maintained an effective hegemony over Eastern Igbo affairs from their comfortable perch with access to the coast via the Cross River at their inland port city of Arochukwu. The Aro Eze acted in concert with a council known as the Okankpo, delegating certain powers to a resident Aro Consul (or Mazi) living among the diaspora settlements. The Mazis were originally often state-sponsored agents of trade expansion but evolved to become the largest trader or the most important Aro personality in the relevant diaspora community. From headquarters, regular migration continued across the countryside, with armed trading caravans able to guarantee safe passage everywhere in the hinterland, a most valuable and unique privilege. News, information, and trade goods thereby flowed through the Aro - from the coast, back through Arochukwu to the inland diaspora and vice versa. In many ways, the Aro trade and information system was not too dissimilar to the itinerant and diasporic Fulani intelligence linkages across the old Hausa country and even to the broader Niger-Benue area, the Arab and Mediterranean worlds, which we have seen already.

Arochukwu and the Igbo Country

The primary objective of the Arochukwu franchise system was to maintain the economic dictatorship and hegemony of the Aro as a group, without attempting to interfere directly with the autonomy of any settlement or community. The means of Aro interference was insidious, carefully calibrated, and - at least until the arrival of the British with an alternative option - largely acceptable to the leadership elite in most of these interior communities. Aro military might was sustained by a monopoly on the arms trade with the coast and a well-established permanent standing army, which provided the muscle to ensure the trade roads remained in Aro hands. More importantly, the standing Aro army was also made available as a mercenary force on an 'as-negotiated' basis to whichever Igbo community sought it.

The annual Igbo fighting season which is perhaps best memorialised in Chinua Achebe's eternal classic novel about a pre-European Igbo community, *Things Fall Apart*, commenced as soon as the planting, harvesting and celebration seasons were attended to. For most communities and villages in the Igbo country, the annual wars and battles were relatively mild local affairs intended to settle small disputes, affronts, border claims and for bragging rights. This was the nature of the battles recalled so evocatively in Achebe's genius short fiction. One actual eyewitness to the Igbo fighting season described it well. George Thomas Basden, later Archdeacon of the Niger from 1926-1936 was a notable Igbophile, who lived in the country and among the people for nearly 40 years from 1901. As Archdeacon Basden cheekily put it: 'Battles are fought in a haphazard manner, there is little attempt at leadership or organisation. Each unit follows his own devices, advancing, firing, or turning tail exactly as he feels inclined. Those whom one would naturally expect to lead their soldiers in battle, i.e. the chiefs, are never present. It is convenient for them to retire to a remote spot in the bush, well away from the fray, where they can in quietness (and security) invoke the help of the gods. When there is no further need to pray they return home'[7].

For many other communities however, wars were less prosaic, more vicious, larger in scope and intensity, and involved more devastating scorched earth tactics. It was in these wars that the Aro standing mercenary force - a dreaded sub-tribe of their own, known as the Abam - specialised. It was also from these battles that the majority of ethnic Igbo human beings embarked as cargo for slavery in the Atlantic world emerged. An excellent first-hand account of this latter kind of battle can be found in the narrative of Olaudah Equiano (more correctly: Ekweano), who lived in the Igbo country up till about 1745: 'When a trader wants slaves, he applies to a chief for them, and tempts him with his wares. It is not extraordinary, if on this occasion he yields to the temptation with as little firmness and accepts the price of his fellow creature's liberty with as little reluctance as the enlightened merchant. Accordingly, he falls on his neighbours, and a desperate battle ensues. If he prevails and takes prisoners, he gratifies his avarice by selling them; but, if his party be vanquished, and he falls into the hands of the enemy, he is put to death: for, as he has been known to foment their quarrels, it is thought dangerous to let him survive, and no ransom can save him, though all other prisoners may be redeemed. We have firearms, bows, and arrows, broad two-edged swords and javelins: we have shields also which cover a man from head to foot. All are taught the use of these weapons; even our women are warriors, and march boldly out to fight along with the men'[8].

Between their booty from wars of attrition among rival communities and the kidnapping of any unfortunates who attempted to breach (without prior permission) the Aro monopoly on internal long-distance travel; a sufficient inventory of bodies was originated to ensure that Igbo slaves constituted by far the largest majority of those exported from the coastal-city-states of the Bight of Biafra to the Americas. But there was one other source of slave inventory, less relevant from the perspective of volumes, but all-important from the perspective of the maintenance of Aro supremacy. This was the *Ibini-Ukpabi* or so-called (by the confounded British) *Long Juju* of Arochukwu.

Perhaps without parallel anywhere else around the Niger (possibly not even among the ardent African followers of the Prophet Mohammed north of the rivers), Ibini-Ukpabi exercised a thoroughly uncontested mental, intellectual, spiritual and judicial control over the people in its area of influence. This spiritual and judicial oracular institution was accepted as a kind of supreme court across the polytheistic Igbo country for the final albeit terribly expensive adjudication of major disputes. Again, Archdeacon Basden provides us with the most graphic account of the Ibini-Ukpabi adjudication process, following the disputants from their faraway village, through multiple expensive journeys over several weeks with a costly retained Aro counsellor, all the way to the terrifying moments of encountering the oracle at Arochukwu. Carefully orchestrated to maximise its psychosensory effect, the dramatic delivery of final judgement and the immediate implementation of the declared sentence completed the mystique and power of the Aro justice system.

Between their river port headquarters, their feared oracle, their standing mercenary force and their control of the main roads, the Aro were able to quite effectively maintain their economic dictatorship in the country, without needing to deploy any governance infrastructure or administrative state resources outside Arochukwu. Rather than govern the inland Igbo people who lived in self-governing autonomous communities engaging in fishing, farming, artisan metal and woodwork, performance arts and trading, the Aro relied on their network of *Mazis* as franchise agents. These agents were settled in each community and responsible for sourcing information, litigating disputes, coordinating the export (of humans, then later palm oil) and import trades, and generally maintaining their hegemony.

For the most part, it is not clear that the general Igbo population (particularly the wealthiest elite, titled men) objected much to this state of affairs. Egalitarian as it was, Igbo society relied on strongly enforced common beliefs and practices for maintaining civil rule, law, and order. The most prominent men and women in society earned those positions by investing the wealth from their commerce in the purchase of 'titles', each of which permitted the bearer certain benefits and privileges in their community, including a proportionate share of future receipts from new title joiners. In the absence of a standing government, occasional recourse to this politically disinterested but militarily powerful external arbiter would have been in the long-term best interests of this self-sustaining financial aristocracy. Therefore, religious, traditional, and cultural superstitions played important roles (perhaps to an unusually higher degree than in other societies) in maintaining social cohesion among the Igbo. The Ibini-Ukpabi oracle was just another manifestation of the strong connection between supernatural beliefs and temporal social and economic practices among the Igbo.

In this way, the Aro were not the only game in town by the early twentieth century. On the western side of the Igbo country (Arochukwu is on the eastern side of the country, just behind the Cross River) another secretive, militarised society known as the *Ekumeku* existed, with their own standing armed forces, elaborate supernatural pretensions and their headquarters across the Niger in Asaba. Of more recent provenance than the ancient *Abam*, the *Ekumeku* forces were accused by the British of random banditry, kidnapping and plunder across the country; but in reality, they were an armed, indigenous organised resistance to the emergence of European enterprise in the inner country at the end of the Clapham Sect Era. Probably known originally as the Ekwunuoku (roughly translated as 'The Silent Ones') prior to the anglicised version Ekumeku, the Silent Ones were a feared but loosely organised fighting force raised among the people of the western Igbo country as a reaction to the British reduction of Aboh, a long-standing trading town on the Niger. Ekumeku fighters were known for assembling in stealth mode from around their country and moving quietly to inflict damage or destruction on whichever target had been pre-selected for the purpose, often a British-affiliated trading location or concern, a perceived ally of Europeans, or other such enemies. Directed by the leading Eze title holders (the highest titled men) of the different towns and villages in the western Igbo country, Ekumeku wreaked havoc where necessary and returned quietly to their various homes until the next mission. This armed resistance movement served as the tip of the spear for the western Igbo civil society, a wealthy elite seeking to protect its interests in the lucrative palm oil trade, sustained as it was by their ownership of human laborers in this slave-dominated society.

By the late nineteenth century, the Igbo country west of the river was as deeply defined by the political, cultural, and economic dichotomy between slaves and free men as the antebellum southern United States. Every important social activity from human rights and political representation, to commercial and financial transactions, marriage, property rights, and even religious rites was governed by strict laws and customs differentiating slaves from free persons. People held as slaves even lived in separate villages, *Ugwule*, in social units established and controlled by their owners, living there as tools of production in the labour-intensive palm oil production trade. The Ekumeku were called upon by the elite Ezes of the country to defend this way of life, in a not entirely dissimilar manner to the United States Confederate Army decades before them. Ultimately, British force would be called upon to break the Ekumeku and subjugate the western Igbo country to the rule of new laws and customs. Across Nigeria, the Western Igbo elite were not unusual in their dependence on slaves for economic prosperity. They were perhaps however unique in the extent of their dependence, and in the guerrilla tactics they adopted as their armed response to the existential European threat to their way of life. Domestic slavery remained a critical institution across all of Igboland at this time, as it was everywhere else in the broader country, even in liberal Abeokuta. Superstition, violence, and fear were essential tools for maintaining a large population in bondage. Hence human sacrifice was still not uncommon across the country, (as was cannibalism) even up to the early 1900s, according to Archdeacon Basden.

Moor and his Marauders Make their Move

These were the summarised conditions in the interior of the Niger Coast Protectorate when - without the direct blessings of Joseph Chamberlain - Sir Ralph Moor sanctioned the entry of his army into Igboland. Moor's stated reason for the expedition was to end the atrocious practices of the Aro, which according to him held the people in effective captivity, prevented efficient trade flows and allowed domestic slavery to thrive. With this rationale, Moor was activating the international legal cover of the Brussels Act. This same rationale was utilised in the justification of the Benin expedition in February 1897, which we will come to shortly. For their part, the Aro were organised for internal domination rather than for defence against external aggression and were a much looser confederation of franchise partners than external observers could discern. The Aro were no doubt aware of the emerging British economic and political force at the coast. The Oil Rivers protectorate had been established nearly 20 years before, one of their coastal partners - Jaja - had been removed in 1887. Further, as our narrative will soon show, their ancient neighbouring country Benin had been taken by the British, and Brass had been reduced after the RNC Akassa attacks. Even the international slave trade of their ancestors had all but vanished, replaced by palm oil. Yet, they either did not expect this trend of White man's interference to affect their economic hegemony in the inland affairs of the Igbo country or they were confident in the ability of their intricate system to resist external threats.

As we have already seen at Gobir, Lagos and Ilorin, and as will soon see elsewhere, local politics provided the beachhead for external influence in the affairs of a long-standing domestic power. Several Igbo communities (notably the *Akwette* whom we already mentioned) were grateful for the opportunity to escape from under Aro dominance by allying with these foreign usurpers from the coast, with their large guns and numerous troops. These communities were beginning to accept emissaries and even residents, including the later so-called native political agents sent by the Niger Coast Protectorate. One such community, called *Obegu* appeared to have taken the lead in resisting the Aro, refusing to pay certain trade debts and attacking the Aro *Mazi* and market traders living within their town. The leaders of Obegu were acting in the same way as Akwette, who had recently been presumptuous enough to fine a wealthy Aro trader named Okori Toti very heavily (8,000 manilas) for a trade dispute in relation to intercourse with Bonny and Opobo. The emboldened Akwette, from their vantage point closer to the coast were now presumed to be acting as middlemen for those city-states, long established partners of Aro traders.

It is not inconceivable that the expansionist Niger coast Commissioner (Sir Ralph Moor) and his agents, having already determined to reduce the Aro for the broader reasons of controlling the Igbo hinterland, instigated the Obegu and Akwette leadership into taking these particular decisions, to give a proximate cause for an already planned mission. In the event, the Aro took the bait and Okoro Toti summoned the Abam mercenaries, led by a certain Uchendu to the scene. Obegu was raided and destroyed. Following this assault, the British Travelling Commissioner consoled and assured the oppressed inhabitants of what was coming: 'We white men are like a big tree, it takes time before we fall, but when we do fall, the surrounding countryside will know of it.'[9] The fate of Arochukwu was sealed, in the same manner as the ancient Benin kingdom just four years before. Ralph Moor had also orchestrated that outcome, but by comparison to the reduction of Benin, Arochukwu would prove to be an anti-climax that we will return to shortly. In the meantime, it is now necessary to explore Moor's work in Benin.

An Impregnable Autarky

The once powerful Benin kingdom had declined from a widespread empire encompassing huge inland areas, to essentially a hard to access, autarkic, self-sufficient city-state by the late nineteenth century. The relative impregnability of the Benin capital was widely known even to the earliest European visitors. Yet, none of this deterred the ambitious British men of the Chamberlain era, led by the glory-seeking Moor. One of Moor's colleagues, Claude Macdonald's vice consul for the Benin River named Captain H.L. Gallwey had first visited the ancient kingdom in 1892, to conduct reconnaissance as much as to enter into a treaty with the Oba Ovonramwen. Upon his return to headquarters, Gallwey tantalised his audience with an exaggerated report of rich trading opportunities in 'ivory, rubber, gum, copal, gum Arabic, fibres, mahogany and hardwoods, and probably coffee and cocoa,' and with tales of the wonderful treaty of 'protection' he had entered into with the 'most powerful' Ovonramwen[10]. The prior year, Gallwey had been in the outlying states subject to Benin, among the Itsekiri and Urhobo, doing the same economic, political, and military reconnaissance. One outcome of this trip was Gallwey's selection of an attractive site with deep anchorage as a police post for the new Protectorate, where present-day Sapele lies.

In 1884, the British officials in the area first came into the acquaintance of a prominent Itsekiri chief named Nana Olomu from a village called Ebrohemie. The Itsekiri lived in an independent principality founded by Benin in ancient times and nominally ruled since then by a chief (or Olu) who had become a figurehead ruler only, relative to the powerful trading chiefs like Nana. By the sixteenth century, the Itsekiri had displaced Benin as the main suppliers of slaves to Sao Tome, first, and then to the Americas. Nominally under the suzerainty of Benin, they owned long and powerful war canoes with which they dominated the lower Benin river[11]. By the time of Gallwey's visit, Nana, the Ebrohemie chief whose father had also been a prominent trader named Alluma and whose mother was Urhobo, maintained a strong monopoly over the palm oil trade on the Benin river. Nana was the undisputed overlord of the area and owned up to 2,000 humans working on his plantations. Nana had worked in alliance with successive British consuls and trading concerns on the river for decades - even being named the 'British Governor' of the Benin River - taking advantage of his mixed heritage to consolidate the palm oil aggregation trade in the Urhobo hinterland.

Nana Olomu gets the Jaja Treatment

By 1895, the entrepreneurial Nana had achieved the same position on the Benin river that Jaja had managed to attain at Opobo: that of an absolute monopolist in relation to inland trading activities. Inevitably, it became the desire of the European traders down the river and the acting Consul (Ralph Moor replaced Macdonald temporarily in the summer of 1894) to dispose of Nana in the same manner as Jaja before him. It is notable that up to this point, British political control had yet to be extended by force on any area in the hinterland of the river. The unfortunate actions of the incompetent French Lieutenant Mizon in the upper Niger area - attempting to induce the Fulani Emir of Adamawa into a protectorate by providing him with armed forces for a Christmas day raid on a Jukun village in 1892 - would have been one of the first cases of force being utilised around the Niger for political rather than trade purposes. That French-supported attack left up to 50 dead, about 100 wounded and more than 200 women and children enslaved. On the Benin river, Major Macdonald aimed to continue in the tradition of limited use of force for 'trade facilitation' purposes only, but his reticence would not be shared by any of his successors, starting with the impatient Moor.

Nana's base, Ebrohemie was located behind a maze of swampy, muddy creeks and impassable morasses, an ideal defensive position north from the bank of the river. Thus, the local chief was confident in his ability to resist domination from the sea-bound British. This did not deter Sir Moor, and local politics once more provided him with an alternative route to reducing Ebrohemie. On 21 June 1894, Moor addressed a letter to Nana, summoning the chief to Sapele, to 'answer charges against him' ostensibly for reducing Urhobo villages who had attempted to trade directly with the British, bypassing the Itsekiri monopolist. In reality, the objective was to remove the wily chief from his privileged trade position on the river. While Nana was not a local ruler in the way that Jaja had been, his wealth and prominence in the trade around Itsekiri and Urhobo had extended a lot of de facto powers to him and his followers. Many Urhobo chiefs and even some Itsekiri opponents were unhappy with this situation, including some of Nana's primary trading rivals. Of these, the leading opponent was a chief named Dore, who was also the son of a past trading rival to Alluma, Nana's father. After an exchange of letters, Nana made it plain to Moor that he was not prepared to attend a meeting at which the fate of Jaja would befall him.

In short order, the field guns and warships ordered by Moor from Lagos arrived, carrying 350 troops under the command of an Admiral named Bedford. Informed from the safety of his base of this force amassing at the coast, Nana attempted to play for time, proceeding to issue an apology letter; 'Please forgive me, I don't want to fight the Government.' But the irate Moor was not in the mood for apologies, especially as an earlier reconnoitring mission he had foolishly sent out had been rebuffed by Nana's fighters, with casualties. In the event, Ebrohemie was reduced after several months of fighting during which rockets, and artillery were liberally employed. Nana fled to Lagos, where he would be tried and sentenced to exile in the Gold Coast. The fate of Jaja had befallen another important merchant-chief around the delta of the river, and a pattern was forming. Brash, young, newly arrived British officers inflamed by Imperial passions, often men of the 'anthropological sort' as the great Bishop Crowther had deadpanned, immediately set about deposing chiefs who dared to assert their independence and collaborating with the local elite to achieve their aims.

The removal of Nana from Itsekiri created immediate administrative and internal stability issues in his former area of control, significant enough for his British conquerors to assume near-direct political rule for the first time in the hinterland of the rivers. To this end, so-called 'native political agents' were appointed. These were the precursors to later Warrant Chiefs selected in Igboland, with Nana's rival chief Dore becoming one of the first such appointees in the Niger area. When in 1895, Macdonald departed finally for China, Ralph Moor assumed authority as the British Commissioner and Consul for the Niger Coast Protectorate. It was in this capacity that he would be sending the four columns of nearly 4,000 men into the Igbo country in December 1901. But before we can return to the Aro Expedition, we must continue finally to Benin, which was also famously reduced under the political authority of Ralph Moor in 1897. Isolated and unreachable by most of the world, we have already discussed how much the closed-off kingdom had declined from its palmy days in prior centuries. Following the successful visit of Gallwey in 1892, developments around the Benin river, including the British reduction of Nana Olomu, had made the leaders of the already reclusive nation even more reluctant to engage externally.

Enter Phillips, the Glorious Incompetent

In a similar pattern to one we must now be familiar with, a young British officer named James Robert Phillips arrived at the delta of the river in October 1896 as an acting Deputy to Moor, who was back home in Britain on leave. Born in 1864, Phillips was 33 years old at the time and this unbelievably bumptious young man must be recorded as being quite simply the biggest European ignoramus ever to set foot in Africa. Evidently intelligent as he attended Trinity College at Cambridge and studied Law, the energetic and sports loving Phillips had spent a short amount of time at the Gold Coast (present-day Ghana) serving as a lawyer for the colonial government before his spectacular promotion to high office in the Niger coast protectorate. Not *one* month after his arrival in November, this mindless fellow determined that he would proceed to Benin and calmly depose the ruler of a several centuries old kingdom. This ridiculous decision would be funny were it not to have resulted in tragic consequences still reverberating over the following 200 years. It is worth quoting his words on the subject in some detail, to capture his exact thinking about what he intended to do. Thankfully, his words are preserved in a letter dated November 1896 to the Foreign Office, which must be one of the most remarkable letters ever to be received at that office. Young Phillips wrote to Lord Salisbury:

'The King of Benin has continued to do everything in his power to stop the people from trading and prevent the Government from opening up the country. By means of his Fetish he has succeeded to a marked degree. He has permanently placed a Juju on (Palm) Kernels, the most profitable product of the country, and the penalty for trading in this produce is death. He has closed the markets and has only occasionally consented to open them in certain places on receipt of presents from the Jakri [Itsekiri] chiefs. Only however to close them again when he desires more blackmail.

I feel so convinced that every means has been successfully tried that I have advised the Jakri chiefs to discontinue their presents. I therefore ask for his Lordship's permission to visit Benin City in February next, to depose and remove the King of Benin and to establish a native council in his place and to take such further steps for the opening up of the country as the occasion may require.

I do not anticipate any serious resistance from the people of the country – there is every reason to believe that they would be glad to get rid of their King – but in order to obviate any danger I wish to take up a sufficient armed Force, consisting of 250 troops, two seven-pounder guns, one Maxim gun, and one Rocket apparatus of the Niger Coast Protectorate Force (NCPF) and a detachment of Lagos Hausas 150 strong, if his Lordship and the Secretary of State for the Colonies will sanction the use of the Colonial Forces to this extent. PS: I would add that I have reason to hope that sufficient Ivory may be found in the King's house to pay the expenses in removing the King from his Stool'.

This stunning letter emanated from the mind of a man who

had achieved exactly nothing in his career to this point, to justify confidence in being capable of doing anything at all, never mind his stated intent. In the event, the letter was politely forwarded to Ralph Moor for his comments, which the more experienced (but still gloriously incompetent) officer eagerly provided, endorsing the hare-brained idea. The Foreign Office, which ought to have killed the idea immediately declined to do so, only pointing out that due to the ongoing Ashanti War, the Niger coast force could not be reinforced by troops from Lagos and the Gold Coast. Several safeguards having failed, the stage was set for disaster.

Young Phillips assembled an unfortunate party of six European officers and two trading executives (one each from the African Association and Miller Brothers), alongside 220 African carriers (mostly Itsekiri and Kru), and some ancillary staff (interpreters, clerks, storekeepers and servants), sallying forth in December 1896. The jovial Phillips intended to also travel with the Protectorate marching band but was dissuaded from this, luckily for the members of that band. The happy party proceeded from Old Calabar into the creeks on the approach towards the Benin mainland. On their march inwards, Chief Dore, the recently appointed native political agent met with Phillips in his camp and politely entreated the young officer to retreat, because the Oba was at that very moment engaged in some traditional rites that did not permit foreigners being present in the city. Whether or not this was accurate is not relevant, but Chief Dore's was the wisest counsel Phillips had received probably in his life, and certainly since penning his incredible letter. Presents were sent to the Oba, who acknowledged receipt, and sportingly invited the party to return at a later date. Again, Phillips declined this advice, insisting on visiting Benin at this exact point in time.

Massacre and Retribution

On 4 January 1897, this large travelling party that had just been advised by the king that he was unavailable followed a group of 'guides' purported to have been sent by the same Oba. The guides led Phillips and his followers directly into an ambush, a bloody massacre which left Phillips and most of his unfortunate party dead, apart from two European officers (named Boisragon and Locke) and a handful of troops. Within the royal court at Benin itself, it is clear that multiple voices were raised for and against the massacre, but the Oba and his counsellors remained confident that the city remained impossible to breach by an invading force, given its remoteness from the creeks and rivers where the White men ruled. It was a fatal gamble for the Benin kingdom to take. Ill-advised as Phillips' ridiculous mission was, it was still a party of emissaries representing the most important military force in the Niger area by 1897, and this was not information unavailable to the well-informed Benin court.

Once the news of the massacre reached London, the wheels were immediately set in motion to assemble what turned out to be the most diversified British imperial armed force ever to be organised for an African fighting expedition up to that point. The retaliatory force came together within a month, pulled away from multiple active engagements globally to converge on Benin and avenge the foolishness of the intrepid Mr. Phillips. Placed under the command of an Admiral named Harry Rawson, sophisticated British vessels arrived from South Africa, Malta, Brass and England itself. One ship already on its way out of the North Sea was recalled, urgently requisitioned, and repurposed for Benin. Stores and provisions were assembled urgently, including a fully functional hospital ship, pre-packaged travelling kits for hundreds of troops and carriers, dissembled Maxim guns, and potable water carrying gear.

By early February, the most sophisticated armed force ever to visit the river arrived in the Forcados river, near the mouth of the Niger, en route to Sapele which would be the forward operating base. An incredibly detailed plan of war was drawn out, recorded for history by multiple participants including most memorably in a book titled *City of Blood* by a Commander Reginald H. Bacon, who served as an Intelligence Officer on the mission. Shock and awe were deployed by the invaders, with large rockets being fired into the city indiscriminately once within range. An eyewitness reported to Bacon that one such explosive apparently landed right in the middle of a Benin planning meeting, which promptly dispersed in alarm. En route, the Maxim gun was deployed, 'played' continuously and heavily on bush paths and suspicious corners throughout the march up to Benin. Two separate divisions approached Benin from its two gates to keep the defending forces busy while preventing the escape of any notable persons.

City of Blood and Bronze

In the event, the city lived up to the gruesome title of Commander Bacon's book, with hundreds of Benin lives lost before, during and in the aftermath of the 'retaliatory' attack. The invaders themselves lost seven European officers and three native troops in fierce fighting, with 31 White men and 20 Black troops injured. Scores of dead bodies were discovered across the city, apparent victims of intense human sacrifices by the defending Benin army during the few days the fighting lasted. The Oba's palace was set upon with explosives, and a sudden fire erupted within the city the day after the fighting had concluded, burning down a significant portion of it. Luckily, and perhaps most famously, in one storehouse near the Oba's palace, 'buried in the dirt of the ages,' to use the immortal words of Commander Bacon who was there, were found 'several hundred unique bronze plaques, suggestive of almost Egyptian design, but of really superb casting, castings of wonderful delicacy of detail, and some magnificently carved tusks.'[12] The Benin 'bronzes,' a treasure trove comprising thousands of brass and ivory sculptures, including king heads, queen mother heads, leopard figurines, bells, and a great number of other sculpted images, all of which were executed with a mastery of the lost-wax casting method, had been found by the invaders. The conquerors of Benin made sure to cart the entire loot away to Britain.

Only a few months after the discovery, the artistic significance of the works would be recognised by the rest of the world, dating as they did well into antiquity, and representative as they were of the once great cultural and artistic emporium that Benin was. Ever conscious of public relations management, a graphic art journalist from *The Illustrated London News* had been commissioned by the military to follow the British expedition into the 'City of Blood,' and tasteful pictures of the stunning African art (then placed in the Horniman Free Museum at Forest Hill, London) soon found their way into that newspaper in August, 1897. This valuable collection still remains scattered across dozens of public and private locations in Europe and America, lost to their original owners, for whom they held great spiritual as much as aesthetic value, but now serving as an international testament to the ancient Benin civilisation.

The proud and handsome young Oba Ovonramwen himself escaped the city, and a manhunt ensued, with the Royal Niger Company agents joining in the chase. Eventually, the king gave himself up and returned to the city, where he was arrested. The humbled Ovonramwen was submitted to a very public trial, presided over by the victorious Moor in Benin, among other grave physical and symbolic humiliations for a royal considered divine by his people. The former Oba was exiled to Calabar, and upon his death was succeeded according to Benin custom by his son, Aiguobasinwin, who ruled as Oba Eweka II, and whose descendants continue to serve as the respected Obas of a modern Benin city in the present-day Edo State of Nigeria. Prior to the succession, a European Resident and a Native Council was appointed by the British to govern Benin, including a leading chief called Agho Obaseki. This important figure in the interregnum period between legitimate Obas was an ambitious trader and close childhood friend of the deposed king. Obaseki was later to be much derided in Benin tradition for accepting a role that must have been essential to some form of continued intelligent governance of his country following a humiliating defeat. While Obaseki collaborated with the invaders, another young Benin chief named Ologbosere led a guerrilla resistance effort over the next two years. He was eventually arrested and executed in mid-1899, putting an end to the last embers of defensive action mounted by the Benin against the British colonisers.

So it was that the ancient Benin Empire, dating back to the eleventh century - which the famous Ekweano had described around 1745 as being '...the most considerable [country in West Africa] is the kingdom of Benin, both as to extent and wealth, the richness and cultivation of the soil, the power of its king, and the number and warlike disposition of the inhabitants' - was reduced to a small appendage of the rapidly expanding British Empire in the Niger area. This spectacular collapse was the fall-out from several centuries of decline and a series of precipitate actions in 1897 by the boldest and most glorious incompetent ever to set foot in Africa, the unlamented and now forgotten James Roberts Phillips. Eight years after the trial of Ovonramwen, Sir Ralph Moor was found dead in his home near central London. He was only 49 years old. The coroner's report determined that he had poisoned himself, during a period of insomnia and temporary insanity. He had suffered from fevers and other maladies since his return from Nigeria, symptoms that in modern times might be associated with Post Traumatic Stress Disorder; but among the superstitious Benin would be diagnosed more simply as strong Juju delivering a just revenge on behalf of the offended, desecrated ancestors.

Igboland is Placed in Formation

And so, we can now finally return to the Igbo country, where the attacking party sent by Moor - conqueror of the Oil Rivers - fanned its way via four separate columns into the country, intending to encircle and destroy the Aro. As it turned out, the Aro Expedition was not worth the trouble. It was a failure of intelligence and another gloriously incompetent adventure, the cost of which was later queried by a member of the British parliament, Edward Moon, in a question to Joseph Chamberlain[13]. There was barely any fighting to be done, as the much-feared military force the British were expecting to meet did not emerge to engage in a head-to-head battle with troops bearing Maxim guns. The disappointed invaders even arrested, tried, and imprisoned two old men for providing misdirection to one of their desired locations, indicative of the sheer lack of action on the so-called expedition. The old men were later released. The cunning Aro had maintained their hold on the Igbo country for centuries using the barest amount of armed force, and the maximum degree of political savvy, trickery, psychological manipulation, and logistical organisation. They would continue with that approach under the new regime of the British occupants, who would soon realise that the real battle could not be won simply by force of arms alone, but by a long-term project of development, just like the Clapham Sect had predicted long before the glorious incompetents arrived.

Following the invasion, the physical manifestations of Arochukwu hegemony were reduced to rubble by the new powers in the country. Okori Toti and Uchendu were publicly hanged at Obegu. The much-treasured shrine of Ibini-Ukpabi was destroyed, the internal trade routes and roads to the coast were opened and warrant chiefs introduced as native colonial agents. Native courts were created, and Christian missionaries welcomed to settle among the people. Archdeacon Basden was probably the first one to arrive inland, in 1901.

The British imperial project of Chamberlain's ambitions was now underway, but it would be a much more difficult enterprise than any of the ideologues might have imagined when they conceived of it. Hundreds of British young men would follow Macdonald, Moor, Phillips, Gallwey and all the other Oil Rivers government pioneers into the country as District Officers, or into other military, administrative and political roles. They were following through with Chamberlain's earnest '...duty of a landlord to develop his estate' and in the process creating an entirely new country out of enclaves previously closed-off from each other and the world. A glorious incompetent like Phillips, abetted by the doomed aggressor, Moor had succeeded at once in erasing and creating history; deliberately altering the direction, lives, livelihoods and cultures of several millions of people now attached to the increasingly choate country, Nigeria.

---

1. Headrick DR, Professor of Social S, History Daniel RH. *The Tools of Empire: Technology and European Imperialism in the Nineteenth Century.* Oxford University Press; 1981.

2. Theresa May – 2016 Speech to Launch Leadership Campaign – UKPOL. CO.UK. (Available online)

3. Untold stories: Birmingham, the British Empire and Bangladeshi Curry 2017/12/7 https://advisor.museumsandheritage.com/features/untold-stories-birmingham-british-empire-bangladeshi-curry/.

4. Hansard - CLASS II. 1895/8/22 1895.

5. Robinson RE, Gallagher J, Denny A. *Africa and the Victorians: The Official Mind of Imperialism.* Macmillan; 1961.

6. Dike KO. *Trade and Politics in the Niger Delta, 1803-1885: An Introduction to the Economic and Political History of Nigeria.* Oxford University Press; 1956.

7. Basden GT. *Among the Ibos of Nigeria.* Seeley, Service & Co.; 1921.

8. Equiano O. *The Interesting Narrative of the Life of Olaudah Equiano Or Gustavus Vassa, the African.* G. Vassa; 1794.

9. Anene JC. *Southern Nigeria in Transition 1885-1906: Theory and Practice in a Colonial Protectorate.* Cambridge University Press; 1966.

10. *Ibid.*

11. Thomas H. *The Slave Trade.* Hachette UK; 2015.

12. Bacon R. *Benin, the City of Blood.* Creative Media Partners, LLC; 2018.

13. Hansard - Nigeria Protectorate-Aro Expedition. 1902/11/20 1902.

CHAPTER 8

Game of Thrones in the Niger Heartland

The Battle of Bida

On 13 February 1897, *The Spectator* (Britain's longest running weekly magazine) carried an editorial titled *The Battle of Bida*[1]. The story described how the European-led armed forces of a private company made up of 500 Africans and 23 White men had stormed Bida on 29 January and taken the town after a four-hour battle, describing the accomplishment grandiloquently as '...a really grand feat of arms, a victory at odds of one to forty, accomplished with the loss of only one European.' Based on this breathless news account, the Battle of Bida appeared to have been a quite straightforward encounter, with the Emir of Bida and his forces electing to run away, rather than face down the foreign invaders with their fearsome Maxim guns. There was a lot more to the story, as is often the case. The highly militarised Nupe kingdom that owned Bida did not simply give up its territory to these European intruders. A more complex political and economic history was at play.

The story of how these armed foreigners came to sack Bida at a canter during the harmattan of 1897 began nearly 80 years before. In the early nineteenth century, Nupe was a prosperous and well-established kingdom at the heart of the immediate Niger hinterland. Nupe was described by later observers as the *Black Byzantium*, in favourable comparison to the late capital of the Eastern Roman Empire. However, after the death of the nineteenth Etsu, Ma'azu in 1818, things began to fall apart. Ma'azu's son and legal heir, the crown prince Jimada, was challenged for the title by his cousin Majiya II. The usurper Majiya made the preposterous claim that, according to Nupe traditional law, as his own father was the late king Ma'azu's *older* brother, he had a stronger claim to the throne than anyone else. This was contrary to the rules of royal succession which were then current at the Nupe court which specified that only sons born *during* a king's reign ('Born in the Purple') were eligible for succession[2].

An outrageous claim of this nature was never going to be resolved over a friendly palava and thus the Nupe kingdom temporarily split in two, in anticipation of hostilities. The crown prince and the loyalist party stayed put at the old capital of Gbara in the western half of Nupe, while the pretender and his supporters went east, establishing a new capital at Rabbah on the banks of the great river. As the armed followers of both parties were evenly matched, an opportunity for a tiebreaker to step into the dispute presented itself. This was duly exploited by a wily court veteran who may well have been a primary behind-the-scenes instigator, as later events will show. This skilful political operator was a Fulani Mallam named Muhammad Bangana, but better known as Mallam Dendo - derived from the Nupe phrase dan yan dondon meaning 'The man on whose shoulders hang all sorts of bags containing herbs'[3].

Two Princes and a Mallam

About a decade before the feud between the princes Jimada and Majiya erupted, Mallam Dendo had arrived in Nupe from Kebbi, a former Hausa city controlled by the Fulani. As was often the case, the Mallam came as a visiting preacher and teacher, settling among the southern non-Muslim countries as an emissary from the Caliphate. Here, Dendo's fame grew as he became known for his wisdom and the quality of his charms and divinations. The Mallam soon built up a considerable following at Nupe, made up primarily of Fulani cattle nomads and various other migrants in the country, but also including members of the indigenous elite. Now, Nupe was a militarised state, dependent on conquest and slave raiding for its power. And so over time, a significant population of the Hausa-speaking mercenary soldiers who had been attracted to Nupe as fighters for the crown also became followers of Mallam Dendo.

Islam predated Mallam Dendo's arrival in Nupe and there was already a community of indigenous Nupe Islamic clerics working in the country before the Fulani teacher arrived. One of such clerics was a certain Abd al-Rahman al-Nufawi, who at the time of the jihad had travelled to Sokoto to pledge his allegiance to Dan Fodio and received a tuta flag in return, recognising him as the leader of the Muslims in Nupeland. On this basis, al-Nufawi launched a Nupe jihad in 1810, which very nearly succeeded. The local jihadists occupied the Nupe capital for six months but were unable to hold it[4]. Several years later, the newly arrived Mallam Dendo had now risen to become the head of the existing Muslim party at Nupe. In due course, Dendo's forces would later eliminate al-Nufawi, paving the way for the Fulani party to assume authority as the undisputed Islamic leaders in the Niger Heartland.

This dynamic would soon come to act strongly on the affairs of the kingdom once the feud between the contending princes escalated. Crown prince Jimada was not a Muslim, but his usurper Majiya had come under the sway of Mallam Dendo, was a student of the preacher and had developed a kind of political relationship with his party at court. Seeing Dendo and his armed Fulani supporters as having the key to tipping the scales in his favour, Majiya sought an alliance with the Muslim party to defeat his cousin. Eventually, Dendo assented and Prince Jimada's forces were routed in 1820, leaving Majiya the newly unchallenged king of Nupeland. The unfortunate Prince Jimada himself was killed in the battle, while his son and heir to his claim, Idirisu, took what was left of his father's forces and fled west to Ilorin, which was still under the rule of the Yoruba secessionist, Afonja.

This turn of events meant that Majiya was now indebted to Dendo and he initially returned the favour by promoting him within his court as his private counsellor and cleric. He also showered him with gifts including two slave girls, one of whom gave birth to the Mallam's most famous daughter, Gogo Habiba. This remarkable girl went on to become the most powerful businesswoman and female leader in Nupe. Gogo Habiba traded slaves extensively throughout her career, dealing with leading merchants all the way down to the coast, including the ubiquitous Madam Tinubu[5]. As we already saw with Dan Fodio at the court of Gobir, alliances like the one between Majiya and Dendo tended to be unstable, and subject to rapid deterioration. This was particularly so in the case of this convenient anti-Jimada alliance, which was in substance practically a power sharing agreement. The situation was not helped by the justified paranoia of the illegal King Majiya, who was eventually overcome by his fear and loathing of Dendo's influence in Nupe.

Once Majiya determined that he could stand on his own feet, he turned his forces on Dendo's Hausa-Fulani Muslim party. In due course, this group also fled across the river to Ilorin, where Idirisu (son of the late crown prince Jimada) was now camped in exile. The Nupe party at Ilorin was expanding, with important consequences for the future as we will soon see. At Ilorin, the exiles came into the sphere of influence of the other important Fulani Muslim cleric we met earlier in our story - Mallam Alimi. Majiya had a decision to make - he could leave things that way and get on with the business of ruling Nupe or pursue Dendo and his forces across the Niger to finish them off. In the event, paranoia got the better of the insecure usurper and he decided to go after the exiles. As it turned out, Majiya was quite right to be obsessed with his enemies abroad, because the Nupe party at Ilorin had resolved their differences and agreed to team up against the illegitimate king now ruling their homeland.

Intending to kill two birds with one stone, Majiya put together an army of 4,000 cavalry and 10,000 foot soldiers (many of them Yoruba) and sallied forth in the direction of Ilorin[6]. The Nupe telling of the ensuing battle is that Majiya's forces ran into a sandstorm just outside Ilorin and in the confusion the horses trampled all over the foot soldiers, killing many of them in the process. Right on cue, the Ilorin army pounced on the weakened Nupe posse leaving Majiya to flee homewards with 1,000 cavalry and 1,000 soldiers as the remnants of his original force. Now it was the turn of the united Nupe exile force to assume the offensive. They pursued Majiya's depleted army across the river back to his capital at Rabah, which they sacked, with Majiya fleeing further north. The Game of Thrones was just beginning. If the victorious Prince Idirisu thought he would now become king of all Nupe, he was mistaken. His party had a weak hand to play as there were several other Mallams in the united Nupe coalition who had been exiled with Dendo. Upon return from exile, the balance of power in the kingdom had shifted decisively in favour of the Muslims. The outgunned Idirisu was installed as a puppet king in the smaller Nupe town of Egga, while Dendo assumed power at Rabah, disguised as a cleric but in reality, the de facto power in the country. Nupe now had at least three power centres with Dendo at Rabah, Idirisu at Egga and the not quite defeated Majiya still scheming at a Northern town called Zuguma. Dendo, the skilful Fulani politician, found it easy to play off one Nupe against the other in this scenario.

Born in the Purple

Some of the events we have already followed back at Ilorin would come to affect this uneasy truce at Nupe. In 1824, Afonja was displaced and murdered by his Fulani co-conspirators, who declared the former Oyo stronghold an Emirate of Sokoto. Seeing the writing on the wall, the puppet king Idirisu attempted to eliminate the Muslims in his putative domain. But he had underestimated Dendo's skill and craft. The Nupe Muslims reversed course and allied with their recent enemy, Majiya to face down Idirisu - who was put in his place. By October 1830, Richard Lander, travelling through Nupeland, was able to report that 'Dendo has sent his messengers both by land and by water to collect the taxes and tribute throughout the country of Nouffie [Nupe], which was last year paid to Ederesa [Idirisu].'[7] The plot thickened a few years later when the old Mallam Dendo died in 1833. While the relentless Majiya had continued to bear the title of Etsu Nupe in his small Zuguma territory, Dendo had been titled Sarkin Fulani Nupe (leader of the Fulani in Nupe) and this title was now passed to one of his sons, Usman Zaki. Following in the path of their Ilorin allies, the Fulani of Nupe under Usman Zaki declared an Emirate over Bida, along with four other Emirates in the surrounding Nupe kingdom (Agaie, Lapai, Lafiagi and Shonga). These latter chiefdoms were established by some of the Mallams who had fled to Ilorin and returned with Mallam Dendo. Bida was by far the largest of these five, spilling across the river into parts of the present-day Edo and Ondo states in southern Nigeria.

With the progression of time, Usman Zaki went on to name one of his younger brothers, Momadu Gborigi, as the Shaba (Crown Prince). But one important new player in the Game of Thrones was not going to stand for this. Muhammad Saba 'Masaba,' Mallam Dendo's youngest son, who was born in the purple and raised under the same roof as Gogo Habiba, was an ambitious prince with designs on the throne himself. Masaba anchored his claim on the fact that he was the rightful heir to the throne of Nupe and not Usman Zaki who was pure Fulani. Masaba's claim was not harmed by the fact that he was born of a Nupe mother, adopted, and raised in the Etsu's court by the old king Majiya when he and Dendo were still on good terms. Recent history soon repeated itself as the house that Dendo built now turned against itself. Usman Zaki drove Dendo's son and his supporters out of Rabah, and they went to settle across the river in another Nupe town, Lafiagi from where Prince Masaba built up a following and intrigued against his brother.

The ambitious prince was not short of allies in this now multi-generational Game of Thrones, as Tsado, successor to the former illegal King Majiya was now reigning as a toothless Etsu at Zuguma. Taking over from his father who died in 1835, Tsado had tried to kick out the Fulani without success. The deposed legal crown prince Idirisu, meanwhile, was still seething at Egga. In due course, all three Nupe pretenders (Masaba, Idirisu, and Tsado) eventually managed to make common cause against the Fulani party at Rabah.

Notwithstanding the common front against the Fulani, Masaba and Idirisu still managed to find time to face off against each other over territorial and trading rights in their various domains. In 1835, the united coalition of disgruntled Nupe princes launched their first attack against Rabah but were repelled by Usman Zaki's forces. They switched tactics for a while and instead targeted the smaller Emirates of Lafiagi and Shonga led by Usman Zaki's acolytes. Here they met with better success and the Emirs of both settlements took to their heels. Not long after, a second attempt was made to sack Rabah. This time, after a year-long siege of the city, Usman Zaki fled to Sokoto. This finally allowed the united Nupe forces, which now included one descendant of the Fulani Mallam, Dendo, to declare victory over their homeland. The problem of which of the victorious claimants was to then become the undisputed Etsu Nupe was fortuitously solved when Tsado died not long after the fall of Rabah, removing the Majiya claim from the scene. This left Masaba - described by one traveller who met him as a 'fine looking negro [...] with a dignified deportment and immeasurably superior to the so called 'kings' on the sea-coast'[8] - as the undisputed king of Nupe, for the first time since the death of Ma'azu.

We the Nupe

Located right in the centre of Nigeria, the kingdom of Nupe might be said to contain multitudes. Populated by a dazzling array of diverse people and cultures, Nupe has tripped up many an ethnographer trying to unravel the complex origins and categorisations of the people living there. Adding to this puzzle was the fact that the Nupe kingdom was situated quite literally in the middle of what was already one of the most diverse countries on earth. Bordered on all sides by an equally diverse group of people, the befuddled Heinrich Barth who travelled here extensively called the entire central Niger area 'A Labyrinth of Kingdoms.' Like the river Niger which flowed through their lands, the Nupe came to be known by multiple names.

The Yoruba to their west called them *Tapas*, the Hausa to their north called them *Nufawa*, and the Gbagyi to their east knew them as the *Anupeyi*. For their part, the Nupe called themselves *Nupeci*[9].

This geographical heirloom had multiple consequences that can be easily imagined. For one thing, like the Abeokutans as we have seen, the Nupe were surrounded by enemies, at risk of being sitting ducks for raids from all sides by hostile and powerful states. And in a sense, they were exactly that. But just like their southern comparator nation, the Nupe also gave as good as they got, raiding and dominating the weaker groups surrounding them until they were the main trading counterparty and emporium for the larger Hausa and Yoruba kingdoms in their area. In this way, Bida, for instance, became a thriving slave market where Nupe middlemen purchased human bodies from the north and sold them to the south, for onward transmission to the Americas. Sitting at the confluence of the rivers Kaduna and Niger did not hurt, since those waterways were the natural system of transport and communication to and from the interior. The Nupe took due advantage and regulated trade flows to their own benefit - the Rabah ferry service across the Niger charged Nupe passengers 100 cowries, half of what it charged the Yoruba (200 cowries) and cheaper still than what the Hausa paid[10].

Apart from slaves, Nupe also did a roaring trade in kola-nuts, illustrated by the large and popular Labozi variety of nut which was sold everywhere across the Niger-Benue hinterland. The trade in this particular commodity was the monopoly of the Etsu Nupe, and growers were forbidden from selling to anyone except the rulers' agents[11]. The Nupeci combination of trade and geography worked to create something fascinating. Even though the Nupeci were conquered multiple times in the Game of Thrones, the underlying Nupe identity remained resilient. Till this day, the three ruling houses of Nupe trace their lineage back to the sons of the Fulani Mallam, Dendo. Yet, any Fulani markers that might have once distinguished the ruling elite have long been localised[12].

Returning to our retelling of the Game of Thrones, by the

time of Masaba's eventual ascension as undisputed king, everyone of consequence in Nupe was already maintaining an armed force of their own with Gogo Habiba even commissioning slave raids using her private army. The implication of this was that Masaba's uncontested reign as Etsu was never going to last for long. Furthermore, nothing had changed in terms of fundamental justice for the average Nupe citizen under Masaba, compared with the time of Usman Zaki or his other predecessors. The underlying conditions responsible for triggering unrest remained intact. Usman Zaki had put in place an exorbitant tax of 100,000 cowries per annum on the citizens and when they couldn't pay, their goats and unfinished clothes (the Nupe were excellent cloth makers) were taken instead of the tax. All of this was done in collaboration with Masaba and so oppressive was their reign that the Sultan of Sokoto wrote to them asking them to go easy on their tyranny[13].

In 1850, when the revolt against the ruling regime finally came, it was from an immigrant military General named Umar Bahaushe; and it found ready local support. Before long, Etsu Masaba had been driven out of Rabah. But perhaps because Bahaushe originally hailed from their common rival, Bornu, the former Fulani enemies could form a united front against him. Usman Zaki who had been cooling his heels in Sokoto brought Fulani reinforcements to the scene against the latest usurper. It still took three years for the brilliant Bahaushe to be defeated even though he inflicted several defeats on the Fulani in the process. The cameo role of this brave, noble general from the north in the Game of Thrones came to a gory end in 1857, when his head was cut off and displayed publicly on a stick at Rabah, *pour encourager les autres*[14].

That same year, Nupe formally accepted to join the Caliphate, like Ilorin, under the Gwandu branch. Emir Usman Zaki became the first Fulani-nominated Emir of a united Nupe Emirate, which would remain in place under Masaba and his successors until the present day. Usman Zaki died after a couple of years on the throne in 1859, with Nupe now finally united under Fulani suzerainty.

As there was no obvious rival to the throne, he was succeeded by Masaba and the new Emir could afford the luxury of switching focus from enemies within to wars of expansion against border tribes and beyond.

Masaba had some experience with this. After he was driven out of Rabah by Usman Zaki following the death of their father, he spent some of the considerable time he had on his hands raiding the towns and villages to his south. While attempting to open up the route to the sea and corner some of the growing trade with Europeans for himself, he marched his army down to a place called Adamugu (near today's Onitsha) but came upon a swamp that gave him pause, since his forces were mostly horse-mounted. He turned back in annoyance and on his way looted and destroyed all the Kakanda villages, located in today's Kogi State of Nigeria.[15] This failure notwithstanding, it offered a useful glimpse into what would become Masaba's trade policies, underpinned by slavery under a system called Tungazi - which he deployed when he became king of Nupe. Tungazi were slave labour plantations owned by the Nupe ruling elite, growing everything from peanuts to shea butter which were then exported to other countries. As a result of the permanent instability over the previous 50 years in Nupeland that we have just followed, at the time of Usman Zaki's death, there were only about 55 Tungazi in Nupeland. Masaba ramped things up 13-fold with just under 700 Tungazi by the end of his reign in 1873.

Further, while almost all of the Tungazi were worked on by Nupe labour at the time of Usman Zaki's death, under Masaba things changed dramatically with Tungazi populated by Yoruba, Hausa and even previously non-existent Afemai slaves from today's Edo State appearing in Nupeland. The Nupe melting pot was being swirled by the Emir's imperial ambitions and expansionist raiding practices[16]. These policies were continued by Masaba's successors - Umaru Majigi, who reigned from 1873 to 1882, Maliki (1882 to 1895) and Abubakar (Masaba's son, 1895 to 1901). In the end, Masaba's expanded Tungazi policy would come to play a big part in the downfall of the Nupe dynasty.

White Men on the River

While the Nupe princes had been engaged in their Game of Thrones, much had changed in the world and on the river Niger. A new power had arrived literally at their back door, following the opening of the river to European influence. The ship-wrecked William Balfour Baikie had settled at Lokoja nearby, in the domain of their river rivals, the Igala kingdom. Soon after in 1861, Lagos was ceded to the British, and the Atlantic slave trade was becoming more difficult to safely undertake. Even Madam Tinubu was diversifying into other commodities, exporting cotton from Abeokuta, from where more than 1,000 bales had been exported to Britain in that same year. The West Africa Company of Thomas Clegg, Henry Venn and Samuel Crowther was formed a few years later in 1863 as we have seen, and Nupeland was one of the main markets targeted for export of produce. Bishop Crowther struck a friendship with Masaba, who quickly became a great ally of the British traders now calling at his ports on the river.

In 1871, W. H Simpson, a British government official, was sent to Nupe to secure an agreement with Masaba for free and continuous trade with his people and within his domain. Regular trading intercourse with Europe began to develop. The Europeans wouldn't sell him alcohol, as they did not want to upset the Fulani Muslims in his domain, but they did sell him weapons and ammunition. Masaba specifically requested that the guns be very loud, the better to terrorise his enemies[xiv]. The Nupe monarch was already very powerful, but had his hand further strengthened by

---

xiv In 1864, William Baikie, as the British Consul in Lokoja, wrote to the Foreign Office in London, on behalf of Emir Masaba, requesting a shipment of Enfield rifles and muskets. The muskets, he wrote, were 'for noise, a very important element in warfare here' (See Joseph P. Smaldone's "Firearms in the Central Sudan: A Revaluation" in *The Journal of African History* Vol 13 No. 4 (1972) pp 591-607).

his enthusiastic attitude to trading with the Europeans on the river. He specialised in ivory and shea-butter, which was a substitute for palm-oil in soaps for the newly rich Europeans. Ivory and shea-butter exports grew significantly under Masaba's reign from £13,500 and £4,800 in 1871 to £24,000 and £25,460 by 1876, respectively. Ivory prices increased 60 per cent between 1871 and 1878 and the amount of shea-butter exported increased more than tenfold from 120 to 1,500 tonnes in the same period[17]. In those days, ivory began its journey in today's Adamawa State, where Hausa traders bought them from hunters and then sold some in Kano while the rest was despatched south to Nupeland. The benefits of the Clapham Sect era were beginning to accrue under Masaba, to this long-disturbed country - at least until he died in 1873.

As we have seen, the British monopolist Goldie Taubman arrived on the river in 1877, and immediately conceived of his grand vision to unite all the trading interests in the area into one company with official sanction. We have also followed the corporate financial manoeuvres and political shenanigans of this ambitious capitalist. We have seen the resulting grant of a British government charter to his Royal Niger Company (RNC) in March 1886, the starting date for the Imperial Era in Nigeria. In addition to its trading monopoly, Goldie's charter required the RNC to establish an effective political and administrative basis for governing the very limited areas on both sides of the river where it owned factories, trading stations, mini-ports and jetties. These assets were mostly inherited by the RNC from its various mergers and acquisitions. The company was also authorised on a limited basis to enter into trading agreements (but not complicated political treaties) with the chiefs and rulers of the various settlements in its trading area.

To achieve these objectives, the RNC would establish its private armed force, originally known as the RNC Constabulary (or the CST) in 1887. This force was equipped with modern marine infrastructure, including several steamers and yachts for traversing the river. The force boasted several hundred native troops under a

European commandant, armed with Snider-Enfield rifles and the soon-to-be ubiquitous Maxim gun, which was now being gradually put into active service. Goldie and the RNC had to move quickly, as other actors were seeking to establish dominance over the lucrative river trade. As we have already seen, a collective of Oil Rivers palm oil traders known as the African Association had come together to secure a similar charter in the Oil Rivers area. Goldie opposed this and attempted to instead convince the British government to *extend* the RNC charter to those other rivers near the Niger's delta. In the event, both parties were thwarted by British officialdom's reluctance to interfere, and by stringent lobbying from multiple private firms. This rear-guard action was led by the most important European shipping company in West Africa, Elder Dempster, which was loath to allow a monopoly to emerge over the entire area, as that would severely damage its powers of negotiation for freight rates.

Also resisting Goldie's company were the other European traders and imperialists on the river. On the one hand, a renegade French explorer named Lieutenant Louis Mizon would fail in his energetic attempts to create a protectorate for his country over Adamawa and other areas in the upper Benue. On the other hand, the German merchants on the river were using their diplomatic channels to protest loudly against what they called the company's monopolistic actions. One particularly troublesome German merchant at Nupe named Jacob Hoenigsberg had created a diplomatic incident in 1887 by inciting Emir Maliki (the leprous son of Usman Zaki with an ego the size of the world) into repudiating his country's treaties with the RNC.

The concerted local and international pushback against the RNC was so effective, that in January 1889, the Foreign Office instructed the highly regarded British army officer we have already met (later, Sir) Claude Macdonald to proceed up the Niger and investigate the company. The riveting, painstaking but also often sadly racist account of Major Macdonald's travels in Nigeria during 1889 provides one of the best contemporary reports on the state of the country immediately after the Game of Thrones in the Niger heartland. Written in colourful and descriptive prose by his chief of staff and private secretary, the grandly named Captain A.F. Mockler-Ferryman, *Up the Niger* was first published in 1892. In it, Mockler-Ferryman regales us with countless anecdotes and graphic personal descriptions of characters, events and affairs up and down the rivers and their hinterlands, from Nupe, Igala, Idah, Lokoja, Adamawa and Rabbah, all the way down to Ilorin which was then in the throes of an unending war with Ibadan.

Through the racially insensitive lens of Captain Mockler-Ferryman, we can view the personalities, concerns and political affairs of major and minor chiefs around the country, in the aftermath of the Nupe Game of Thrones. Through Mockler-Ferryman's foggy prism, we can recount critical observations like the extreme caution and refusal of successive well-informed and sceptical Emirs at Adamawa to trade with the Europeans at Yola. True to form, the reigning Adamawa sovereign in 1889 flatly refused even a complimentary visit from Macdonald, Queen Victoria's much-heralded envoy.

From Mockler-Ferryman we also learn more about the stubborn ignorance of Emir Maliki at Bida, who responded with profound incredulity to the idea that the premier Muslim in the world, the Ottoman Sultan had stooped to visit the Christian Queen of England in London. To this observant foreign envoy, we also owe some of our insight into the governance constraints of the intelligent but hapless Emir Alihu at Ilorin. This confused monarch was beholden as much to his powerful war chiefs south of the capital, as to the Nupe warrior-princes living on his northern border, as well as to the influential Borgu fetish-woman stationed in his court. It was also to Macdonald and Mockler-Ferryman's visiting party that Emir Alihu deadpanned in open court when he was informed that Victoria had reigned for over 50 years in England that: 'It was incredible that one person should govern for so long a time without enemies arising to plot against her life'[18].

Weary of the unending 'Yoruba Wars' and desirous of peace with the Ibadan, Alihu allowed Mockler-Ferryman to travel as a diplomat to Offa, the border town where Ilorin's armed forces were then camped. This journey in turn allowed the diligent captain to report extensively on everything he saw. From his excursion, we meet the commercial farmer, Chief Braima who was one of the most significant landowners in the Ilorin Emirate but lived in Lagos. We also meet the impressive Ilorin war-chief Gimba, who was an athletic and astute horseman and Alhaji Abdul-Salami, both cut from the same cloth as the martial princes of ancient Oyo. The latter was a clever and well-travelled politician, who had been to Mecca and spoke some English, having worked with several Europeans around West Africa. From Macdonald's travels we also observe the turmoil and confusion across the Yoruba country in the late nineteenth century, still reeling from the early century collapse of Oyo and the aftermath of the slave export trade being disrupted. Several times in his journey, the captain records reports of recent raids on a settlement, or raids in the process of being planned and implemented. Mockler-Ferryman's boss Macdonald dutifully reported on all these affairs in a balanced manner that was most satisfactory and illuminating to their superiors in London.

High Noon in Akassa

Major Macdonald was the same person who later (as Ambassador to China) played an instrumental role in securing the Second Peking Convention, which granted the British Government a 99-year lease of Hong Kong. His terms of reference in Nigeria required him to investigate complaints that the RNC was charging excessive duties, using its administrative powers to create a monopoly, and extending its jurisdiction beyond its territories. Macdonald was also charged to evaluate the suggestion that the RNC charter be extended to the Oil Rivers. Following his thorough investigation, Macdonald's report, which was never made public at the time, indicated that there was some level of truth to the allegations, particularly concerning the excessive duties and monopoly behaviour by the RNC.

Macdonald's findings would in short order have significant consequences for the company, for the nominally Fulani Emirates at Bida and Ilorin, and ultimately for the future country, Nigeria. Meanwhile, the RNC continued its financial consolidation by buying out the interests of the African Association on the river. Soon after, the British government took action and appointed Macdonald as its Commissioner and Consul General for the Oil Rivers based at Brass (Nembe). It is to this coastal city in the Niger delta that our story must now turn briefly if we are to understand the fall of Bida on the Upper Niger in 1897.

At about 9pm on 27 January 1895, Macdonald's vice-consul at Brass in the Oil Rivers received an anonymous message: 'Brass people leaving tomorrow to destroy Royal Niger Company's factories at Akassa on Tuesday morning. Be sure you send at once to stop them. An observer.' This cryptic but disturbing missive was forwarded at once to the Agent-General (the chief executive officer) of the company at the Akassa port, a man named Joseph Flint. The port of Akassa was the most important operational location of the RNC, situated as it was near the centre of the southernmost point in the Niger's delta. It was from this base that most of the company's activity on the river was coordinated and supplied. Akassa was the take-off point for most of the company's travel up the Niger. The critical storage facilities as well as other infrastructure were located there, including vessel repair yards, administrative offices, and most importantly for the intending attackers from Brass, customs revenue collection points.

Akassa was also a hostage holding depot of some sort. The RNC had developed an unusual system of enforcing its agreements with chiefs in the interior lands behind the river. Young boys, the sons of these chiefs, were arrested or offered up as part of trade dispute settlements between the chiefs and the company then brought them to Akassa for 'safe-keeping.' Here, they were taken on for most of the year as servants of European agents working for the company. Mockler-Ferryman, who visited Akassa, commented about these boys in his customary racially tinged pithy manner that 'after a few months, one sees them waiting a table as if they had been reared in a Strand restaurant'[19].

As already noted, the Macdonald report corroborated the allegation of excessive duties on export trade being charged by the company. For the indigenous traders at Brass who had been traditional coastal middlemen for centuries, these RNC customs duties essentially froze them out of the palm oil markets they had hitherto dominated. Worse, their loss was the gain of larger operators like the soon-to-be-acquired African Association, who could afford the charges. The RNC monopoly was tightening. The ruler of Brass, the grandly named Amanyanabo Frederick William Koko, Mingi VII of Nembe (more briefly, King Koko) was a Western-educated former school teacher who had already launched multiple written complaints against the RNC to the British authorities. Koko's complaints on behalf of his Brassmen were included in Major Macdonald's report and were considered to be fair and valid even by European traders in the area. Yet, these protests had met deaf ears for over three years, and King Koko was beginning to lose face among his people, who demanded more assertive action. Several prior threats of attacks by the Brass on RNC facilities and assets in the area had already been made, and so Agent-General Flint was quite certain that this latest anonymous message was yet another bluff. This was to prove a serious error of judgement, and the entire affair a tragic miscalculation for all the parties involved.

As predicted by the anonymous writer who was likely a European or Saro missionary living among the native people, the Nembe Uprising proceeded exactly as forewarned first thing on Tuesday morning. More than 40 massive war canoes carrying nearly 1000 armed Brassmen appeared out of the dark into the channel at Akassa. Slipping easily through the unprepared defences of the company, the warriors opened fire on the depot, using the

12-pounder cannons that were mounted on their war canoes. Flint and the luckier members of his staff were able to escape the scene, hastily casting off inside any functioning dinghy or vessel they could find, as most of the boats were under repair. The Brass attackers proceeded to thoroughly plunder and destroy the base, sinking two vessels (the *Argus* and the *Vigilant*). Virtually all the furniture, stock and equipment at the yard were removed or destroyed, and some clever sleuth among the Brassmen even arranged a ransacking of the RNC records office, carrying away the administrative books and confidential files of the previous years.

Most importantly, about 24 RNC staff were killed on the spot, and another 60 or so were kidnapped and taken back to Nembe with the rest of the loot, never to be recovered. The RNC would later allege (and their version of the story would find its way into all historical accounts), that the Brass chiefs ordered for the hostages to be killed *and eaten* at a celebration to mark the successful destruction of RNC's Akassa port. It is not clear how much of this vicious accusation was true, although a Catholic priest resident at Nembe was said to have witnessed the hideous bacchanal. What is clear however is that the RNC had a very strong commercial incentive to inflame opinion back in Britain against the Brassmen, who had delivered a disastrous defeat for the company and were justified in their opposition to excessive tariffs. The unpalatable alternative for the company would be to accept criticism of *both* its lax defence of its base, *and* its aggressive customs duty policy. Introducing cannibalism into the narrative served a useful purpose of switching the conversation to a more sensational headline, guaranteed to deny the Brassmen any public sympathy in Nigeria or Britain. The Nembe Uprising was the official opening scene of the British armed colonisation project in Nigeria. From the perspective of the company, such a travesty simply could not stand, and Nembe had to be reduced to rubble immediately.

Goldie applied great pressure on the Foreign Office to approve the retaliation expedition. In short order, a certain Admiral Frederick

Bedford, a Crimean war veteran and then chief of the West Africa Naval Squadron, was summoned to the Oil Rivers, accompanied by three warships, 150 troops and 50 RNC constabulary. This fearsome force set sail on 20 February, proceeding to blow up the well-crafted barriers and defensive obstacles sunk by the Brassmen into the approach channel to Nembe. During the next week, Admiral Bedford's force systematically razed several Nembe towns and villages to the ground; with the residents fleeing into the bush. Several hundreds of Nembe and other local people were killed by British armed forces in reprisal for the Nembe Uprising. This grim death toll was worsened by a smallpox epidemic then raging, which was exacerbated by the upheavals. While his city burned to the ground, King Koko escaped into the bush behind the creeks. He committed suicide a few years later.

A parliamentary investigation into the entire tragic affair was commissioned, undertaken by Sir John Kirk, the Scottish abolitionist-explorer, a contemporary of David Livingstone. Sir Kirk's report indicted the RNC for its 'inadequacy' and a 'virtual monopoly, which had caused reasonable resentment among African traders.' Kirk further reported that the RNC should 'confine itself to a purely administrative role by selling off its commercial interests to competitors,' essentially recommending direct responsibility for the Niger area by the British government[20]. This report was the final death knell in the coffin of the Royal Niger Company, and its charter would be revoked in July 1899. The Brass people had dealt the killer blow that ended the RNC's tyranny over their country, even if it was to be replaced by colonial rule in short order.

From Akassa, the Road to Bida

The events at Akassa in 1895 were the precursor to Bida in 1897. A few months after the gruesome killings at the coast, the Conservative government of Lord Salisbury was returned to office. As we have seen already, Salisbury was the well-informed analyst of affairs in the Oil Rivers during the time of King Jaja's removal by the British. Perhaps more important than Salisbury, the new government brought Joseph Chamberlain into office for the first time as Secretary of State for the Colonies. Joseph Africanus, the former President of the Board of Trade, was originally a radical Liberal and later an arch-imperialist Conservative and was now the powerful Colonial Secretary. Chamberlain was an unrepentant believer in the virtue of Empire, specifically, the British Empire and his views and actions would come to have a defining impact on the formation of Nigeria in this Imperial Era. To start with, when Chamberlain resumed office on 1 July 1895, he made it quite clear that he would like to see armed action taken against the Fulani Emir of Ilorin. Whether the action was taken by the government of the Lagos Colony, or by the Royal Niger Company, it was all the same to Chamberlain in London.

We will come to Chamberlain's problem with Ilorin very shortly but suffice to say that Goldie and the RNC quickly recognised that they must become more active militarily in Nigeria, given their poor showing at Akassa, and the new demands for action from London. Preparations for war began in earnest including the purchase and transportation of ships, troops, horses, Maxims, and other essential stores like tinned food and electric searchlights, a tool that the RNC army was one of the first to deploy in combat situations. Nothing was left to chance, as Goldie respected the adversaries he was preparing to encounter. The 50-year-old Goldie also took care to manage the public relations outcomes of the impending actions by getting a reporter from *The Times* of London to join his party in covering the war on the spot and telling the story as he wanted it told.

By 1895, Ilorin, under the Fulani successors of Mallam (later, Emir) Alimi had become an important economic and military power in central and western Nigeria. Notwithstanding this economic profile, our contemporary reporter on the spot, the tactless Mockler-Ferryman (the one who visited Alihu with Claude

Macdonald in 1889) was exceedingly disappointed with the place, describing this proud emporium as follows: 'We had heard the place described as the Mecca of West Africa - of immense size, possessing fine buildings, wide streets, magnificent mosques and handsomely clothed inhabitants. What we find today is a town certainly of considerable size, but in appearance not to be considered with Bida and Yola. The buildings are dilapidated-looking erections, irregularly roofed with palm fronds and untidy thatch; the streets are filthy and unsanitary; the mosques are mere barns, and the people are decidedly the dirtiest Mohammedans I have encountered anywhere in the world'[21].

Fortunately for him, the hard-to-please Mockler-Ferryman kept his negative opinions to himself for the moment and retained enough objectivity to provide us with a good sense of the late nineteenth century conditions in this thriving metropolis. At the time, Ilorin was still in a low-intensity boundary war with Ibadan - concentrated at the border camp called Offa, where a clearly eccentric but also apparently half-mad Fulani warrior-prince named Karara ruled. Karara owed his position in theory to the Emir at Ilorin, but in reality, was an independent operator focused on sporadic raiding and irregular sorties into Ibadan territory. A primary entrepot for trading caravans travelling from the interior across the river towards the thriving port of Lagos, the economy of Ilorin was built on commercial agriculture and trade intermediation. The trade goods included cloth, ivory, cattle, horses (on a limited basis), livestock, leather and slaves flowing outwards on one hand; and textiles, European manufactures, spirits (on a limited basis), arms, ammunition and cowries in the opposite direction. In 1895, Ilorin was ruled in theory by the Emir Moma dan Zubayru, but the reality was quite different.

As illustrated by the recalcitrant Karara at Offa, who was the nemesis of his supposed lord, the Emir Alihu ruled at the behest of the powerful baloguns of the five tribal wards into which his capital city was divided: *Fulani, Gambari* (Hausa), *Alanamu* and *Ajikobi* (both Yoruba). The Emir's ward made up the pentarchy, all of which were together divided into a total of 18 sub-wards. These baloguns controlled trade directly through the markets of each ward or sub-ward, and a critical factor for their commercial success was open access to markets regionally but especially at the coast. Slaves for domestic utilisation formed a substantial part of the Ilorin trade flows. This was because human labour was in great demand to achieve increased commercial agricultural production in western Nigeria, driven by the demands of the growing commodities export trade at the coast. Furthermore, slave porters were still the primary means of transporting trade goods in all directions.

As much for boundary protection or political conquest, as for keeping the southern trade roads open and safe for its merchants, Ilorin was constantly embroiled in wars with the rest of Yoruba. As we have seen, the Yoruba wars had continued for decades until the British as new rulers of Lagos desired them to end. This had to happen so that profitable trade could flow, as trade was the only sustainable means of paying the Imperial costs of holding and administering Lagos. In the early Protectorate, British interference to end these wars had initially been through the use of diplomacy and moral suasion, but it subsequently evolved to active armed participation. Starting with the rout and expulsion of Egba forces from Ijebu-owned Ikorodu to end the Ijaiye War in 1860, followed by the 1886 multilateral treaty to end the 16-year Ekiti Parapo War, the British were now engaged in all-out combat. They had defeated the Ijebu in 1892 using 400 troops, rockets and the now ubiquitous Maxim gun. Reading the future pragmatically, Ibadan had accepted protectorate status and a British government resident, by a treaty signed in 1893. Even the head-strong, notoriously ungovernable but forward-thinking Egba had observed the fate of Ijebu and loudly signed a 'Treaty of Independence' with Britain, reluctantly accepting a commissioner in exchange for nominal self-rule. The stubborn Ilorin however was not prepared to submit, and remained an independent operator outside of British influence, an undesirable state of affairs from the perspective of the overlords at the new regional power, British Lagos.

Chamberlain's long-held desire to subjugate Ilorin, even if under the guise of ending the continuing slave trade, was finally coming to effect. At this point, the slave trade was a domestic affair, following the collapse in foreign demand. Slaves were essential for porterage and industrial-scale cash crop production everywhere in the Niger-Benue country, like the Nupe Tungazi and the palm oil plantations among the Urhobo and western Igbo. As foreign demand for slaves disappeared, their local price remained steady in real terms, rising from £1 (around £130 today) for a male slave in 1850 to £7 (same amount, after accounting for inflation) in 1895. Female slaves cost slightly more than these sums. This phenomenon of market prices staying firm despite a decades-long collapse in export demand was probably best explained by the growth in local demand, and by indiscriminate slave-raiding creating a supply glut.

Two for the Price of One

Goldie understood the political mathematics at play, and the fate of Ilorin was probably already sealed by the time of the events at Akassa. However, to get to Ilorin, he needed to pass by their close friends and historical allies at Nupe on the river, with whom the RNC was beginning to have serious commercial disputes following the death of their long-time friend, Masaba. Thus, Goldie planned for two career-defining battles in quick succession, firstly at Bida - subduing Nupe and securing the river route - and then shortly after, at Ilorin - satisfying the desires of the powers that governed his charter, in Lagos and London. Major Alfred Arnold, commandant of the CST was appointed to lead the expedition. The transport ships were purchased, stocked and sailed up the river, the dismantled Maxims and artillery were packed, native troops were recruited, marshalled and drilled under seconded European officers. Nothing was left to chance; local political matters were also taken in hand.

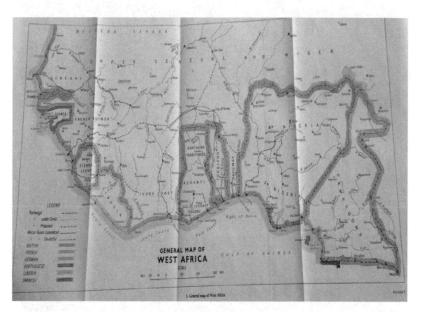

Map of West Africa

*Lugard and Commanders in camp before the battle of
Sokoto 1903. UK National Archives*

*St Peters Ake built 1861. Image captured in 1897
Walter Egerton Collection UK National Archives*

*Railway train heads out of Lagos to Abeokuta
1900 UK National Archives*

*Siging of the Yoruba peace treaty between the
Oyo, Ibadan, Ijebu, Ijesa, Ido, Otun, Ife and
Modakekean, Ijesha and the British 23rd Sep-
tember 1886*

*Royal Niger Company Armed Force at Lokoja c.1895
Royal Niger Company Collection. UK National
Archives*

Nigeria Regiment Carriers

*Lugard at Zungeru 1903, receiving a courtesy visit
from some Fulani representatives. Also in shot is one
of his African staff possibly Obed Azikiwe C.1903*

Old Supreme Court Building, Lagos 1897. It was replaced by a new building in 1905. The latter housed the amalgamation ceremony in 1914. UK National Archivesjpg

Lugard and commanders breakfast en route to battle

Eshugbayi Eleko and Chiefs outside Iga Idun-ganran c.1920

Nigeria Railways Train at a Provincial Railway Station. 1914 Alamy

Henry Townsend and CMS Missionaries at Abeokuta c.1862

Fred Pepple of Bonny former Regent of Bonny, with his children - c.1893 Brass River Photo by Jonathan Adagogo Green

Fulani Horsemen at a Durbar early 20th century. UK National Archives

Jos Market and Native Town c.1912 Bartlett Hughes + Sons Postcard - UK National Archives

Corpse of a Sokoto warrior after the battle of Sokoto, in 1903. A British soldier bears the body of a colleague in the background. UK National Archives

Lagos Harbour 1897 from photo taken on the Church Tower of Government Steamers Gertrude and Ekuro opposite Government House Lagos. UK National Archives

Hugh Clapperton Scottish Naval Officer and explorer who travelled through Northern Nigeria in the early 19th century Painting National Gallery of Scotland

Lord and Lady Lugard 1925 UK National Archives

*David and Anna Hinderer. German CMS
Missionaries who were responsible for the spread
of christianity at Ibadan. Image_ c.1870. UK
National Archives*

*Bishop Samuel Ajayi Crowther during his visit to
the United Kingdom in 1867 - Lambeth Palace
Collection*

*Bishop Samuel Ajayi Crowther during his visit to
the United Kingdom in 1851 Ernest Edwards tif*

*King Jaja of Opobo in Kalabari ceremonial dress
Image_ c.1881*

Firstly, the French were informed of the intending hostilities, and commitments were made to them by Lord Salisbury that the fighting would not happen in their nearby territories.

At this point, the interests of Imperial Britain found a common cause with Nupe domestic politics. Deputy Agent-General (later, Sir) William Wallace reached out and exploited internal disaffection against the ruling elite within the riverine Nupe communities, chiefly, the Kyadya sub-tribe, which controlled large lots in the middle river. Back in 1881, Umaru Majigi had fallen out with the Kyadya over his attempted appointment of one of his lackeys as Kuta, or chief of the sub-tribe. The Kyadya were a somewhat independent group occupying the strategic river routes through which trade and slaves flowed. But their independence was always untenable for an expansionist Bida. For their part, the Kyadya took very badly to the impostor sent to take taxes and slaves from them and pass them on to Bida. They had tolerated the previous Kuta imposed by Masaba as the former Etsu had opted for diplomacy, knowing he had no power to overrun them. But when the Masaba-installed Kuta - Prince Zhiri - died, the Kyadyas saw another opportunity to assert their independence, figuring out that a Kuta appointed by Umaru Majigi, who they had come to detest, was unlikely to be an improvement[22]. This proved correct as the hostility between them descended into a full-blown war which Umaru Majigi eventually won. He promptly publicly executed their preferred leader and his army commander in 1882. The Kyadyas never forgot or forgave this, although ironically it was the RNC who had helped suppress the ensuing revolt of the Kyadya by supplying Nupe with steamers.

Similarly, across the river from Nupe proper (in the North-East regions of Yorubaland, and present-day Kogi state), the long-suffering communities from Nupe's rapacious slave harvesting also harboured multiple decades-long resentments against their overlords at Bida. The British's decision to reduce Nupe was a once-in-a-lifetime opportunity for these long-suffering communities to strike back and regain freedom from their oppressors. For them, the arrival of a new, foreign power in the country was heralded with joy, for it was their moment of historical emancipation, irrespective of the provenance of this new potentate. Prominent among these groups were the Kabba-Owe, who volunteered their support of and participation on the side of the British forces, supplying them with food and soldiers. In the event, the jubilant Kabba were the first imperial Nupe domain to be 'liberated', in January 1897. This was achieved before any fighting had yet happened, as the Nupe army previously camped at Kabba vacated the area before the invaders arrived.

Things Fall Apart

In organising his defence of Nupe, the then reigning Etsu Abubakar (son of Masaba) unwisely sent out a force led by a certain Prince Muhammadu Makun who he had passed over as Shaba when he became Etsu. Given that Bida was now in a state of heightened alert over imminent British occupation, Prince Makun saw an opportunity to strike a deal for himself with the incoming usurpers. Rather than obey the Etsu's orders, he instead sought out William Wallace and negotiated a Faustian bargain with him: *if I stand down my forces and you take Bida, will you make me Etsu afterwards?* Wallace shook hands with him on the deal.

Ultimately, it was the Kyadya who delivered the decisive blow against Bida. Their de facto leader, Marike, had also negotiated a postbellum autonomy with the RNC. In exchange, the Kyadya supplied the Europeans with pilot canoes while also guarding the river to ensure the Bida army could not retreat or regroup elsewhere. This strategy also had the effect of stopping reinforcements from reaching Bida. The British force marched north from Kabba unhindered, crossing the river safely in the company's ships[23]. Following an arduous 40-kilometre march, during which heavy artillery was dragged by the heroic porters over this marathon, the little force arrived on the outskirts of Bida. Here, the 30,000 strong Nupe army awaited, some of them armed with breechloader rifles. The fighting commenced before the artillery arrived - Nupe cavalry versus the six Maxim guns and CST forces holding a square formation - continuing until late at night when the heavier guns arrived. However, poor training meant that most of the Nupe soldiers ended up firing over the heads of their adversaries. The following day, the RNC forces continued fighting their way towards the city, still formed as a square, until they reached within easy artillery range of the walls. Hardly ten days after reaching Bida, the invaders were departing, their grim work done.

In that infinitesimal period, the ancient Nupe Empire, resulting from an 80 year-long Game of Thrones was reduced by modern political, economic and military considerations. Abubakar was deposed and Wallace kept his promise to Prince Muhammadu Makun, installing him as Etsu. The Kyadya also got the autonomy they desired, and they were granted semi-independent status directly under the RNC, bypassing Bida. 'The arrangements which brought about the [...] capture of Bida appear to have been admirably devised and brilliantly executed' Lord Salisbury later wrote in a telegram to George Goldie[24]. Gratuitously, the Etsu Nupe's palace was blown up just before the victorious troops departed, marching back to the Niger where the four ships (named *Liberty*, *Empire*, *Soudan* and *Florence*) were waiting to ascend the river up to Jebba Island, across from the banks of Ilorin's domain. Here they rested for a few days and even had time to organise a horse racing competition which they called the 'Bida Cup' before picking up their guns and starting for the next phase of the war[25].

Another death march followed, this time over 52 kilometres, hauling heavy weapons all the way. Buoyed by the Bida victory, Goldie felt confident enough to drop two of the Maxims and proceed inland with only four, bound for the banks of the *Oyun* River, where the Ilorin cavalry was assembled waiting for the invaders. The square formation was employed again, with artillery and the Maxim being deployed to devastating effect. The following day, the offensive party crossed the Oyun and marched to the city walls, which were reduced by rockets and heavy guns. The unfortunate Emir Zubayru, who did not intend to fight but was forced into it by his baloguns, was only too eager to organise a surrender once the city was breached. A new treaty was signed on 18 February 1897, reinstating Zubayru as Emir, a fact that would earn his loyalty to the British for the rest of his life. Some accounts indicate that Goldie sought out a descendant of the long departed Afonja to install as Emir but found no suitable candidate.

It was over in less than three days; the excised limb of the centuries-old great Oyo Empire was reduced to an appendage of a stock market listed company in faraway London. For good measure, Goldie toured the river with his victorious army, showing force at Idah and Patani, which were major RNC depots. At the former, the normally imperious Attah fled before their arrival, while the Patanis were quick to guarantee future good behaviour. For his final trick, the capitalist turned conqueror Goldie issued at Asaba a proclamation abolishing the legal status of slavery in the Niger Territories. This gesture was more a political and public relations gimmick with an eye on news reporting than real, enforceable legislation.

That was how Bida and Ilorin, the southernmost and most recent Emirates created due to Dan Fodio's 1804 revolution were removed at a canter from the direct control of the Sokoto Caliphate, in less than one calendar month of hostilities during 1897. These historically and politically important nations were now placed into the Formation of the now relentless Nigerian story that was rapidly taking shape. The international, local and regional political, economic and diplomatic forces that brought about this summary reduction were only escalating as the turn of the century approached. The fall of Bida and Ilorin was not a story of military valour as gleefully reported by *The Spectator*; it was the opening shot in a new political and economic counter-revolution on and around the Niger, which was about to halt the progress of Dan Fodio's original religious movement.

By this time in the Niger Game of Thrones, it ought to have been clear to the local players that the game had changed, and that new strategies would be needed to remain in control of their political and economic futures. Their summary defeats should have given pause to Emirs Moma dan Zubayru and Abubakar dan Masaba's Fulani overlords at Sokoto[xv]. But as we will see, they learned the wrong lessons. With the benefit of hindsight, the ruling elite at Sokoto were not alone in this regard. In almost all cases around the river - the Egba being perhaps the notable exception - this game-changing realisation did not lead to a discernible change in local elite political and economic policy. The world was changing rapidly, and the country soon to be known as Nigeria would not be left out of it. The opening of the River Niger had erased that possibility for all times, and the only valid question henceforth was *how* the local population would adjust to change, and not *whether* or *why* change must occur.

One senior British soldier who was visiting the river on a separate mission at the exact moment of the Akassa disaster would later come to embody that forceful movement towards change in Nigeria. A genius, but also a functional megalomaniac, this military-minded successor to Goldie in Nigeria shared a lot in common with the imperial-capitalist state-backed entrepreneur, including the most intimate possible of unifying experiences: a shared lover. Our story will now turn to the long life and storied career of this controversial military officer, including his short period in Nigeria, during which time he attempted and failed dramatically to mould an already choate country into a rigid form that was completely inconsistent with its chaotic history.

---

xv To be exact, Bida and Ilorin were under the suzerainty of Gwandu – carved out for Abdullahi dan Fodio – which administered the western part of the Caliphate.

1. The Spectator Archive - The Battle of Bida. 1897/2/13 1897; (Available online).

2. Nadel SF. *A Black Byzantium: The Kingdom of Nupe in Nigeria*. LIT Verlag Münster; 1996.

3. Falola T, Jennings C. *Sources and Methods in African History: Spoken, Written, Unearthed*. University Rochester Press; 2004.

4. Lovejoy PE. *Jihād in West Africa during the Age of Revolutions*. Ohio University Press; 2016.

5. Idrees AA. Gogo Habiba of Bida: The Rise and Demise of a nineteenth Century Nupe Merchant Princess and Politician. *African Study Monographs*. 1991 1991;12(1):1-9.

6. Nadel SF. *A Black Byzantium: The Kingdom of Nupe in Nigeria*. LIT Verlag Münster; 1996.

7. Hallett R. *The Niger Journal of Richard and John Lander*. Routledge; 1966.

8. Knowles C. Ascent of the Niger in September and October, 1864. *Proceedings of the Royal Geographical Society of London*. 1864 1864;9(2):72-75.

9. Nadel SF. *A Black Byzantium: The Kingdom of Nupe in Nigeria*. LIT Verlag Münster; 1996.

10. Crowther S, Taylor JC. *The Gospel on the Banks of the Niger: Journals and Notices of the Native Missionaries Accompanying the Niger Expedition of 1857-1859*. Cambridge University Press; 2010.

11. Nadel SF. *A Black Byzantium: The Kingdom of Nupe in Nigeria*. LIT Verlag Münster; 1996.

12. Daily Trust Newspapers, Nigeria - Meet the Royal Ndayakos of Bida. 2018/7/28 2018; (Available online)

13. Crowther S, Taylor JC. *The Gospel on the Banks of the Niger: Journals and Notices of the Native Missionaries Accompanying the Niger Expedition of 1857-1859*. Cambridge University Press; 2010.

14. Glover JH. *The Voyage of the Dayspring: Being the Journal of the Late Sir John Hawley Glover, R. N., G. C. M. G., Together with Some Account of the Expedition Up the Niger River in 1857*. J. Lane; 1926.

15. Baikie WB. *Narrative of an Exploring Voyage up the Rivers Kwóra and Bínue (commonly Known as the Niger and Tsádda) in 1854. With a Map and Appendices. Pub. with the Sanction of Her Majesty's Government.* J. Murray; 1856.

16. Mason M. Captive and Client Labour and the Economy of the Bida Emirate: 1857-1901. *Journal of African history.* 1973 1973;14(3):453-471.

17. Flint JE. *Sir George Goldie and the Making of Nigeria.* Oxford University Press; 1960.

18. Mockler-Ferryman AF. *Up the Niger: Narrative of Major Claude MacDonald's Mission to the Niger and Benue Rivers, West Africa (Classic Reprint).* Fb&c Limited; 2018.

19. Mockler-Ferryman AF. *Up the Niger: Narrative of Major Claude MacDonald's Mission to the Niger and Benue Rivers, West Africa (Classic Reprint).* Fb&c Limited; 2018.

20. Kirk J. *Report by Sir John Kirk on the Disturbances at Brass.* H.M. Stationery Office; 1896.

21. Mockler-Ferryman AF. *Up the Niger: Narrative of Major Claude MacDonald's Mission to the Niger and Benue Rivers, West Africa (Classic Reprint).* Fb&c Limited; 2018.

22. Idrees AA. *Domination and Reaction in Nupeland, Central Nigeria: The Kyadya Revolt, 1857-1905.* E. Mellen Press; 1996.

23. *Ibid.*

24. Orr CWJ. *The Making of Northern Nigeria.* Macmillan and Company, Limited; 1911.

25. Flint JE. *Sir George Goldie and the Making of Nigeria.* Oxford University Press; 1960.

CHAPTER 9

Frederick Lugard, The King in the North

Mahdis and Messiahs

By pure coincidence, it was Sudan that gave two Imperial Era Britons named Fred Lugard and Flora Shaw their first taste of Africa. British entanglement in Egypt - that vital waystation en route to the much beloved India of the Empress Victoria - meant that the imperial government's resources were also inevitably drawn into the brutally harassed far-southern domains of this historical Ottoman possession. British involvement in the long-Islamised Sudan was beginning at a time when Mahdis, the long foretold martial redeemers of Islam, were constantly rising around West and Central Africa.

One such Mahdi to have popped up in Sudan around 1882 was Muhammad Ahmad, a former Egyptian government official and also an experienced slave trader. Ahmad was proclaimed by his followers to be the leader of a jihad, in much the same manner as Usman Dan Fodio with whom our story began. The primary complaint around which the followers of this Mahdi rallied was that Islamic Egypt was succumbing to Western influence under British occupation.

To them, this meant it was only a matter of time before Sudan came under the same influence, threatening their vision of a theocratic Sudan under the rule of Ahmad, if they did nothing to stop it. Matters came to a head in November 1883 when Mahdi Ahmad's followers obliterated an Egyptian army of 10,000 men led by a British officer named Colonel William Hicks aka Hicks Pasha. William Gladstone, then in his second of four stints as British Prime Minister, was reluctant to intervene in Sudan and so decided that the best course of action was to send in a force on strict orders to evacuate the remaining British officials there. The mistake he made was that he sent Major General Charles Gordon to lead the evacuation. Gordon, who was semi-retired in 1883 doing biblical reseach in Palestine, to put it delicately, was a weirdo with a storied military career behind him. A man deeply obsessed with religion; Gordon was a tortured soul who believed himself to be a vessel through which God's purpose might be fulfilled.

In January 1884, the messianic Gordon left for Sudan and it did not take long for the government to realise that it had made a recruitment error. Sir Charles Dilke, a member of Cabinet who had lobbied for Gordon to be appointed, wrote with regret in his diary in March, after receiving several bizarre telegrams from Gordon, that 'we are obviously dealing with a wild man under the influence of that climate of Central Africa which acts even upon the sanest men like strong drink.'[1] In short, the half-mad Gordon arrived in Sudan and decided to be a hero. After evacuating a significant number of people from Khartoum, he decided that it was his Christian duty to fight and defeat the Mahdi. He then refused offers of an expedition to remove him from Khartoum because it had been named the 'Gordon Relief Expedition'.

Eventually, Gordon's martyrdom was secured when the attacking Mahdi's forces surrounded his garrison, destroying the entire contingent of armed men and 10,000 civilians, before decapitating Gordon himself. His severed head was the only part of his body discovered, the rest having been cut to pieces and taken away. News of this spectacular massacre caused such a sensation in late Victorian Britain that the reluctant government decided to send in a much larger punitive force. The new Sudan offensive army assembled by the British was drawn from all around the world and a young officer named Frederick Lugard (garrisoned in India at the time) signed up as part of what came to be known as the 'Suakin Field Force.' Their objective was to defeat Ahmad's brilliant army commander, Osman Digna, who Winston Churchill would later describe as 'immortal'[2].

Young Lugard arrived in Sudan and joined in several fierce

battles against the Mahdi's forces, sustaining his first ever wounds in battle. He also got to see the Maxim gun in action for the first time, as it was employed with brutal efficiency against the Mahdists. This made a profound and lasting impression on the young officer, as we shall come to see in our story. Imperial Britain however did not manage to finish this battle - the punitive armed force was pulled away to Afghanistan where the Russians were once more threatening - and so Lugard was sent back to India with his unit. He had tasted blood in Africa, and not for the last time. He had also formed an opinion on the dangers posed by Mahdists which would shape his future reactions to them. Meanwhile, revenge against the Mahdists was served cold by Britain more than a decade later, in 1898 at the bloody Battle of Omdurman.

A Lady's Interview with a Captive Chief

A gallows humour joke among media professionals till today is that 'For your sun to rise as a journalist, it must first set over Africa.' Flora Shaw's journalism career took off at the same time as her first African excursion, even if it occurred in the unlikely setting of Gibraltar, where she had been invited on holiday. While walking around the southern European coastal town one day, the curious young woman saw a group of Black men guarding a house which she was told, after persistent enquiries, was holding a notorious Sudanese slave trader named Zubayr Pasha. Famous in England as the Black nemesis of the mad General Gordon, Zubayr was under house arrest for reasons that were not immediately clear to Shaw. The aspiring journalist got permission to interview the Sudanese captive and began by asking him what he knew about the sensational murder of Charles Gordon. Zubayr angrily blamed Britain's arrogance for Gordon's death, claiming that Gordon had tried to bring him in from Egypt to calm the situation down, but the British authorities had refused. Flora Shaw visited Zubayr several times and interviewed him on various subjects ranging from his slave trading to his relationship with the Mahdi. He proved to be an interesting subject who held strong opinions about the world and himself. Flora now had an interesting story and by some coincidence, she had only recently been introduced to a well-connected editor named William Stead. By June 1887, her first article titled "A Lady's Interview with a Captive Chief" was published, kick-starting a long and distinguished career which would culminate in her much-celebrated appointment as one of the first women editors of a major newspaper in the world.

The Making of a Megalomaniac

Frederick John Dealtry Lugard suffered a quite traumatic childhood. Born to Reverend Frederick Grueber Lugard and Mary-Jane Howard in January 1858 at Fort St. George, Madras, India, Lugard's father was the descendant of Protestants who had arrived in Britain from Central Europe via Holland. His first wife had abandoned him (with three children) for another man, which left him humiliated and permanently short of money. Nine years before the birth of his son, he met and married a fellow missionary and they had another two daughters in three years, after which she caught cholera and died. Now approaching 50, saddled with five children and still desperately poor, Lugard senior met Mary-Jane (also the daughter of a Reverend) in 1855 and married her. This patchwork family proceeded to expand further with five additional offspring (Frederick was the second) but only three survived. As revivalist members of the CMS, the Lugards were what might be called 'born again' Christians today. As doctrinaire Baptists, the crowd of children in the poor Lugard home were steeped in the revivalist Christian dogma of the time, abolitionism being a big theme, alongside ethics of frugality.

When little Frederick was five, his mother took him and the four youngest children back to Britain, leaving the Reverend behind in India. About a year later, Lugard senior returned to

Britain to join them and the year after his return, the latest Mrs. Lugard fell pregnant again, an unwanted outcome that she had feared once she heard that her husband was on his way home. She gave birth to another son, named Edward or 'Ned' as he would be more popularly known. In a matter of weeks, tragedy struck the Lugards again when Mary-Jane died from complications brought on by Ned's birth. After losing three wives and with a large company of children to tend, Reverend Lugard collapsed under pressure - he suffered a nervous breakdown and abandoned the children to themselves. Fred's older half-sister became his de facto sole parent and looked after him until he was ready to leave home. By 1878, after an itinerant schooling career and with his family still reeling from all the trauma, Lugard was advised by an older relative (an Uncle who had also served) to join the army. Barely passing the qualifying examinations, he enrolled in the Royal Military Academy at Sandhurst from where, after only a couple of months of training, he was commissioned and joined a battalion in Ireland. Not long after, the young officer was on his way to India, part of a force deployed to defend the fraying Empire from multiple aggressors, while continuing his military training for several years. While in India, he missed out on any real fighting because he was down with fever. He however learnt a lot about logistics and transport systems that would prove useful in his later career, and eventually rose to the rank of Lieutenant. Lieutenant Frederick Lugard's tragic childhood would however continue to haunt him into adulthood, affecting his emotional capabilities into maturity.

Love and Heartbreak

Upon returning to Lucknow, India from his service with the anti-Mahdists in Sudan, Lugard met a woman who would wreak further havoc on his already unstable emotional health, sending him back to Africa in search of war. She was the wife of a much-admired army officer in the city at the time. Lugard fell hard for Francis Catherine

Gambier and by the end of their six-month affair, he no longer cared that most people knew he was having sexual relations with her. But the tempting Mrs Gambier was much more worldly than the lovestruck young officer and spurned his offers of a permanent match. Her marriage at the time was already the second one, and Lugard was almost certainly a virgin when he met her. The affair ended when Lugard was posted to nearby Burma as part of a force detailed to deal with a local Prince named Thibaw. This ruler had come to power in 1878 by murdering almost 100 members of the royal family, to ensure he reigned without any challenges, and was determined to push Britain out of the lower half of his country. While in Burma, Mrs. Gambier came back into Lugard's life, via a destabilising letter telling him she had been in a terrible accident which she went on to blame on his abandonment of her. The lovelorn Lugard abandoned his duty post and headed back to India to look for Gambier, arriving there to find she had already sailed for Britain. Lugard continued at once onto a ship for England, in hot pursuit of his former lover, only to arrive in London and find her living with another man. Even worse for the unfortunate Romeo, Gambier received him very coldly and showed no interest in rekindling the old romance.

Heartbroken and disoriented, Lugard wandered around London for a few months (including a stint working as a fireman) before deciding that he needed a new adventure to a place that had held no memories of his lost love, ruling out a return to India. A less sensitive commentator might have observed that at this stage of his life, the traumatised and heart-broken young soldier was in the firm grip of a death wish and was seeking to plunge into a war that might provide a glorious avenue for its fulfilment. In due course, after much travel Lugard ended up at Zanzibar where he thought he would help fight the Arab slave traders on the coast of East Africa and put a stop to the trade. He arrived there in 1888 and teamed up with the African Lakes Company, a trading concern founded about a decade before by Scottish businessmen and run by a couple of brothers - John and Frederick Moir. Lugard's first expedition in East Africa pitted him against a great slave trader known as Mlozi bin Kazbadema, a Swahili man who called himself a Sultan and did a brisk trade in capturing humans from the interior near Lake Malawi and transferring them to the coast for sale. Mlozi also maintained a side business dealing in ivory, which pitted him against British traders like the Moir brothers. Suffice to say that defeating the formidable Mlozi did not provide an answer to Lugard's death wish, nor did it prove as easy as he originally thought. He departed for Britain in 1889, with plenty of wounds he had sustained in the fighting, to return to East Africa[xvi] later in the year. In East Africa, Lugard had better acquainted himself with the Maxim gun, which at that time was still somewhat unreliable. He also experienced the discipline of trekking hundreds of miles in a tropical country, two more lessons that would feature heavily in his later adventures.

Fame and Prosperity

More importantly than trekking and war-making, however, Lugard the avid writer had kept a meticulous diary in Uganda, a document that would soon prove to be influential in shaping British policy in East Africa. His memoir, *The Rise of Our East African Empire* which was published in 1893, became a successful contribution to the 'African Expedition' genre of British travel writing, in the well-worn tradition of previous Mad Men in Africa like Mungo Park on the river and Henry Morton Stanley deep in the Congo. Lugard's bestseller went a long way towards convincing the British government to commit more resources to the eastern sections of the continent, ostensibly to control access routes to Egypt via the Lower Nile, in the protection of the Imperial jewel, India. Such was the success of his advocacy that by 1894 Uganda would be colonised,

---

xvi   His journey took him through today's Kenya, Uganda, Tanzania and Malawi, hence the use of 'East Africa.'

and not long afterwards, the East Africa Protectorate created out of what is present-day Kenya. Mlozi was eventually defeated in 1895 when the British government put together a large armed force for the purpose. While back in London, the now influential author also began to meet important and famous African adventurers like Harry Hamilton Johnston (later, Sir) who had served as Vice Consul in the Niger delta around 1886 and helped to shape the British government's colonial policies.

Thus, commenced Lugard's other stellar career as a self-promoting public relations guru; adept at using the media, and his influential friends, to his professional advantage. The newly minted influencer on all matters Africa wrote several newspaper articles and gave talks across the country. His speeches proved so popular that no lesser a personage than the Prince of Wales once wrote to him to apologise when he could not attend his talk in London. It was while on a media tour promoting his book that Lugard was introduced to the rising star journalist Flora Shaw in November 1893, at the office of The Times. Shaw had been assigned by the newspaper to review his book and after overcoming his initial disappointment that a woman was chosen to interview him, Lugard got on quite well with his future wife. Their shared interest in African affairs provided the initial basis for regular correspondence between them, which blossomed with time into a real friendship. Needless to say, Shaw gave Lugard's book a glowing and detailed review, which was published on 22 November 1893 in which she glorified it, without any irony, as '...the most important contribution that has yet been made to the history of East Africa'[3].

Even though Lugard did not know it at the time, he had met his lifetime personal cheerleader and life-coach. Over the years, Shaw would do more than anyone else to promote Lugard's career, burnish his credentials and cement his legend. Boosted by Flora Shaw, Lugard expanded on his flourishing celebrity, receiving invitations to dinner parties held by artists, writers, and politicians, including Joseph Chamberlain who would go on to become

Colonial Secretary in 1895. Of all the notable Africa personalities with whom he was now au fait, it was the capitalist George Goldie that would give Lugard his first taste of blood in Nigeria.

Goldie and Lugard: Marching for Treaties

As we have already seen, Goldie had managed to consolidate trading activity on the Niger by 1884, seven years after he first visited the river. Once he obtained his much-treasured charter for the RNC, Goldie set about signing treaties with various rulers along the banks of the river and as far inland as he could muster and march safely. These treaties were of course worthless pieces of paper, as they were not backed by any potent force. This put Goldie at a disadvantage to the well-funded French armed forces who were making determined advances into the West African interior. Unlike the British who often had to wait for direction from London, the French forces were funded directly by their government and then left to their own devices; which meant they were able to move much quicker if they needed to. In June 1894, Captain H. A Decoeur was sent by the French government to negotiate a treaty with the King of Nikki (a Borgu town in present-day Benin Republic), to cement French claims to a strategic position upon the banks of the Niger.

Intending to prevent this outcome, Goldie managed to convince Lugard to lead an RNC armed force towards Nikki so they could arrive before Decoeur and sign a treaty - a deliberate provocation of the French for whom Lugard was already a notorious figure after some skirmishes in Uganda. Within four days of each other, Lugard and Decoeur set sail for Nigeria, taking different routes. Lugard took the longer route as he had to travel through areas under the protection of the RNC. The French media had a lot of fun with the 'Race to Nikki,' which they dubbed a 'steeplechase'[4]. In the event, after a long and tortuous journey with only a handful of ill-motivated RNC troops, he arrived at Nikki late in October 1894. Lugard obtained his treaty quite alright but he was tricked with a fake signature. A Mallam had approached him and told him that the king was blind and did not like meeting White men anyway. The Mallam went on to tell Lugard that the king had instructed him to sign any agreements on his behalf. Lugard's interpreter had gone in to see the king and came out 'confirming' the Mallam's story. As Lugard did not have the personnel to use force - Goldie's instructions to him had been 'diplomacy and not conquest is the object of your expedition'[5] - he was left with no choice but to sign the agreement. The Mallam wrote the name of the king on the document as 'Lafia'.

It turned out that Lafia was the name of a long dead King and the actual king's name was Sire Toru. When Decoeur arrived there five days after Lugard had left, he was able to 'reopen' the agreement as he had a force of almost 300 Senegalese infantry with him. This time, on 26 November, the king personally signed a treaty placing himself under the 'exclusive Protectorate of France.' King Sire Toru would later also sign another declaration that he had never instructed any Mallam to sign an agreement with Lugard on his behalf. This Anglo-French posturing and treaty-making rivalry on the upper Niger would continue for several years, much to the initial amusement and later alarm of the local chiefs until it was resolved by conquest and summary allocation of territory as we will see later in our story.

Narrow Escapes on the Niger

This first experience of Nigeria did not endear Lugard much to the country, which he found much more hostile than East Africa, so much so that he considered turning back on a couple of occasions. Upon leaving Nikki, Lugard and his army were attacked nearby in Neshi (present-day Niger State). The celebrity officer with a former death wish ended up with the poisoned arrow of a Borgu warrior stuck in his skull after it pierced through his standard-issue helmet. In attempting to remove the arrow, one of his Hausa soldiers dragged Lugard across the ground, the stubborn missile refusing to detach from his head. Luckily for Lugard, the rudimentary but highly effective munition was eventually dislodged, but only after taking a decent amount of his skull flesh with it. His life was probably saved by the intervention of the intrepid native soldier, and the cocktail of local antidotes that native troops applied to the open wound. It was Lugard's first taste of blood and near-death experience in the country that would come to be known as Nigeria. It would not be the last.

Leaving the area and travelling into the relatively safer Yoruba country, Lugard arrived in Iseyin (present-day Oyo State) around Christmas 1894. He carried on his journey and after a few days of rest was able to secure a meeting with the incumbent Alaafin of Oyo, Adeyemi Alowolodu who was rather amused to see that the White man had made it that far alive. After marching nearly 1,200 kilometres in a little more than 100 days, Lugard arrived at Jebba in January 1895. He took a boat to Akassa, where the RNC maintained an important base, to await further instructions from Goldie as he considered his mission complete. After waiting a few days and hearing nothing, the impatient Lugard elected to return up the Niger to Lokoja. History turns on these seemingly marginal decisions and Nigeria's story may well have been different had Lugard remained in Akassa for even one more day. It was the very next day after his departure that King Koko's Nembe forces launched the devastating raid on Akassa that we saw earlier in our story.

Had he remained, Lugard may well have been one of the 24 RNC staff killed, or the 60 kidnapped, that day. Ultimately, he was stuck in Lokoja for a few more months in the fallout of the raid and the British Navy's reprisal in February. It was not until March 1895 that Lugard was finally able to sail back to Britain, with his dizzying experiences in Nigeria occupying his mind back to Liverpool, where his ship docked in May.

The Romance of Empire

About two years before Flora met Frederick, she was asked as one of the leading colonial journalists at the time to write an article about the Niger delta and its 'Oil Rivers' for the *Guardian* newspaper of Manchester. Shaw dutifully went off to interview the leading capitalist of the Niger area, George Goldie for his take on the subject. She left with more than a story - Goldie, a handsome and married but notorious philanderer, charmed her, and they began what turned out to be an eight-year love affair. Shaw hoped that Goldie would leave his wife for her, but to him, she was just another one of his many women, even if he greatly admired her intellect. Soon after, the first major political crisis of Flora Shaw's career was triggered in 1895 when Leander Jameson (a Scottish politician with imperial ambitions) came up with the hare-brained idea of overthrowing the nominally independent Boer government then ruling South Africa. Equipped with no more than a private army made up of a few hundred amateur armed imperialists, Jameson and his motley crew attempted what came to be known as the 'Jameson Raid'.

They were summarily routed, captured by the Boers and the fortunate Jameson was sent back to Britain for trial rather than executed. But the failed raid had caused a sensation in London and further greatly embarrassed the government when the plot was linked to Cecil Rhodes, the wealthiest entrepreneur and most prominent British public officer in South Africa. As the scandal unravelled, it emerged that Flora, who was friends with Rhodes, had known about the raid in advance and had been communicating by telegram with him. Shaw had even published the manifesto of the raid - which the plotters had produced in the event that they were successful - in the *Times* the day after the raid. For this particular attempted contribution to British imperialism, Shaw found herself in front of the British South Africa Committee of Parliament, set up to 'Inquire into the origin and circumstances of the incursion into the South African Republic by an Armed Force'.

The enquiry began early in 1897, with Chamberlain and the government properly dragged into the ensuing hot media mess. An attempted British putsch in the resource rich country of South Africa was particularly newsworthy, as the country had already produced large quantities of diamonds for decades, and a significant gold deposit was discovered on the Witwatersrand in 1884. Flora was eventually called to give evidence before the committee in May 1897 but was let off in the end when the members agreed that as a journalist, she was protected by the privilege of confidentiality she enjoyed with her sources. Still, it was a chastening experience for the high-flying journalist. Later the same year, George Goldie's wife, Mathilda, who was the former family governess, had travelled with him to Nigeria and even owned a house in Calabar, died. As much as Goldie had been serially unfaithful, her death devastated him. Flora offered her support and after a while they continued their relationship, leading ultimately to a marriage proposal which she delivered to him by letter. At 45 years old, and after seven years in the off-and-on extra-marital relationship, Ms. Shaw felt entitled to the honour. Goldie replied by sending her a book titled *Rosmersholm*, which is still going on as a stage play in London's West End today. This tragic play was about a man who lost his wife and then carried on an affair with a woman who lived in his family home. Eventually, this protagonist asked his lover to marry him and she refused. This was Goldie's melodramatic way of rejecting Flora's marriage proposal. The rejection, and the impersonal manner in which it was done, devastated Shaw. She was also frequently ill at the time and she suffered a near mental breakdown, unable to eat properly and confined to her bed for weeks. She was only shaken out of it when her editor offered her a trip to Canada to report on the Gold Rush there at the time, a task for which she summoned all her energies.

All of this was happening around the same time that the ambitious and energetic Chamberlain was perfecting his plans to finally apply some muscle behind Britain's claims to its West African paper possessions. In a debate in the House of Commons in February 1898, Chamberlain told Parliament in relation to West Africa that 'if we are to occupy, as evidently it is necessary that we should occupy, these territories over which we have assumed a protectorate, we must have a force capable of that duty.'[6] The import of this was that the French who had been making inroads into the West African interior were about to be challenged for the territory. Chamberlain went on to announce the creation of the West African Frontier Force (WAFF) to be commanded 'on the Lagos side' by none other than the famous Colonel Lugard. At the centre of this turn of events was Flora Shaw, who counted as her three closest friends George Goldie, Joseph Chamberlain, and Fred Lugard. Flora Shaw's role in shaping Nigeria went beyond her heavily mythologised and much talked about responsibility for coining the country's name. Shaw popularised the use of the name to refer to present-day *Northern* Nigeria only when she wrote her famous article about the still inchoate country. Published by the *Times of London* on 8 January 1897, her article is the best-read document that uses the name, but it is quite doubtful that she can be rightfully credited with originating the term[xvii].

For his part, the media 'influencer' Lugard was desperately looking for a real job by this time. He had complained to his brother that he was only surviving by dipping into his savings, but his preference was to go back to the scene of his past glory in East Africa. But his frequent public utterances on all things East Africa meant that he had put off many of the people who might have made it possible for him to get the job. Moreover, East Africa was by then under the supervision of the Foreign Office and thus outside the influence of his admirer Chamberlain at the Colonial Office. In short order, Parliament voted £161,500 (£21 million in today's money) for the WAFF effort and by March 1898, the 40-year old Lugard was on his way back to Nigeria as 'Commissioner and Commandant of the West African Frontier Force,' at the rank of

xvii The Nigerian historian, Edward Keazor, has credibly documented that the name 'Nigeria' had been used long before Flora Shaw committed it to print in 1897 (See Keazor's 2014 paper "Nigeria: The Journey to Amalgamation")

Lieutenant Colonel, and on a salary of £1,500 per annum.

A Golden Sunset

As for Goldie, he had enjoyed a good run and the show was inevitably coming to an end for the RNC. Chamberlain's muscular approach to imperialism meant that it was only a matter of time before he saw Goldie and his RNC as no longer fit for his 'chessboard' strategy in the Niger area, which consisted mainly of infiltrating the French held areas and confronting them but never firing the first shot. He began to make demands on the RNC for their men and resources and Goldie, reading the writing on the wall, resisted as much as he could, which had the effect of merely delaying the demise of the RNC. Chamberlain, in September 1897, wrote to the Prime Minister that it was time to 'expropriate the Company [RNC] lock, stock and barrel.'[7] The nationalisation of the RNC was not completed until 1899, but because it was a matter of public knowledge that the government was in negotiations to buy out the company, speculation in its shares drove them up from £10 per share in 1897 to £20 per share in 1899. Goldie had also cleverly split the company into two different companies - one administrative and one focused on trading. The administrative arm had been losing around £20,000 per annum while the trading arm was profitable and was paying out dividends to its shareholders. This trading arm also had assets made up of buildings, trade debtors and stock worth around £416,000. After long debates in Parliament, Goldie was able to exit his 22-year-old start-up for more than double his money after Parliament voted (181 to 81 votes) in favour of buying out the company for £865,000 (£110 million in today's money). The now fantastically rich Goldie turned down job offers from the Colonial Office, cashed his cheque and went on a long holiday to China to enjoy his money and try out a new adventure but he was disrupted by the anti-foreigner Boxer Rebellion which broke out there in late 1899. Goldie would later serve on a few obscure commissions when he returned to London but is most remembered, ironically, for burning all his papers and placing a curse on any of his children who wrote about him after he had died. One of the original names proposed for Nigeria was Goldesia, after Goldie, but he flatly rejected the usage of his name. Goldie also politely declined an unofficial job offer from Colonial Office, which had assumed he would continue in a soon to be created role of High Commissioner of Northern Nigeria, after clearing his cheque, a snub that was held against him for many years after by senior officials.

The atheist who found himself out of place in religious Victorian England had finished his pioneering part in the story of Nigeria.

From Commander to High Commissioner

Lugard set about his task at the WAFF with the incredible energy and personal dedication which would later come to characterise his Nigerian regime, for good and bad. He handpicked the weapons (six Maxims included) and men he wanted, turning down some men who had been assigned to him by the Colonial Office, claiming they were rejects who had failed in other postings. He tapped Colonel (later, General Sir) James Willcocks, a logistics expert who had distinguished himself in Afghanistan and India, as his second in command and they sailed together for Nigeria. He also sent some officers ahead of him to Lokoja, led by Colonel FitzGerald, to start recruiting and training local soldiers. When Lugard got to Lokoja in April, he found that the '1st Battalion' - made up of Yoruba and Hausa recruits - already had more than 1,000 soldiers undergoing training. Quite possibly one of the greatest bluffs in history, colonialism, looked at in the cold light of history, was as remarkable as it was absurd.

Provided with only a handful of British officers, Lugard was able to proceed to the country confident in the knowledge that they could recruit the locals who would help them do the work of taking over their own country. A single one of the six 75-mm heavy artillery guns Lugard took with him required 32 people to move - one person to carry all the spare parts, four people to carry the gun itself, two people to carry one wheel each, one person to carry the axle, four to carry the cradle and another four to carry the two trails. The whole thing weighed close to 300 kilograms[8]. There were also various other non-soldiers employed by Lugard such as porters, servants, and labourers which helped the British officers to concentrate on strategy and military tactics. Without this local support, it would have been impossible for any reasonable number of Europeans to carry the heavy weapons and supplies, in stifling heat, while fighting against highly motivated opposition. History has not been kind enough to preserve the names and thoughts of these indigenous people, who played such a critical role in reshaping Nigeria, leaving a gaping hole in the story of the country that can only be filled by speculation and educated guesses. Many of them were freed or runaway slaves who were not tied to any particular town or home and as such were happy to tag along with the newly arrived restless White men who were seemingly intent on touring the whole country. The least that can be said about them, however, is that they had good reasons for fighting, and were fully formed humans making rational decisions.

Lugard quickly commenced his task of sending the French packing and making Nigeria the property of Britain. He divided his army into three groups and dispatched them North, South and West of Lokoja, where the French were located. What followed was a series of manoeuvres that now look like silly games between Britain and France. 'You will advance rapidly from Fort Goldie, on the Niger, until you come in contact with the French outposts. You will then move on into the interior of Borgu, avoiding towns and villages over which the Tricolore is flying, and which are garrisoned by soldiers properly armed and in uniform. With these exceptions, you will occupy any places you may decide on, and there hoist the Union Jack. Once this is done you will consider it British territory, and take any steps you deem necessary to safeguard our interests'[9] were the precise instructions given to Lugard and Willcocks by Chamberlain for his 'chessboard' policy.

As it turned out, both countries ended up supplying amusement to the locals who watched them arguing over who got there first and then raising their flags within a few metres of each other. One can now look back at Nigeria as a British creation but at the time Lugard and Willcocks were trying to take possession of it, they ran into the French everywhere they went. That the French got to Nigeria first, had ambitions to connect all their West African colonies from Senegal to Dahomey, and yet lost out to the British is one of the great what-if questions of history. We can only suggest that the British - via the RNC - focused their energies on the richest and most commercially important parts of the country that enabled trade, while the French simply went after territory almost for territory's sake. In the end, control of trade won over sheer physical presence.

At the same time that all the flag-raising was going on, the British and French governments were in negotiations in Paris which gave birth, in June 1898, to the grandiloquently named 'Convention between Great Britain and France for the Delimitation of their respective Possessions to the West of the Niger, and of their respective Possessions and Spheres of Influence to the East of that River' which gave to the British Kaiama and all of northern Nigeria from Sokoto to Bornu. The French took Nikki, in modern-day Benin Republic. All of a sudden, Lugard who had arrived in Nigeria as a soldier found that the battle he was sent to fight had ended without a shot being fired and as a consequence, he was transformed from soldier to administrator almost overnight. Chamberlain then told him of his plans to nationalise the RNC and turn the whole of the north into one British Protectorate.

This time there was no reticence on Lugard's part - Chamberlain offered the job and the former lovelorn soldier with a death-wish accepted his first major administrative assignment. By

1899, Lugard the administrator was in full flow. He went back to London to personally interview staff (he did not want the Colonial Office to just send him anyone as was the normal practice) because he wanted to be frank with them and let them know the task in Nigeria was by no means an easy one. At the same time, he was negotiating the transition of the RNC's properties and resources to the government. That same year he was promoted to Brigadier General and on the very last day of the nineteenth century, he was formally installed as the High Commissioner of the 'Protectorate of Northern Nigeria,' a vast country, home to some 24 million souls.

Another Kind of Jihad

The obsessive-compulsive soldier was not one to engage in half-measures. As soon as the RNC take-over was offered as his next mission, he plunged into it with full vigour and arrived at Lokoja on December 31 full of ideas and plans for expanding the limited areas along the banks of the river controlled by the company. Having negotiated the best possible deal in terms of operational assets to be transferred from the company to the Government; and having been himself the pioneer commander of the government-sanctioned armed force established for the area, Lugard was very well informed about the country and just the man for the job.

One of Lugard's first actions after being ceremonially sworn in on New Year's Day 1900 was a legal pronouncement abolishing the institution of slavery in the new protectorate, an important political statement but a largely meaningless edict as of that date. Even the very boundaries of Lugard's new political territory were still only ambiguously defined. By referring to theoretical spheres of interest, and some local but mostly international treaties of very little significance to the actual rulers and people on the ground, Lugard's paper protectorate was a chimera that would have to be substantiated by conquest.

By the anti-slavery proclamation, which it had no powers

yet to enforce, the newly arrived power in the country was publicly identifying itself as fully allied with the lowly, oppressed and disenfranchised across the dominions of Dan Fodio's successors. In a sense, Lugard was borrowing a political leaf from the former revolutionary jihadis themselves, 100 years before him. Seen this way, the seemingly superfluous anti-slavery proclamation was not merely about creating an international justification for British rule in this faraway country. Perhaps more importantly, it was also about signalling to the local population that the usurping White men were allied with the weak and downtrodden, against the prevailing ruling elite then pressing down on their necks. It was Dan Fodio's jihad all over again, only this time presided over by a European revolutionary whose own radical theology was a mixture of imperial capitalism and paternalistic humanitarianism. Evaluated alternatively, Lugard was intending to complete and continue the work of imperial consolidation in northern and central Nigeria that was commenced by the ideological Sheikh in 1804 and faithfully continued by his less capable descendants for one hundred years.

Annoyingly for the intending conqueror on the Niger however, serious fighting broke out nearby at the Gold Coast during 1900, diverting the attention of British officialdom, and the troops of the WAFF to the more pressing challenge of the Ashanti War. Lugard therefore, spent most of the year in planning, diplomacy and organisation, as well as seeking out a site for a new capital. He would ultimately settle on Zungeru, a pleasant clearing located deep in the hinterland, alongside a bend in the Kaduna river - within fighting distance of his future adversaries but still well connected to the major Niger waterway. Fighting would begin in earnest the following year, but the early priorities were logistical and strategic, perhaps contributing to an under-estimation by his adversaries of the available British military capacity.

However, among his enemies in the Caliphate, it was well understood that war was coming, and confidence was high that these White men, isolated as they were so far from their comfort zones at the coast and on the rivers, were beatable. Nonetheless, preparations for war in the Caliphate began in earnest, including the placement of spies among the recruits of the WAFF. These spies typically joined and later deserted, with the intention of understanding the capabilities and methods of the British force. Among the established powers in the country, frontline opposition to this new anti-slavery force in their homeland was led by a notorious, gratuitously violent raider, Ibrahim Nagwamatse, the Emir of Kontagora, but more popularly known as Nagwamachi ('the destroyer') or Mai Sudan to the Hausas he terrorised.

Nagwamatse was the pithy commentator who famously deadpanned when asked to stop raiding the local communities for slaves: 'Can you stop a cat from mousing? When I die, it will be with a slave in my mouth!'[10] A renegade operator even within the Caliphate; he was a grandson of Abubakar Atiku, the second Caliph of Sokoto, and a son of Umaru Nagwamatse who founded the town of Kontagora in today's Niger State. This Emir of Kontagora was a borderline psychopath, even by the low standards of late nineteenth-century slave-raiders. Sadly, for all concerned, he was now at the peak of his powers, devastating all the areas surrounding Lugard's new base, all the way to the Adamawa country. Not even the Sultan at Sokoto seemed able to check this marauding bandit. 'Mai Sudan came to Kaya and Fatika and Danmahawaye, he laid them all in ruins, he carried off the people and sold them'[11] was how Baba of Karo, the Hausa Muslim woman, with the book of the same name, described what it was like to live in his shadow. The Destroyer could not have known it of course, but with the arrival of Lugard, his days of glory were now numbered. And they could not have ended sooner. Like the slave hungry Kosoko at the coast half a century before him, Nagwamatse would shortly become an early casualty of British intervention in Nigerian politics.

Opening Shots in Lugard's War

So, Lugard chose to start his fighting with this particular opponent who grandly called himself 'King of the Sudan' and was universally feared for his potent supernatural powers. The appropriate moment for arresting the slippery Emir presented itself when internal Caliphate politics resulted in a blockade of Zaria by Nagwamatse and his forces. Having escaped from Kontagora when it was previously sacked, Nagwamatse settled in a camp with thousands of his warriors near Zaria, sallying forth from there to capture any undefended people in the villages around the walled metropolis. The Emir of Zazzau appealed to Lugard, as the newly arrived power in the country, for assistance, aware that internal dissent within the city would soon lead to the gates being breached in favour of The Destroyer. In one of the more astounding cases of British bluster overwhelming an unexpecting enemy, a small party of 40 Black troops and four White officers answered the call and rode 200 kilometres hell-for-leather from Zungeru to Kaya, where the camp of Nagwamatse with nearly 10,000 men was located. According to the telling of Captain George Abadie who led the mission, this small force utilised the element of surprise and rode straight through the camp, surrounding the largest tent, which they suspected would house their target. They entered it, proceeding to immediately arrest and handcuff the 'King of the Sudan' with barely a shot fired.

Turning to the rest of the force surrounding them, they announced that their problem was only with Nagwamatse, and everyone else could go home. This remarkable tale would appear untrue if the historic evidence did not exist of a captured slave chief interred at Zungeru for several months until he was released and 'given another chance' by Lugard. Separately, opening shots in Lugard's war were fired in another more conventional British expedition, led out against the stubborn Adamawa by a colonel named Thomas Morland. This led to a bloody battle, with 41 British-led troops dead and more than 150 Adamawan casualties.

The conquest of the Caliphate had commenced in earnest.

Financing the New Caliphate

Apart from the determined enemies surrounding the intending conquerors, another major challenge to any putative new government in Northern Nigeria was revenue. While the newly declared 'Southern Protectorate' controlled customs revenue from booming coastal trade that could be relied upon to fund its government, the landlocked country in its hinterland had no efficient single point or similar trade volumes from which such revenues could be charged. This meant that Lugard's Northern Protectorate would have to rely on a combination of customs revenue sharing with its southern neighbour, as well as funding from Britain. The first annual budget drawn up by the new 'High Commissioner' for the running of his administration came to just under £86,000 (£11 million today) covering everything from medical expenses, running of a police force and prisons and payments to local chiefs as compensation for losing their livelihoods following the crackdown on slavery.

London accepted Lugard's budget and added £50,000 for infrastructure spending. Thus, of his total inaugural budget of £136,000, London sent down £75,000 or 55 percent, while the balance was obtained by a grant from the Southern Protectorate as a pro-rata share of customs revenue[12]. William Wallace, whom we met at Bida, was chosen as Deputy High Commissioner to assist Lugard, for his deep knowledge of the country gained from the years he spent working for the RNC.

Lugard had a total of nine political officers 'administering' the vast territory he purported to govern. With what little resources he had of men and funding, he decided to concentrate his efforts on the security of the routes for conducting import-export trade in the country. This meant that any marauding chieftain would be the first to know there was a new king in the north. One such Emir would be Etsu Abubakar, whom we met in the previous chapter.

Although he had been removed from office and replaced by Prince Muhammadu in 1897, he soon returned to Bida, kicked out his successor, and continued his slaving business from where he left off. Lugard showed up at his palace one fine day in January 1901 with a handful of troops only to meet the place empty - Abubakar had read the writing on the wall and fled. Muhammadu was re-installed as Etsu Nupe for the second time in four years. Another warning shot had been fired and it was going to be the Sokoto Caliphate or Lugard left standing, but not both.

War and Insurgency in Bornu

Yet another test of a different kind showed up in Bornu. It was one thing for the British to claim to govern 'Northern Nigeria' as a protectorate, it was quite another to do so in practice. While theoretically defined as part of Lugard's paper protectorate, Bornu at this point had no British presence whatsoever. The North-Eastern portion of the putative protectorate was unprotected by any European and was under the control of a warlord named Rabeh. Rabeh az-Zubayr ibn Fadlallah was so named because he made his name as a Lieutenant of Zubayr Pasha, whom we met earlier through Flora Shaw at Gibraltar. Rabeh had been enslaved as a child but had learnt the slave-raiding trade under Zubayr, becoming a fierce slaver himself. When Zubayr's forces tried to break Sudan from Egyptian control in 1878, they were roundly defeated but Rabeh refused to submit and fled with a few hundred of his fighters to the Darfur area. There he continued his slave-raiding and made enough money to build up his army such that by the early 1890s, they numbered over 5,000 men.

In 1893 Rabeh rolled into Bornu, sacked the Shehu, a man named Ashimi, and established his new capital at Dikwa. In case anyone was in doubt that he meant business, he let loose his army on the former capital, Kuka. The troops proceeded on a two-day rampage of murder and destruction. When the dust settled, over

3,000 people had been killed[13] and Kuka, which is located in today's Kukawa local government area of Nigeria has never been the same since. Rabeh proceeded to govern the territory as a brutal military dictator and launched attacks on anyone near him, including the Emirates under the domain of the Sokoto Caliphate. These he claimed to be seeking to 'liberate' from oppression. In reality, most of Rabeh's fighting was to raise money for the upkeep and happiness of his army. The only trouble for this brutal ruler was that the European powers France and Germany were also operating in the same neighbourhood. Before long, these rivals would come to blows. In 1898, French armed forces were advancing north from the Congo and Rabeh decided to suspend all his other wars and take them on directly. In the first battle between them that year, he destroyed the French party. A few months later, the French put together a much larger force and went back for Rabeh. This time, after some brutal fighting, they managed to defeat him.

A truce between them followed for the next two years while the French tried to establish control over the areas around Lake Chad. By 1900, the Europeans felt confident to recognise former King Ashimi's nephew – Mohammed el-Amin, better known as Kyari - as the new Shehu of Bornu, effectively deposing Rabeh[xviii]. More fighting was inevitable. The third and final battle between Rabeh and French forces took place in April 1900 when he launched an attack on them. Again, after much heavy fighting, in which the commander of the French forces, Major Amadee Francois Lamy, was killed, Rabeh was finally defeated. The French had offered a bonus to any soldier who managed to kill him and so one of them decapitated Rabeh for good measure. A picture of his separated head on a pike still exists on the internet for the morbidly curious modern reader.

---

xviii The ease with which Rabeh had sacked Kuka was considered a disgrace by Kyari and other members of the Bornu ruling elite. To right this, Kyari had his uncle, Ashimi (who had been reluctant to fight), assassinated and declared himself Shehu to take on Rabeh. He then led an army to Kuka but was defeated and captured alive. He refused to beg for his life as Rabeh demanded and was summarily executed.

Quite apart from France expanding into what was supposedly British territory, the situation was further complicated when Rabeh's son, Fadlallah, who had inherited the rump of his father's army, appealed to the new colonial power for help. The trouble was that it was impossible to offer any help at the time as Northern Nigeria's forces were on loan to the over-staffed Aro expedition, as well as in Ghana helping to face off the Ashanti. Nevertheless, one officer was sent down to meet with Fadlallah who received him lavishly. He took this as a sign that the British were ready to back him even against the French and so not long after he attacked French forces, suffering obliteration in the ensuing battle. His brother immediately surrendered to the French and handed over what was left of their army. Thus, Britain watched as the French pranced around its supposed 'territory,' unable to do anything about it. Following much diplomatic wrangling, France withdrew from this territory, which was accepted as a British 'sphere of interest,' leaving Bornu in a state of complete lawlessness. It would not be the last time that this state of affairs would ensue. Anyone who thought that governing Nigeria was going to be easy would have been quickly disabused of the notion at this point.

Sir Frederick Weds Miss Shaw

In line with colonial office policy, Lugard proceeded on leave to London in April 1901 for six months. Earlier that year in the Queen's honours list, he had been made a Knight Commander of the Order of St. Michael and St. George (KCMG) and thus became Sir Frederick, a rather eligible 43-year-old bachelor. Flora Shaw meanwhile had finally broken off her relationship with Goldie for good, and Lugard had gotten to know about their long affair. He took Flora's side, seeing how much damage the heartbreak had done to her. Perhaps it was also because he could empathise, given his own experiences with Francis Gambier. The knock-on effect was that he broke off his friendship with Goldie and spent a lot of time with Flora. Later that year he asked her to marry him and she refused but not 'in terms which preclude hope' as he wrote to tell his sister later.

He duly proposed again a few weeks later and this time she accepted. Theirs was an unusual kind of love (she was six years older than he was) that was born out of a friendship sparked by a mutual interest in Africa. He was about to return to Nigeria, so they decided to get married the following year. On June 11, 1902, on the island of Madeira off the coast of Portugal which was a popular colonial rest and recreation spot, Fred Lugard and Flora Shaw were married, and they shortly after sailed forth to Nigeria as husband and wife. The aspiring conqueror had won his most important battle yet, securing the highly accomplished newspaper editor as his wife and partner.

Corresponding with the Enemy

Just before Lugard left Nigeria to get married, the Sultan of Sokoto, Abdurahman dan Abubakar - the Danyen Kasko we met earlier - finally replied to the letters Lugard had been writing to him since January 1900. In the last of the letters sent in March 1902, Lugard told him what he had done to Nagwamatse in Kontagora and Abu Bakr in Bida - after the fact - both of whom had disobeyed his orders to stop slave raiding. Further annoying the Caliphate, Lugard also posted a Resident, with a garrison in tow, to Zaria, again only informing the Sultan after the deed had been done. He then sought to flatter the Sultan by trying to claim they were on the same side: since the Sultan had also sent cease and desist orders to both Emirs he had deposed, which they ignored. Lugard's letter also let the Sultan know that he was putting Nagwamatse on trial for his crimes. 'Peace be with those who seek peace and trouble on those who make trouble' he concluded.

The Sultan might have been equally alarmed and amused at this new non-Muslim foreigner presuming to administer justice and deposing Emirs of a hundred-year-old Caliphate as he saw fit.

His now-famous uncompromising reply read - 'From us to you, I do not consent that anyone from you should ever dwell with us. I will never agree with you. I will have nothing to do with you. Between us and you, there are no dealings except as between Muslims and unbelievers - war, as God Almighty has enjoined on us. There is no power or strength save in God on high. This with salutations'. Almost entirely based on this one letter which was received in May 1902, the crafty Lugard set about building the case for his war against the Sokoto Caliphate with a skeptical British government in London.

But who or what had the Sultan been replying to? None of Lugard's letters to him had said anything about anyone going to 'dwell' with them in the manner that the Sultan's letter suggested. Furthermore, the very next month, Lugard received another letter from the Sultan that was less hostile and made no mention of war except to say that 'Be it known to you that I did not call on you to enter on the pacification of Bauchi or any other place whatsoever [...] I seek help from no one except God'. This was a direct reply to Lugard's March letter in which he had also informed the Sultan what he had done in Bauchi. By the time this restrained letter arrived however, Lugard had already decided (based on the May letter) that the Sultan was spoiling for war. Yet, for a letter of such importance, Lugard did not show the latter communication to London until several months later. The original of the letter also mysteriously vanished.

When Lugard had been on holiday in London in 1901, William Wallace, acting on his behalf, had written to the Sultan informing him that the British wanted to place a resident in Sokoto. The letter was either not delivered or got lost and Wallace did not receive a reply. It is not a giant leap to conclude that the Sultan eventually got the letter and his reply refusing anyone from the British to 'dwell' among them was a direct response to Wallace's request to place a resident in Sokoto. There was also something else going on around Lugard at the time. As with many 'cabinets' before and since, the leader was often surrounded by one faction of hawks and another faction of doves. Lugard was no different and this distinction could be best seen in two of his residents - Captain George Abadie, the resident in Zaria (the hawk), and Major John Burdon (later, Sir), the resident in Northern Nigeria (the dove). In the end, it came down to who was Lugard's favourite and the relationship he had with Abadie was like that of father and son[14].

Where Burdon brought him reports of one Emir or the other offering a chance of diplomacy, Abadie told him tales that were often made up about Fulani hostility and imminent danger. In the febrile atmosphere of the time, and with Lugard only having a small force to hand, Abadie's scare-mongering found much purchase in the fertile mind of his father figure. Lugard's assessment of the situation was that since His Majesty's Government (Queen Victoria had died in January 1901 and was succeeded by Edward VII) had declared a protectorate over the area now known as Northern Nigeria, it was his job, as the man on the ground, to turn that declaration into a reality, by any means necessary.

The Dodgy Case for War

By the end of 1902, Lugard had concluded detailed plans to take Kano first, and then Sokoto. Kano's ostensible offence originated at Keffi, in present-day Nasarawa State of Nigeria. In October 1902, Captain Moloney, the British Resident in Keffi, had gone to see the Magaji of that town, Ibrahim dan Abd Allahi, in his palace to try to reach some kind of understanding for his submission to British rule. He went to the square in front of the Magaji's palace and sent his assistant resident, Webster, to ask the Magaji to come for a meeting (Moloney had been crippled in the Akassa raid). When Webster got inside the palace, Abd Allahi's guards attacked and beat him within an inch of his life, but he narrowly escaped. Moloney then told him to go summon some troops to come to their aid while he waited behind.

Abd Allahi, knowing he was going to be arrested and deposed, then came out of the palace and attacked Moloney, killing him with his sword. Moloney's interpreter, Audu Timtim, was also killed. Timtim appears to have deliberately misinterpreted Moloney's message to Abd Allahi when it was discovered that some native officials had been blackmailing local women into slavery claiming that Moloney had requested this of them. An infuriated Lugard would, in the aftermath, bring in a Hausa language course as compulsory for all his political officers, without which no officer would be promoted. There is still a Moloney Hill in Keffi today where the resident was buried.

The Magaji thereafter fled to Zaria and then later to Kano. In Kano, the Emir, Aliyu ibn Abdullahi-Maje Karofi, better known as Aliyu Babba (whom we already met earlier), gave the Magaji Keffi a state welcome and rode through the town with him on a horse. This played into Abadie's hands as he had been claiming to Lugard that Aliyu Babba was putting together an army to attack the British garrison in Zaria, a made-up tale. For Lugard, Moloney was the second resident to be killed in a year and this meant that it was open season on his officers if he did not respond immediately. Yet, within a few days of Moloney being killed, Sultan Abdurahman died at the age of 74. Even if Lugard had been making a case for an expedition based on Abdurahman's hostility, a change in Sultan surely offered reason to pause or at least open discussions with his successor on a clean slate. But Lugard carried on like nothing had happened and did not even reach out to the new Sultan, Muhammad Attahiru I, son of Sultan Mu'azu Ahmadu.

By January 1903, Lugard was ready to mount expeditions against Kano and Sokoto without informing the Colonial Office. He must have known that they would refuse to sanction the raids, given the way the recent Boer War had left Britain fatigued. He planned to commence the expedition and present its success as a fait accompli for the government, who would also be forced to support him if things went wrong - to save British prestige. But his plans were somehow leaked by the Reuters news wire service and the story appeared in newspapers in Britain[15]. The blindsided Colonial Office was furious and sent angry telegrams to Lugard asking him to abandon his plans. In December 1902, Sir Charles Dilke, who was against any war of expansion in Nigeria, raised the issue in Parliament to Austen Chamberlain (the son of Joseph Africanus) demanding assurances that Kano would not be attacked[16]. Telegrams flew back and forth between Nigeria and London in which Lugard cleverly hinted at his plans without fully revealing them, preserving plausible deniability for himself. In the end, the determined Lugard ordered Colonel Thomas Morland (later, General Sir), who had earlier in 1901 led the expedition to depose the Emir of Adamawa, to take 722 infantry soldiers, 24 British officers and 12 NCOs and march from Zaria, where they were stationed, to Kano. The guns were not left behind - 4 Maxims and 4 75-mm guns also made the trip. Before embarking on the journey to join Morland, Lugard took some time to write his will.

Kano Falls

In the event, the great city of Kano - described by one visitor as the 'Manchester of Tropical Africa' for its manufacturing and thriving commerce[17] - with walls as high as 15 metres and as thick as 12 metres, fell relatively easily. This was because Aliyu Babba had taken 2,000 of his horsemen with him a few weeks before to Sokoto to 'pay homage' to the new Sultan Attahiru I, leaving the town undefended. But he had a good sense of what the British were up to and so he took most of the possible claimants to his throne with him on the trip, knowing that Lugard would want to install one of them as his successor to give any deposition some credibility. After some pounding, Morland's men were able to make a hole in the thick wall and entered the town. Lugard set off from Zungeru and arrived in Kano late in February to see things for himself. The first order of business was to reopen the markets and allow trading to continue. This seemed to please the Kano residents who immediately went about their business as normal. Lugard later wrote to Flora that he had never seen anything as magnificent as the Kano palace in Africa, 'It is a marvellous place,' he wrote. The conquerors installed Muhammadu Abbass, the Wombai and one of Aliyu Babba's brothers (the man who had pursued and dispatched Tukur during the Kano Civil War), as the new Emir. This was after Abbass reached out to Lugard and they held lengthy talks agreeing on how Kano would be governed under British rule. Thousands of slaves were freed, and a new tax system was established.

Up next was Sokoto and the expedition now began the 16-day march westwards. A small advance party led by a 28-year-old officer new to Nigeria, Captain Wallace Wright, had been sent out. On their way, Wright's little force ran into an ambush laid by Aliyu Babba's army, who were now on their way back to retake Kano. Somehow, this small advance party made up of 45 Yoruba and Hausa soldiers and one other British officer, held their own against Aliyu Babba's 1,000 horsemen and 2,000 soldiers on foot, without losing a single soldier. The Kano army was now led by Aliyu Babba's older brother and Vizier, Ahmadu. On the night before the fight, Aliyu Babba himself had a change of heart and headed for the border disguised as a salt trader. Ahmadu was killed in the fighting while Aliyu Babba was later captured by anti-Caliphate rebels in Gobir as he attempted to escape to Mecca through their territory - in today's Niger Republic. He was handed over to the British who sent him on internal exile in Yola and later to Lokoja where he died, humiliated. Wright for his part was later personally awarded a Victoria Cross by King Edward VII for his exploits and went on to be elected a Member of Parliament.

The Battle for Sokoto

A debate began in Attahiru's palace as the British advanced on Sokoto - do we resist, or do we submit to them? As one might expect, opinion was divided down the middle. Some of the smaller towns between Kano and Sokoto had made their choice and decided that submitting to Lugard was not the worst thing in the world. The tall and aristocratic Attahiru, who always wore white clothing, introduced a third option into this debate: why not embark on a Hijra like Dan Fodio had done a century before, rather than submitting to the British infidels?[xix] This was an idea earlier suggested to him by Aliyu Babba, which might explain why the Caliphate nobleman chose to flee rather than fight. With no seeming consensus, the unfortunate Attahiru, who had inherited all the problems of his predecessor, ordered his men to saddle up and wait for the White men outside the city gates. The British force duly arrived on 15 March 1903 with nearly 600 carriers who helped to carry the Maxims and 75-mm guns, another 656 Yoruba and Hausa soldiers armed with rifles and 25 British officers and 5 NCOs.

This would have been a novel experience for many of the Yoruba and ethnic minority porters and soldiers fighting on the side of the British. For context, just three years before, a group of unarmed CMS missionaries advanced up to the north to spread the Gospel. They soon found that their Yoruba porters had fled as they approached Kaduna, recognising that they were entering into an area where they were very likely to be captured as slaves. This time, with the heavy guns and British officers in front of them, there were no Yoruba desertions. Perhaps even more telling as a source of Yoruba motivation was that, shortly before he died, Sultan Abdurahman had chased out all the Yoruba traders in Sokoto claiming that they were British spies[18]. These kinsmen of Afonja were now at the gates of Sokoto, ready to serve a cold dish of revenge under the command of British officers.

---

xix   Islamic eschatology would also have played a role in the adoption of the hijra. This allowed for heading in the direction of Mecca as a response to the world seemingly coming to an end and the imminent arrival of the Mahdi. The coming of the unbelieving white men would have intensified the sense of foreboding in the mind of Attahiru.

The infantry square had become popular in the British Army following its effective use at the Battle of Waterloo in 1815. As we have already seen, Dan Fodio's jihadists also used it to a devastating effect against the Gobirawa at the Battle of Tabkin Kwatto in 1804. There are variations to this fighting formation, but in general, it involves soldiers forming a square, allowing the advancing forces to see and defend all areas around them. The key discipline required was in advancing together without breaking the square formation. This formation was so effective against cavalry because horses are simply unable to run directly into sharp objects. Thus, a square needed only to have a second line with soldiers holding long bayonets to put off the advancing cavalry, who would throw off their riders rather than run into such an arrangement. Dan Fodio's jihadists did not have bayonets, but their archers had played the same role against the Gobirawa. The irony is that having used such innovation to great effect in the early jihad, the Caliphate then abandoned it in favour of a predominantly cavalry force. Nearly one hundred years to the day they had taken Kwatto, roles were now reversed with Lugard's forces arriving on foot and the Caliphate meeting them on their horses. Now, as then, the square won.

2,000 of Sultan Attahiru's horsemen charged at the British square repeatedly and hundreds of them were mercilessly cut down by machine gunfire. At this point, the outstanding General Marafa Mai Turare, whom we last saw saving the Caliphate with a brilliant counterattack against the Kebbi diehards in 1892, took one look at the futility of the unfolding fight and his pragmatism took over. Marafa asked Attahiru to call a halt to the fighting. Poor Attahiru must have been incredibly confused at this stage. He did not want war, but events had forced it on him. Now he had reconciled himself to fighting, he was being asked to quit by no less a person than his army commander. He initially rejected General Marafa's advice, but the Vizier chimed in with a veiled threat that the blood of every man who died in the pointless battle would be on him. With no way to advance the argument any further, Attahiru took the rest of his army and retreated eastwards to the sacred town of Burmi while the British forces occupied Sokoto. From a personal point of view, General Marafa had made a profitable choice - in 1915, this crafty General would become Sultan Muhammadu Mai Turare and reign over the affairs of the British Caliphate for nine years.

A triumphant Lugard arrived in Sokoto a few days later and could now announce to the Colonial Office, who were still furious at his disobedience, that he had been right all along. Declaring 'mission accomplished' over Northern Nigeria, the celebrity soldier of East African fame put on his starched white uniform with all his medals, entered the Sultan's palace square and declared a momentous end to the 100-year-old Sokoto Caliphate. Speaking in English, translated into Hausa, Lugard addressed the Vizier of Sokoto and the Chiefs of Kebbi, Gobir, Zamfara and General Marafa, setting out his stall - 'There will be no interference with your religion nor with the position of Sarkin Musulmi as the head of your religion,' he declared. This commitment in particular resolved a major dilemma for Waziri Buhari who found himself effectively in charge in the aftermath of the invasion's chaos and leadership vacuum. In his famous Risalat al-Wazir 'ila ahl al-'ilm wa'l-tadabbur treatise, Waziri Buhari made the argument that abandoning what was effectively a Muslim land was tantamount to giving it up to unbelief. This left the question of what kind of relationship it was possible to have with people who had the goal of 'seeking for territory and overlordship in worldly matters.' Lugard's aforementioned promise to them meant that the Waziri could then square this circle saying, 'we show regard to them with the tongue and have intercourse with them in the affairs of the world but never to love them in our hearts and accept their religion'.

Lugard went on to give the chiefs the option of deciding whether they wanted Caliph Attahiru to return as Sultan or preferred to nominate someone else to take his place. After conferring among themselves, the Emirs came back to say they had decided on Muhammad Attahiru II as the new Sultan. He was a son of the fourth Caliph of Sokoto, Aliyu Babba (Mai Ciniki who earlier tried to hold the disintegrating caliphate together). This new Caliph held as much a claim to the Sultanate as Attahiru I (who was a son of the fifth Caliph, Ahmadu Atiku) and had only narrowly lost out to him the previous year. Attahiru II went on to reign for 12 years, with the British having removed most of the Sultan's powers, turning him into a glorified figurehead.

Katsina and Zaria Keel Over

Lugard then left for Katsina in the company of 70 Yoruba soldiers and arrived there after six days. He strolled into the town and 'confirmed' Abu Bakr dan Ibrahim - who had been on the throne since 1887 - as Emir. He did this presumably because Katsina had put up no resistance and had welcomed him into their town. Decades later, Muhammadu Dikko, who became Emir in 1906 and reigned until he died in 1944, became friends with Lugard and visited him in Surrey on a trip to Britain. There he told Lugard that the Katsina chiefs, just like in Sokoto, had agonised over whether to resist or submit to him. In the end, they decided against resistance[19]. From Katsina, Lugard went back to Kano and was greeted by a large crowd and the new Emir he had installed. He left Kano and marched for five days to Zaria where on the recommendation of Attahiru II, he installed Ali ibn Abd al-Qadir as the replacement for Muhammad Kwassau. The new Emir was a grandson of the Fulani jihadist who had taken Zaria for the Sokoto Caliphate in 1835. Kwassau himself had come to power in 1897 when (backed by Fulani forces and soldiers sent down to support him from Kano) he had insisted on being named Emir instead of the likelier candidate (who was blind, deaf and dumb and was going to be a puppet of the Hausa *Galadima*, Suleimanu). With his forces massed outside the city ready for war, the Galadima backed down and made Kwassau king. But he would only reign until the new King in the North came and knocked him off the throne. 'In the northern part, Frederick Lugard gathered his people/and said to them the land became "ours" by snatching' was how a Fulani poet would later describe the scale of what had happened to northern Nigeria[20]. The former London fireman with the traumatic, impoverished childhood was now at the peak of his powers: the new King in the North. In less than 40 days, Lugard had marched nearly 1,300 kilometres and brought the centuries-old Emirates of Sokoto, Katsina, Kano and Zaria under British control.

Massacre at Burmi

But Lugard's declaration that the fighting was over proved to be optimistic. Just as Yunfa had watched helplessly a century before as people took flight to join Dan Fodio in Gudu, William Wallace watched in amazement as men, women and children in Sokoto began to heed Attahiru's call to withdraw from the rule of the infidels and join him in Burmi. Abubakar of Bida and Abd Allahi of Keffi also joined him there, forming a coalition of the disgruntled, mirroring the old diehard enemies of the Sokoto Caliphate. The British resident in Kano, Featherstone Cargill, was alarmed at the devotion and fanaticism of Attahiru's followers and thought he was seeing the beginning of another jihad. He called for help, which arrived in the form of Captain Sword and 130 men. The confused Sword reached the gates of Burmi and tried to talk things over with the leaders there who rebuffed him and rained down poisoned arrows at his party.

In the end, Sword and his men retreated with nearly half of them being killed. Attahiru announced that the British defeat was a sign from God that He was still on their side and called on the people to reinforce in anticipation of the British reprisal. Women and children were sent away and the walls of the town were strengthened. The reprisal duly arrived two months later on 27 July 1903, in what proved to be the bloodiest battle the British had so far faced in Northern Nigeria. Where the Sokoto battle had lasted for less than two hours, this one raged from 11am to 6pm with Attahiru himself leading the resistance of 10,000 men. After suffering 80 casualties, the British forces eventually subdued Burmi. Attahiru walked out to meet his death - an honourable man, he had been dealt a cruel hand by fate and the machine-gun fire that cut him down may have come to him as a relief. Abd Allahi and several other leaders of the resistance were also killed. Far from putting an end to discontent and rebellion, this battle merely foreshadowed what was to come as we shall see in the next chapter. We will also see how the same Mahdis and diehards who had haunted the Sokoto Caliphate for a hundred years also came to haunt the British with one of them eventually costing Lugard his job, albeit temporarily.

Peace and Abolition

The King in the North reigned from his self-created new capital of Zungeru, where various Emirs and kings came to pay homage to him. Many of them were awed by the amenities Lugard had set up there, such as running water and electricity. He also continued his energetic touring of his domain, covering thousands of miles to visit each Emir under his authority and remind them of what he, and by extension, the British Government, expected of them. He could now settle down to the business of administration and by his example extracted a fierce commitment and determination from his appointees.

As his territory increased, so did the cost of administering it, which meant he had to find new ways of raising money from local taxes. Having stamped his authority over the various trade routes and cleared them of slave raiders, he could now collect tolls (5 per cent on the value of goods being transported at each toll point and no further toll charges once three tolls had been crossed, i.e. a 15 per cent maximum charge). Receipts from these taxes leaped from just over £600 in 1902 to nearly £8,000 in 1903 and an astonishing £40,000 in 1904. For 400 years, beginning with the slave trade, cowries had been in use in northern Nigeria as a method of payment. In the end, slaves themselves became a form of currency when inflation meant that an ever-increasing amount of cowries had to be carried to make payments - some kings simply embarked on journeys carrying slaves which they sold off during the journey as and when they needed money[21]. The cowry as a currency was swept away almost overnight when it became clear the only way to pay taxes to the new rulers of the country was in British coins.

As we have seen, the institution of slavery was deeply woven into the political and economic fabric of the Sokoto Caliphate, the world's last mass slave society[22]. This presented a golden opportunity to a moralising crusader, who considered himself to be the practical heir of Wilberforce. In one stroke, he could break the financial back of the Caliphate, while performing an important social good in the process. By 1904, Lugard had issued a proclamation which re-affirmed the prior toothless one 'abolishing' slavery in 1901. This time though, he possessed the superior force to go a step further by abolishing slave-raiding. Further, slaves could now walk away from their masters if they so wished and could even give evidence in court. Even more, the government would no longer pay compensation for the loss of slaves. This led to a change of strategy by slave traders who moved to kidnapping and selling children, deciding that they were less likely to run away or give evidence against their captors in court if it came to that[23]. Given that slaves were still the primary store of value, this was quite a far-reaching reform. In the event, the institution of slavery which had existed in Nigeria since antiquity (and had greatly expanded under the Sokoto Caliphate) would not be ended in Nigeria for another three decades. It would take several blows in succession - military patrols on land and waterways, the raiding and shutting down of slave markets, arrest and prosecution of slave traders, and most importantly the local people turning against the practise - to finally bring the institution to submission.

For his part, the boy born in Madras had brought to heel the largest empire in sub-Saharan Africa and made it his own. By ruthlessly exploiting its weaknesses and internal contradictions, Lugard had both altered and reinforced the shape of Northern

Nigeria in fundamental ways that remain with us till this day.

1. Jenkins R. *Gladstone: A Biography*. Random House; 1997.

2. Churchill WS. *The River War: An Account of the Reconquest of the Sudan*. Library of Alexandria; 1933.

3. The Times Newspapers Archive - Shaw F. Captain Lugard's Book. 1893/11/22 1893;

4. Cook AN. *British Enterprise in Nigeria*. University of Pennsylvania Press; 1943.

5. Flint JE. *Sir George Goldie and the Making of Nigeria*. Oxford University Press; 1960.

6. Hansard - COLONIAL SERVICES (SUPPLEMENTARY). 1898/2/24 1898;

7. Crosby TL. *Joseph Chamberlain: A Most Radical Imperialist*. I.B.Tauris; 2011.

8. Muffett DJM. *Concerning Brave Captains: Being a History of the British Occupation of Kano and Sokoto and of the Last Stand of the Fulani Forces*. A. Deutsch; 1964.

9. Willcocks J. *The Romance of Soldiering and Sport*. Cassell & Co.; 1925.

10. Temple CL. *Notes on the Tribes, Provinces, Emirates and States of the Northern Provinces of Nigeria*. Cass; 1965.

11. Baba, Smith MF. *Baba of Karo: A Woman of the Moslem Hausa*. New York, Praeger; 1964.

12. Orr CWJ. *The Making of Northern Nigeria*. Macmillan and Company, Limited; 1911.

13. Johnston HAS. *The Fulani Empire of Sokoto*. Oxford University Press; 1967.

14. Perham MF. *Lugard: The Years of Authority, 1898-1945*. Collins; 1960.

15. Vandervort B. *Wars of Imperial Conquest in Africa*. Routledge; 1998.

16. Hansard - Sokoto. 1902/12/9 1902;

17. Robinson CH. *Hausaland Or Fifteen Hundred Miles Through the Central Soudan*. Sampson Low, Marston & Co.; 1897.

18. Johnston HAS. *The Fulani Empire of Sokoto*. Oxford University Press; 1967.

19. Perham MF. *Lugard: The Years of Authority, 1898-1945*. Collins; 1960.

20. Bashir Abubakar MM. Muslim Responses to British Colonialism in Northern Nigeria as Expressed in Fulfulde Poems. *Islamic Africa*. 2013/6/3 2013;4(1):1-14.

21. Robinson CH. *Hausaland Or Fifteen Hundred Miles Through the Central Soudan*. Sampson Low, Marston & Co.; 1897.

22. Iliffe J. *Africans: The History of a Continent*. Cambridge University Press; 2007.

23. Ubah CN. Suppression of the Slave Trade in the Nigerian Emirates. *Journal of African History*. 1991 1991;32(3):447-470.

CHAPTER 10

Conquest and Discontent

The Wise White Man

On 24 August 1884, a tanned, wise and wizened old White man who had lived in Abeokuta for many years arrived at a war camp in the Yoruba hinterland. The veteran missionary had embarked on this journey North-East a few weeks previously, obtaining permission from his Egba hosts to visit his colleagues living at Iseyin, Oyo and Ibadan. The oldest White man then living in the country, Reverend J.B. Wood commanded the universal respect of the key interlocutors - both African and European - upon whom his safe travels in this divided and war-torn country depended. Invited by the war chiefs at his latest destination to see what he could do to bring about peace between the intransigent enemies currently in the throes of a fight to the death, the old man proceeded on 16 September further inland, to the battlefront where Ibadan's Aare Ona Kakanfo (the title of the Oyo generalissimo traditionally based outside the capital) was camped[1].

The Ibadan army was engaged in a multi-year, seasonal, intermittent, low-grade yet unceasing armed conflict with several adversaries, particularly against the Ekiti and Ijesha, working together in a tight coalition loosely known as the Ekiti Parapo, transliterated, the 'Ekiti All Together'. On the morning after he arrived at the expansive camp located in a flat valley bordering the famously hilly Ekiti-Ondo country more than 100 kilometres from Ibadan proper, Wood was granted an audience with the Aare and his war council. Listening quietly and politely, the old European peacemaker was brought up to date on not only the current position of affairs at the front but the entire colourful history of relations between the contending countries, which had led to the war. It was a long and convoluted history, told of course from the biased viewpoints of these aggressors now camped at the foot of their enemies' border. A more neutral and succinct version of the history lesson delivered by Chief Maye of Ibadan that cold September morning in 1884 is worth repeating briefly here.

Wars Without End

As we have seen already, the final collapse of Oyo in 1824 with the secession of Ilorin had led to an immediate state of chaos and confusion across the domains formerly held by that late, great empire. We have seen how the Dahomey and the Egba immediately threw their shackles off, violently setting upon their Ajele and any other emissaries of the old country and declaring their independence. We have also seen how not much longer afterwards, the secessionist Afonja was hoist with his own petard, usurped and murdered by his former Fulani allies, appending Ilorin forevermore to the empire of Dan Fodio's descendants at Sokoto. The resulting fighting aimed at dislodging the Fulani-led Ilorin army - reinforced by allies from across the river at Nupe and Lafiaji - led ultimately to a conflagration across the North-Central Yoruba country, engulfing neighbours as far as Kaiama, Wawa, and Bussa on the river. Amidst the fighting, a core section of the former Oyo imperial army would migrate southwards to settle from 1829 at a place called Eba Odan.

A strategically located war camp laid out on hills between forests and plains, Eba Odan - later anglicised to Ibadan - became the effective new southern 'capital' of Oyo. In reality, Ibadan was soon to be a new empire by itself. At this new location, some form of order was quickly established over time, with a strict military hierarchy taking shape in line with the martial origins of the settlement. Ibadan was a war empire, based in a city that was established during a military crisis and which existed explicitly for the purpose of waging war on enemies far and near. And so, war was the basis of Ibadan's economic existence, with entire industrial complexes arising out of the requirements for the care, housing, feeding, training, equipment and furnishing of a large fighting force.

The city's most important inhabitants were warrior chiefs and princes, each of whom owned or controlled a corpus of warrior-slaves. Ibadan served at once as a rear operating base and training camp for these fighting forces, as well as a home city for a large civil population that came to settle among the warriors. Even the totally reduced but still 'reigning' Alaafin of Oyo would eventually become himself resident at Ibadan, now led by the former Oyo war chiefs, among whom the principal was a successful General named Oluyole.

Oluyole was a war prince of Oyo, who came up together in life and training with two other important men: the reigning Alaafin, a man named Atiba; and another warrior-prince named Kurunmi. The princes and childhood friends Atiba, Oluyole and Kurunmi combined to form the most important troika in the politics of the Yoruba country, immediately following the collapse of Oyo. To consolidate his power upon assuming the much-weakened throne, Atiba appointed his bosom friends Oluyole and Kurunmi to the critical positions of Bashorun and Aare Ona Kakanfo of Oyo. Bashorun Oluyole held his position of authority at Ibadan nominally (but not in reality) as a vassal of Alaafin Atiba, while Aare Kurunmi replicated the same situation at a place called Ijaiye. These two nominal subordinates of the Oyo suzerain were the most powerful factors in the trade and politics of their country during their lives, with all major commercial parties in their domains aligning under their banners. One of the favourites of Oluyole was his maternal cousin, the woman trader we met earlier at the point of her emigration from Egba to Ibadan, Efunsetan Aniwura.

A viciously competitive operator, Aniwura was said to have been happier for boatloads of humans to be drowned, rather than sold at a loss to her. But Aniwura was also an intelligent entrepreneur with a great deal of industrial acumen, which she applied to an expansive regional export trade in agricultural commodities, fabrics, mats and cosmetics. Her farms, worked by thousands of persons in bondage, produced and supplied the food required by the new empire of Ibadan and its ever-warring armies, an important security consideration during more than a decade of armed conflicts at multiple locations. Efunsetan's trade and export volumes contributed significantly to market levies, toll fares and other official revenues for the growing state. Her commercial power financed the supply of foreign-made arms and ammunition for the private army that she maintained, as well as (often on credit) the many exploits of her loyal overlords.

In due course, Efunsetan Aniwura rose to become probably the wealthiest person in her new country. With this impressive reputation, she was elected to the high office of Iyalode in 1866 and thereafter continued her rise to more wealth and prominence in collaboration with, and under the protection of Bashorun Oluyole at Ibadan. However, her reign would be cut short, as clashes with the other powerful, and mostly male, elite of her adopted home would eventually lead to her humiliation and deposition in 1874. But during her reign, Iyalode Efunsetan Aniwura maintained active supply routes with the interior and the coast, with stations at all the major markets of the time: including bases at Lagos, Badagry, Ouidah, Ilorin and Ijaiye. Of these cities, Ijaiye is the only one that no longer exists in the present day.

Rise and Fall of Ijaiye

Located on the edge of the former Egba forest, about four days' march north of Abeokuta, Ijaiye was an important inland entrepot along the trade route between the Niger and the port of Lagos. A strategically located war camp, Ijaiye was both fortuitously and purposely encircled by a thick forest occupied by wild beasts, a stream moat, a large ditch, and a wall. The town was also famed for its large market, situated right at the centre of the settlement.

The important Ijaiye market was spread out on a piece of land measuring at least twenty acres, where caravans from the interior met those from the coast to trade and communicate. According to an eye-witness account around 1858, 'swords, sandal-wood, red fez caps, silk yarn, paper, beads and other things from interior and northern Africa, clothes of many kinds, cutlery, tin, earthen-wares, guns, gun-powder, rum, tobacco, salt and other things of foreign import' were bought and sold at this great emporium, which met till very late at night three times a week, with about 20,000 people assembled[2]. Traders who had travelled from exotic metropolises as far off as Istanbul, Cairo and Baghdad were to be found at Ijaiye, including foreigners and natives of the land. One dutiful eyewitness was Richard Henry Stone, the Baptist missionary from the southern United States, who lived in Ijaiye for an extended period in the mid-nineteenth century (contemporaneous with the civil war in his country) and faithfully recorded his observations in his *In Africa's Forest Jungle: Six Years among the Yorubans.*

It is to Stone's meticulous records that we owe a great deal of insight into affairs at this now lost but historically important city. From Stone's narrative, we are also able to contrast the personality, leadership style and political decision making of Ijaiye's ruler, Kurunmi, with that of another nineteenth-century Yoruba leader whom we have already met at a nearby country: Sodeke at Abeokuta. Where Sodeke ruled by wise consensus, eschewed despotism and helped found a long-lasting civil settlement that continues to exist to this day, Kurunmi adopted the antithetical approach, with consequences that we will shortly observe. Stone met several times with Aare Kurunmi, and partly from his accounts, we learn more about this former armed bandit turned brutal dictator who held Ijaiye by sheer force of arms and personality. Having murdered the prior rulers of the place, the Aare established himself as a maximum despot with the support of his childhood friend, the Alaafin. Despotism was an unusual political situation in Yoruba, where hereditary monarchs ruled in a power-sharing arrangement with constitutional chiefs, the religious and merchant elite. But by all accounts, Kurunmi and his officers ran Ijaiye with military efficiency; his word was law, and the people lived in mortal fear of this self-declared tyrant. He diverted as much regional trade as was possible to his market through the use of military force, charging throughput tolls on both imports and exports, in so doing amassing significant wealth to maintain his position.

In due course, Aare Kurunmi's wealth and aggressive trade diversion tactics would pose a political challenge to his childhood friends and allies, quite apart from any personal disagreements. During an annual tribute celebration at Atiba's capital, an unsuccessful attempt was made on the life of Kurunmi within the palace walls. Kurunmi valiantly fought his way out of danger and returned to Ijaiye. But his relationship with the Alaafin was destroyed, and a force from Ibadan was deployed to lay siege on the impenetrable fortress that was Ijaiye. The objective of this operation was to choke off supplies to the town and starve its inhabitants to death. Remarkably, Kurunmi's forces stormed their former friends and new enemies outside the city's ramparts, and they fled. When Atiba died soon after, Aare Kurunmi refused to acknowledge the sovereignty of his and Ibadan's preferred successor, the Alaafins first-born son. This prince was considered an illegitimate heir under more recent Oyo custom, which required the Crown Prince or Aremo to 'reign with his father' and then accompany him to the grave by ritual suicide. Based on this political discontent, the bloody Ijaiye War of historical accounts thus commenced, coterminous with the still ongoing efforts by Ibadan to reverse the Fulani-led incursion into northern Yoruba.

The then 21-year old R.H. Stone, the American Baptist missionary provides us with the most dramatic first-hand account of this devastating months-long battle. It is one of the purest, most technically sound, on-the-ground portraits of mid-nineteenth century organised warfighting in western Africa. Stone himself was an active albeit peripheral and inadvertent protagonist in the political matters surrounding the conflict. He was captured near Ibadan, tried, nearly killed, escaped and returned to his American wife at Ijaiye by a very circuitous route through the country. A parsed review of his diligent but self-centred writing reveals to us the consequences of Aare Kurunmi's tyranny in internal affairs and greed in matters of foreign trade. Reinforced by allies from around the country, including mercenaries from as far off as Nupe and Benin, Ibadan laid siege on Ijaiye again, this time more ferociously and with a determined intent to eradicate their enemy.

Under the leadership of a general named Ogunmola, a several-months long siege ensued outside the town walls - which destroyed the flourishing economy of Ijaiye, leading to famine and starvation in the city. Forces from Abeokuta rallied ostensibly 'in defence' of their neighbour against a common enemy, but in reality, the Egba were more focused on maintaining Ijaiye as a protective buffer against Ibadan, stripping the Aare of his power, and denuding the city of all its people and wealth. Soon enough, clever Egba intrigue with the Ijaiye Ogboni led to the deposition of Kurunmi even amidst the bloody fighting. In the end, all three political objectives of the cunning Egba were masterfully achieved, and the effectively dethroned Kurunmi led his remaining loyal troops in a final suicidal death charge, right into the frontlines of the besieging Ibadan army[3].

The accomplished Ibadan warriors would in due course ruthlessly annihilate Ijaiye, just as they had checked the advance of the relentless Fulani-led Ilorin into Yoruba country. This latter victory was sign-posted by a historically important battle at the still-existing town of Osogbo. Ibadan itself had become a powerful successor force to Oyo, with imperial ambitions around the country. Beyond political dominance however, with the erstwhile northern trading roads (to the Niger and the Mediterranean) now closed-off by mortal enemies, access to trading routes leading to all-important seaport locations on the Atlantic coast would soon become the primary driver of much war-making between Ibadan and their neighbours over the next few decades.

The Yoruba Contenders

As we now know, the Niger was opened to European influence in the late 1830s following the surreptitious and remarkably safe passage through Yoruba of the plucky Lander brothers amidst all the fighting. The knock-on effects of this epic journey would in due course determine the future of all the eager gladiators in the region. Once Oyo disintegrated, Ibadan and half-a-dozen other important successor states emerged in the Yoruba country, judged by their comparative advantages in terms of economic organisation and their war-making ability. Just like the unfortunate Ijaiye, each of these powers was focused on maximising its relative geographical and political advantages, for economic success, measured by trade flows and customs rights. They were also as determined as ever to remain independent from domination and enslavement.

The most remote and least threatened of these states - at least from inland military rivals - was Lagos, the slave-power city. Lagos was growing in influence and soon to be made even more powerful once annexed alongside the lesser port, Badagry by the British, those undisputed lords of the sea. Forward-looking Abeokuta also emerged as a regional power, under the liberal Sodeke and his successors chiefs, guided by their Saro and missionaries, helped by British friendship and strengthened by the capitalist enterprise of their leading traders like Madam Tinubu.

Thirdly, the ancient Ijebu kingdom in the eastern hinterland of the Lagos Lagoon also raised its head in regional ambition, in alliance with powerful exiles from Lagos like Kosoko and his successor merchant-chiefs like Oshodi Tapa, Taiwo Olowo and others, who provided important international trading connections. Hemmed in as they were between the expansive lagoon, the northern Ibadan domains, the western greater Egba countryside and a massive forest to their rear; the Ijebu were a politically tenuous but commercially advantageous and eminently defensible position against non-naval military aggression. Fourth among the new powers was the dreaded megalomaniac, Ghezo, at Dahomey. The king of the Dahomeans was controlling Ouidah and Porto Novo from Abomey, and thus maintained good access to global trade flows and connections. Ghezo considered himself the 'Greatest King in Africa,' and had assembled a military fighting force worthy of the title, dominating an increasingly large portion of the country behind his coastal redoubts. The fifth new power in the region was Ilorin, which was now under Fulani ownership, whose post-Afonja military and economic structure we have already discussed in some detail.

Finally, as we have just seen, the Ekiti Parapo also arose from their prior state of subjection to Ibadan, (who had placed Ajele among them) and soon became themselves a military force to be reckoned with. They were allied with the stubborn Ijesha and supported with capital and firearms provided by their Saro diaspora at Lagos. The local leader responsible for this latest new power in the country was a former prisoner of Ibadan, named Orisarayibi Ogundamola but better known as Ogedengbe, an important war-chief who like Sodeke would lead his people to independence by force of arms. Born in 1822 and arrested by the Ibadan warriors in their early days of conquest in the Ijesha-Ekiti country, Ogedengbe learned the art of war among the enemy before escaping and rising to fame as a lightning rod among his people in their military revolt against Ibadan. The Ekiti-Ijesha rebellion triggered the Kiriji War, onomatopoetically named for the sounds made by the more sophisticated munitions and firearms now being liberally imported and employed in warfare for the first time by the Yoruba.

Blessed are the Peacemakers

This was the turbulent history of political matters into which the aged Reverend Woods plunged, bravely and perhaps naively, attempting to broker peace in September 1884. After his conference with the Ibadan chiefs at their camp that morning, the determined old man readied himself and sought permission to be allowed across the front lines under a white flag - to the camp of Ogedengbe who was leading the Ijesha and Ekiti Parapo forces at the front. After a bit of hesitation from the Ibadan chiefs, who did not want to appear weak by seeking peace, Wood was let across with his small party. Travelling alongside him was the Saro CMS priest and later the greatest Yoruba historian, Reverend Samuel Johnson. Upon reaching the frontlines, the entirety of this historically invaluable crew nearly lost their lives on the spot, as the Ijesha vanguard immediately fired upon them, the flag of truce be damned. Saved by the Ibadan who returned fire, the peacemakers retreated for the day. The next day, their unlikely presence at the front was reported to some senior Christian officers in the Ijesha camp, so a deputation was sent to meet with Reverend Wood and his party, to hear what they wanted.

What followed was another extensive conference, this time with Ogedengbe and his frontline war chiefs. After this summit, the missionaries had managed to coax out the initial outlines of a potential peace agreement. The terms for the cessation of hostilities issued by the Ekiti emissaries are recorded faithfully for us by the irreplaceable Johnson in the epic tome, *The History of the Yorubas*. This draft peace agreement provides one of the clearest pictures of the underlying reasons for the so-called 'Yoruba Wars' which continued for much of the nineteenth century. Political independence, border control, ancestral claims to land and political title, and control of trading routes were the headline issues; and these may be safely understood to be the same key issues in all the battles and at all the fronts upon which war was then being waged.

As an interesting aside, Reverend Johnson's priceless history book would have to be posthumously re-written from his copious notes by his younger brother, Obadiah, the pioneering medical doctor who was also educated through the agency of Venn and the CMS. Eventually, *The History of the Yorubas*, which became an instant classic, would only be published through the agency of the CMS in 1921 because the only copy of the original manuscript was 'mislaid' in London by the commercial publisher to whom it was sent. In other similar historical near-misses, Achebe's *Things Fall Apart* was also mislaid by a London agent before its eventual recovery and publication, and George Taubman Goldie's original draft of the RNC charter was lost by Prime Minister William Gladstone when he left it in the pocket of his travelling jacket, forgotten in a train carriage during 1886.

Back at the Kiriji war front, after a significant amount of back and forth, the good Reverend Wood and his team appeared close to reaching an agreement between the parties for peace, except for one point. Ogedengbe flatly refused to accept this key condition precedent; the removal of his forces to a location about a mile away, to allow the Ibadan forces to retreat without fear of being ambushed. The wily Ijesha war-chief cheekily said to Wood with the help of a popular Yoruba adage: 'The dog cannot pursue after a leopard. They are leopards, and we but dogs. White man, do take them away!' But the Aare Ona Kakanfo of Ibadan was not born yesterday and would never take such a gamble. He knew Ogedengbe very well and smelled a rat. Without safe passage, there would be no ceasefire. Thus, the peace talks broke down in early October, and Reverend Wood left the area (with the fighting re-commencing in earnest even while his departing party was still within earshot of the front).

Carter, Conqueror of Ijebu

It was a golden opportunity missed. In less than a decade, the same noble objective which Wood - the Clapham-Sect Era diplomat - attempted to achieve by peaceful intermediation during those few weeks in 1884, would later be comprehensively attained by a culturally disinterested outsider, with the aid of Maxim guns and heavy artillery. In 1892, under the political direction of a less diplomatic British officer named Gilbert Thomas Carter, peace was enforced in Yoruba by a combination of armed forces and political pragmatism. He would later be knighted for his efforts. Born in Devonshire, England to a navy commander named Thomas Gilbert Carter, Carter - who would confusingly change his name later in life to Thomas Gilbert-Carter - joined the British Navy as a clerk aged 16 and spent his entire life in the overseas colonial civil service as the quintessential man of Empire. Before arriving on his historic tour of duty in Yorubaland, the former navy clerk and assistant paymaster of a colonial vessel was a junior civil servant at the Gold Coast. He would later serve in the Bahamas and Trinidad after leaving Lagos. Having married the daughter of a senior navy officer and served as private secretary to a colonial Governor, Carter achieved the highest office of his life when he was appointed (aged 43) Governor and Commander-in-Chief of the Colony of Lagos, commencing 3 February 1891.

Carter was the most important Governor of Lagos since the pioneering efforts in the newly acquired colony of John Hawley Glover, popularly known as Oba Globa. Glover was forced out of Lagos in 1866, defeated by local political intrigue in relation to the future of the settlement between the Saros, the missionaries, the merchants and the traditional chiefs in Yorubaland proper. Between Glover's departure and the five years before Carter arrived, Lagos was attached to Sierra Leone and the Gold Coast as a sub-province, limiting the powers of the nominal British administrators on the spot. Following a pattern of conquest that we must now be familiar with, Carter arrived in Lagos with a clear intention and authority to resolve - by the use of armed force - the political problem that had confounded all his predecessors. By 1891, it was a long-settled British policy in relation to Lagos that the island could not survive economically if its British administration were not the dominant power concerning the affairs of the Yoruba interior. From the tentative days of Glover, who was limited by law from pursuing a 'forward' strategy in the hinterland, to the full-blown Imperial days of Carter, legal and political support had finally arrived from Britain for the strategy favoured by the ambitious men on the ground.

Governor Carter wasted no time in executing his plans for achieving glory in Nigeria. Of the half-a-dozen odd powers in the greater Yoruba country when Carter arrived, it would be the unfortunate Ijebu, with their tenuous perch on the eastern shore of the very navigable lagoon, who provided the perfect opportunity for the first strike by the seafaring British. Kosoko, the former king of Lagos and key economic ally of the Ijebu in the palmy pre-Imperial days of the native agency, had died in 1872. Before his death, the astute trader had settled in exile at Epe, an Ijebu village situated alongside the most strategic chokepoint in the Lagos Lagoon. Kosoko boasted strong international connections and dealt extensively with slave buyers in Brazil. His military power was also significant as the ever-virile warrior-prince maintained a fleet of war canoes and ground troops at all points during his adult life. The former Oba also maintained strong local commercial partnerships even after his removal from Lagos. Taken together, Kosoko had been the best possible broker-advocate for Ijebu interests with the British during his career at Epe, and he had contributed to the post-Oyo rise of the kingdom.

Now, in the absence of this important partner, successive Awujale (kings) of the Ijebu, advised by a council of chiefs roughly equivalent to the Ogboni but known as the Osugbo, had failed to replicate his influence and power on the Lagoon and at Lagos itself. Further, unlike the Egba and Ibadan (both of whom had welcomed missionaries into their fold, early and eagerly) the Ijebu had resisted the establishment of mission houses and Western education within their territory. This resistance would prove a costly and distinct disadvantage in their dealings with European adversaries in the Imperial era. This disadvantage persisted despite the best efforts exerted to influence the Awujale by several eager missionaries. Those who did their best to influence the Ijebu included James 'Holy' Johnson, the Saro CMS luminary and pastor at Breadfruit Street, who was also a member of the Lagos Legislative Council, and later assistant bishop of the Niger Delta and his collaborator, the pioneer Western-educated Ijebu - John Augustus 'Otunba' Payne, who had attended CMS Grammar School at Lagos.

In the event, Carter picked his target and the perfect opportunity presented itself when the Ijebu closed the roads to Ibadan in the first half of 1892, a normal occurrence all through the sixteen-year war. The Ijebu notables further compounded the diplomatic incident by allowing robberies on certain trading caravans and issuing threats to the lives of two CMS missionaries living among the Ibadan. Using this slight provocation as the pretext, the stage was set. On 12 May 1892, the Anglo-Ijebu or Imagbon War commenced. Beginning just over a year after Carter arrived at Lagos, the conflict is named for the border town where much of the fighting occurred. A detachment of 450 troops from Lagos (Hausa Regiment), Sierra Leone, and the Gold Coast accompanied by some specially provided Ibadan warriors were dispatched up the lagoon to Epe, with nearly 200 carriers recruited along the way. Under the overall command of a Colonel F.C. Scott, and equipped with the now customary Maxim guns, rockets and heavy artillery, the armed force made short work of Ijebu defences – the war lasted only seven days.

The victory was decisive and intentionally resounding, Ijebu Ode (the capital) was reduced to rubble, a British resident placed in the city, and the Osugbo council house burnt to the ground. The point of the heavy defeat was not merely the elimination of Ijebu influence on the eastern Lagoon, but a pointed message to the remaining five feuding powers in the Yoruba country that there was a new sheriff in town. This opening gambit paid off in spades. In short order, previously unimaginable political capitulations would follow. Ibadan accepted a resident after much letter-writing and conferencing. The Egba signed their 'Treaty of Independence' which was negotiated with the benefit of much Saro and missionary influence, and which kept Abeokuta nominally free of British rule.

The underdog Ekiti Parapo celebrated their 'victory' over Ibadan aggression. Around the same time, French forces finally managed after a year of fighting to subdue the morbid and colourful Dahomey Empire. Dahomey was then under the rule of Ghezo's successor King Behanzin, who burned his ancestral capital - Abomey - to the ground rather than see it surrender. With the hitherto ruling powers of the country now dramatically reduced, the Yoruba Wars were summarily over, and the period of British rule in the hinterland firmly commenced.

Completion of Formation

Nigeria was now in Formation. As we have seen already, Benin (which is contiguous with the Yoruba country) was taken soon after Ijebu in 1897 following the actions of that Glorious Incompetent, James Roberts Phillips. Phillips was in all likelihood partly inspired on his daredevil mission by the decisive military and political victories of Governor Carter in Yoruba. As we have seen, Ralph Moor and his outsized force seized the Igbo mainland across the Niger from Benin in 1901. Along with the annexed coastal city-states, this effectively established the full boundaries of present-day Southern Nigeria. Meanwhile, the independent Borgu Empire, partly subdued by the French and contested for by the Royal Niger Company was summarily partitioned via the Anglo-French Convention of 1898[xx]

For his part, we have seen how Frederick Lugard would also shortly after (in 1903) crush the expanded Sokoto Caliphate of Dan Fodio's labours while incorporating the many independent, undefeated non-Muslim tribes of the Niger valley into a new empire all of his creation. In doing so, British rule was now established (albeit indirectly in most places) for the first time over nearly all of

---

xx The more correct and grandiloquent name of the treaty was: The Convention between Great Britain and France for the Delimitation of their respective Possessions to the West of the Niger, and of their respective Possessions and Spheres of Influence to the East of that River.

modern-day Nigeria. The final piece of the modern-day puzzle that is Nigeria - the Bornu Emirate - would be divided between British and German control for a while longer, before being incorporated by the English after the defeat of Germany in the Great War. By 1904, the stage was fully set for British rule over a territory ten times the square area of the United Kingdom, assembled piecemeal by an assorted variety of adventurers, glory-seekers and ideologues, under the guidance and political cover of Chamberlain and the new Imperial politicians in London. This gargantuan feat was accomplished over a short decade from the first shot being fired by Carter's forces in the Imagbon War against the Ijebu.

The world had changed while most of the Nigerian native traditional elite were fighting each other and focused on internal intrigue. The nineteenth century had unfolded dramatically: from Dan Fodio's jihad in 1804, to the opening of the river to Europeans in 1832, to the arrival of missionaries at Abeokuta in 1849, through the reduction of Lagos in 1851 and its seizure in 1861, Goldie's emergence on the river from 1877, the Berlin Conference in 1885 and the declaration of the Northern and Southern Protectorates in 1900. It was the most eventful 100-year period in the collective history of the people and countries affected. And it had all happened so fast, throwing up urgent and different reactions by many of the leaders and ordinary people that we have already met in our story so far. The future had now forced its arrival on the doorstep of this new country, formed against the will of long independent neighbours soon to be politically united for the first time in their histories. These neighbours were now to be united under a new foreign leadership with industrial-scale economic ambitions, and an unusual form of government unparalleled in their peoples' long traditions.

Rule Through the Conquered

North of the river, we have seen how the British (led by the new

'King in the North') prevailed by violence over the successors of Dan Fodio, and immediately followed in the tradition of conquerors before them by placing residents at each defeated metropolis, backed by a strong garrison of troops. As the conquest expanded, the British residents, the early cohort of whom were typically former officers of the RNC or the British army and Hausa language scholars, became the de facto political authorities in the country. But there were severe human capacity limitations on the part of these new rulers because there were always only a limited number of non-invalided political officers available, and the contemporaneous Boer War (1899-1902) ensured a scarcity even of military officers. Thus, the so-called 'Indirect Rule' policy that evolved was not so much philosophical or strategic, as imperative. There were no other reasonable means by which British political power could be exerted over such a large country, without co-opting the ready-made bureaucratic infrastructure of the conquered elite. While points might be debated post factum about how extensive the delegation of executive, judicial, fiscal and legislative power from the resident to the local Emir and his council needed to have been; it was never in doubt that delegation would be an essential condition precedent to effective British administration in Nigeria.

In the event, a system was evolved from scratch which met the satisfaction of the exacting Lugard, under which the real decision making authority on all matters large and small vested in the all-powerful British chief executive at Zungeru (later, Kaduna), but was exercised daily via residents by Emirs and chiefs serving at the pleasure of their conqueror. The now agnostic Lugard had supplanted the militant evangelist Dan Fodio, but with broader geographical coverage, alongside a more modern fighting and administrative infrastructure. This solution, designed for the peculiar realities of the Sokoto Caliphate, became - in essence - the form of Indirect Rule that Lugard championed, and which, with limited variations, his successors, loyalists, mentees and advocates would also support for decades to come. The cultural imprint of adopting and reinforcing this form of government would remain deeply engraved on the emerging psyche of the inchoate country for the next 100 years. From the perspective of any careful observer of Northern Nigeria from 1903 therefore, a curious situation had emerged. The former ruling class remained firmly in place, strengthened beyond its former powers in many areas, albeit now under the supervision of a foreign power whose sole pressing concern appeared to be the maintenance of political control, law, order, trade flows and economic expansion.

To accomplish this impressive feat of proxy government by complete foreigners in a still hostile country, Lugard recruited and relied on a cohort of remarkable political officers, best described by one reporter who lived among them and knew them well. Sylvia Leith-Ross was an impressive French-born, British-Canadian Afrophile who first arrived in Northern Nigeria during 1907. She was only the third wife of a White political officer to be allowed to live there. Her Canadian husband died early in his tour, but Leith-Ross, who became a Fulani language scholar, colonial educator, prolific author of Nigeria-related books and pottery curator of the National Museum at Jos, would fall in love with the country. She returned in 1910 and lived in different parts of Nigeria for decades. Her perceptive reporting of the fundamental character of most early residents under Lugard is worth repeating at some length: 'The job the Political Officer was called upon to do was not a static one, a mere question of keeping law and order, stopping slave trading, inter-tribal wars, preventing extortion. He had to be a jack of all trades, administering justice and introducing vaccination [...] They knew the slow talk of the countryside, and understood its resistance to change, its prejudices against new methods. They had also learnt the rights and responsibilities of those set-in authority and they knew how to command, easily, certain they would be obeyed.'[4] These new potentates became the mediums between Europeans and the native population - at once responsible for treasury, accounting, statistics, sanitation, construction, transportation, prison, post office, trade promotion and criminal justice administration. It was imperative to their mission that these former British country boys could rely on a heavily armed garrison of well-martialled Black soldiers to enforce their rule at short notice, but the fundamental character trait of being genuine lovers of local life and administration would come to serve Lugard and the British well in establishing a workable compromise with their new subalterns.

It was an acceptable compromise for most of the ordinary people as well, and the country settled down remarkably well in the immediate aftermath of the conquest. One view of the compromise is encapsulated in the words of a contemporary observer, (later, Sir) Charles Orr, the early British resident at Zaria: 'As soon as the inhabitants realised that no interference with their religion or customs was intended and that the position of their rulers and officials was to be maintained under conditions promising more security to life and property, and less corruption and oppression, the country settled down with marvellous rapidity.'[5] The other viewpoint from which the compromise must be observed is that of the indigenes, best reported by a later historian, R. A. Adeleye in his epic The Sokoto Caliphate and its Enemies. Adeleye's thorough historical analysis points out the fact that relative peace only ensued within the boundaries and surrounding areas of the major Caliphate cities because the more violent opponents to British rule had forcibly migrated with their supporters.

As we have seen, the hijra of the deposed Caliph Attahiru (who escaped from the Sokoto battlefield on 15 March 1903) lasted until late May when the former Sultan, all his key officers from several Emirates and more than 600 other unfortunates were killed by British forces. The price of Orr's breezily observed 'more promising conditions' in the main metropolitan areas of the Caliphate, was the lives of all the stringent opponents who departed on Hijra and were subsequently liquidated. That being said, the acceptance of British rule by the remaining elite and populace was so established that in 1906 when yet another religious revolutionary and his supporters raised their standard against the new order - a challenge to both the British and Fulani aristocracy, they were quickly and violently put down by a joint British-Caliphate armed coalition.

Satiru and Abinshi Set Alight

The story of this revolt is important to the future evolution of the country, and so is worth repeating in summary. Mallam Isa was the son of the chief at a place called Satiru, about 22 kilometres from Sokoto. In 1904, this chief proclaimed himself Mahdi but was arrested by the new British Sultan and killed in custody while awaiting trial. Two years later, the chief's son and successor re-organised Satiru again for revolution, this time encouraged by a blind cleric named Shuaibu Dan Makafo, an outlaw in French-controlled Hausa territory from where he fled after killing two French police officers. Isa's attempted revolution coincided with another violent uprising of Tiv natives against Hausa traders at a place called Abinshi, located far east from Satiru on the Benue River. The violence on the river was triggered in January 1906 by a long-standing quarrel between local natives and traders. The proximate cause was a dispute between a Hausa man and a Jukun woman over petty financial matters. Their disagreement led to the murder of a Jukun man and escalated into a massacre of the Hausa contingent at Abinshi in retaliation, during which 70 to 80 people were killed[6]. Several Hausa women and children were also marched down to the river and drowned. The situation further exploded into an uprising against the hated Royal Niger Company, whose warehouse at the place was set upon by the Tivs and burnt to the ground.

Informed about the Abinshi massacre, Lugard telegraphed his bosses in London. The then 31-year-old Liberal politician, Winston Churchill was the cherub-faced Under-Secretary at the Colonial Office. Lugard requested permission to embark on a punitive expedition against the Tivs. His justification was that their violent actions had led to the Benue River being closed to navigation. This was unacceptable as it was the main trade route into North-Eastern Nigeria, being used by both Britain and Germany. Churchill declined the request. He had fought in the Battle of Omdurman and had come to resent the use of violent retaliation against local populations. Lugard's case was not helped by his previous reputation for manipulating the Colonial Office over Kano and Sokoto - 'It is the Kano business all over again', Lord Elgin later wrote to him. Lugard disregarded his bosses and went ahead anyway - 'How can one run a country like this on such terms? Such orders are applicable to a young novice, not to a H.C. [High Commissioner] entrusted with the government of a country and moreover one who has been here as long as I have', Lugard fumed in a letter to his wife, Flora, after being told not to go ahead with the expedition[7].

British armed troops were sent to the scene to restore order and punish the resisting Tivs. Meanwhile, it was around this same time that Dan Makafo arrived at Satiru, an occurrence that was reported by the Sultan to his British overlord. The agile acting resident unwisely proceeded at once to the scene, to arrest the newly arrived troublemaker, leaving his company of mounted infantry officers following behind him. Tragically for this officer - H.R Preston-Hillary - two of his British colleagues and their 25 armed troops were ambushed and killed by Isa's forces. Rifles and a Maxim gun were seized by the *Satirawa* forces, and there was jubilation in several cities of the Caliphate. Hadejia was particularly festive, as its leaders were already in active opposition. The city would be reduced for this. The character of Lugard was such that he always concluded he needed to react strongly whenever he felt under siege. This was one such moment, with the Satiru news arriving right in the middle of most of his troops being engaged hundreds of miles away near the Benue River. In this particular case, the immediate threat he detected was that the Emirs might smell the weakness of British rule and rise against them in unison.

Under the influence of Flora Lugard, *The Times* of London would later run a series of reports on the incident under the headlines

"The Rising in Sokoto," further contributing to the sense of panic that Britain's five-year experiment in Nigeria might be forced to an abrupt end[8]. Lugard cobbled together all the arms and men he could muster: 100 rifles from Lokoja, 75 guns each from Zungeru and Kontagora and 250 Black troops loaned from Lagos. Sokoto lent its support by deploying the by now familiar Muhammadu Mai Turare with 3,000 troops, although his troops would refuse to attack the Satirawa after being taunted with songs 'Marafa, you have delayed in coming for a fight.' The expedition against Satiru was ready to deploy. In its reaction to these events, the quick response time of the British forces was possible only due to the foresighted rapid laying of extensive telegraph infrastructure, which Lugard had championed between 1903 and 1906. This allowed for fast communication and rapid troop deployments, an invaluable benefit. With this important logistical advantage, an overwhelming force was deployed against Satiru.

Unable to use the Maxim gun which they had seized, the Satirawa simply attacked the British forces and threw themselves at the machine-gun fire in their hundreds. The result was an incredible massacre where at least 2,000 Satirawa were killed. Dan Makafo somehow survived the battle but was captured and taken to Sokoto where he was put on trial. By 22 March - less than two weeks after the British forces attacked Satiru - he had been found guilty and promptly beheaded along with four of his lieutenants. As a message to future revolutionaries, his head was put on display in the market[9]. Satiru was razed to the ground, but this revolt had been too close for comfort to the capital of the Caliphate. The terrified Sultan of Sokoto, living like all his predecessors and successors in mortal fear of popular religious revolutionaries, pronounced a curse on the village and anyone building or farming on it. In 2009, a reporter from Nigeria's Daily Trust newspaper visited Satiru and after describing it as 'one vast cattle grazing field,' concluded that 'the land of Satiru may congeal in the curse forever.'[10] The women and children who survived the massacre were carted off to Sokoto in their thousands, where many of them ended up as slaves.

Despite great efforts to hide it, this was a scandal that could not go unnoticed and met the disapproval of the new British Liberal government and its Colonial Office under Churchill. The affair soon blew up into a wider fight about the whole shape of imperial policy and in short order, Frederick Lugard was asked by Lord Elgin to return to London for three months for 'consultations' - a sacking in all but name. Still, Lugard had lost none of his public relations skills and once back in London, he mended his relationship with Churchill (with the help of Flora) and converted the sacking to a safe landing the following year when he was appointed the new British Governor of Hong Kong. Dan Makafo and his motley crew of Satirawa martyrs had achieved a major political coup, knocking the megalomaniac military conqueror of their country off his perch, albeit temporarily.

Alternatives to Megalomania

Sir Percy Girouard, Lugard's successor was much less a breaker of stones and much more of an infrastructure builder, for the benefit of enhancing the import and export trade. He was an engineer with specific expertise in railways and was appointed by the new Liberal government with the specific intention that he should focus on developing a long-planned railway connection between the Northern hinterland and the coast or the river. Percy Girouard arrived in early 1907 proceeding immediately on a gruelling trek through hundreds of miles in the countryside, covering the intended alignment of the new railway. The line would be built from Baro (a river port on the Niger) up north to Kano, later connecting south to the Lagos-Ibadan line via Abeokuta. For the first time, a direct and seamless communication link was established between these countries, bringing the distant and different neighbours into closer economic and political proximity.

With Lugard's ignominious but temporary departure, we can

turn briefly now to the conditions south of the rivers, following the establishment of British authority in those countries early in the new century. Not much longer after Lugard received his commission over the former territories of the Royal Niger Company, another much more experienced and longer-standing British colonial officer named Walter Egerton also took an oath of office at Lagos as High Commissioner of the new 'Protectorate of Southern Nigeria.' Until the year before (1903), Sir Egerton had been Governor of Lagos, and for 20 years before that, he was a colonial service officer in the Far East. Egerton came from an entirely different school of thought to a situation that could not possibly be more different than the one met by Lugard in his inchoate paper protectorate. The area that came to be politically and administratively described by the British as 'Southern Nigeria' included the island of Lagos, all of the Yoruba hinterlands except for Abeokuta, the conquered Benin kingdom and its riverine neighbours, the former coastal city-states of the Niger delta, and the still barely occupied Igbo country. Abeokuta maintained a nominally independent government, surrounded by the new British territories.

Apart from the Igbo country, by 1903, these were all areas with at least a half-century of experience contending with British power in their territories. While administrative control was only now being forcibly stripped from the local elite, the idea and reality of British power were already firmly entrenched in their minds, since the time of their fathers and in some cases even their grandfathers. By 1903 fully westernised Africans already lived and participated actively in political life everywhere in these Southern countries, as far up the rivers as Lokoja (the confluence city), Zungeru (Lugard's strategic conquest capital), and Nafada (river port of the Bornu country). In short, the nature of the dominant local elite to be contended with following Southern conquest, could not be more different from the feudal, theocratic and culturally homogenous elite who previously sat astride the Caliphate, by right of conquest. By extension, the nature of Indirect Rule that could be exercised in the Southern protectorate by the limited number of British officials living in the country would also be quite different from the Lugardian version.

Egerton and his contingent understood their local reality perfectly and established their government within its constrained limits. Power would have to be shared here, the politics would be messier, consensus would have to be built, and the most potent instrument of British authority would not be the all-conquering Maxim. It had to be administrative and development expertise, and international capital. As a general rule, there were no autocratic rulers in the political traditions of the countries south of the rivers, the Dahomeans now under French subjugation being the clearest exception. Kings and chiefs ruled largely as figureheads, subject to a powerful governing council through which the partisan political and economic viewpoints of the leading factions in the country were frequently and vigorously expressed. Individual wealth and trading power factored in the political affairs of the people. These were also without exception polytheistic societies, and while everywhere religion played an incredibly important role in enforcing societal harmony, there was no widely accepted religion-based political framework. Thus, in the absence of fiscal and administrative structures maintained by absolute autocrats or theocrats armed with both military force and the power of historical acceptance, Indirect Rule in the south had to necessarily be invented with a sense of diversity.

To give a sense of the diversity of systems being dealt with, it is useful to summarise again the socio-political lay of the land. The new rulers were dealing with a highly cosmopolitan and long-urbanised elite at Lagos, a stubbornly independent Egba city-state, established after all precisely for political freedom. There was also a newly conquered ancient Benin kingdom, still under a restless regency. Then there were the hitherto highly decentralised Igbo communities, still barely understood by the first rulers ever to occupy this country using forces of arms. Apart from the unlimited armed forces, the only common language of political dominance that this diverse agglomeration of people and their leaders could accept on a sustainable basis was increased trade and economic development.

Egertonian Governance in Southern Nigeria

Luckily for the British, Egerton was a person whose natural inclination was already set towards economic development as the basis for expanding imperial power and influence. This was probably a legacy of his service in the Far East under a well-known colonial governor named Sir Frank Swettenham. Swettenham's philosophy of development was that governmental revenue and prosperity followed from: 'The liberal but prudently directed expenditure of public funds, especially when they are invested in high-class roads, railways, telegraphs, waterworks, and everything likely to encourage trade and private enterprise. The government cannot do the mining and agriculture, but it can make it profitable for others to embark on such speculations.'[11] It was a simple bargain proposed under the Swettenham philosophy, and now championed by Chamberlain in London: public investment in economic infrastructure and promotion of private enterprise would generate the financial resources and political credibility required to maintain the imperial government sustainably.

This simple idea went against the grain for the permanent officials at the Colonial Office and Exchequer, who rather believed that colonies should live from hand to mouth, with no forward public investment in their infrastructure. Before Egerton's arrival, the excess of expenditure over revenues (a fair measure of how much investment Britain put into its Southern Nigeria Protectorate), illustrates the point starkly. From 1892 to 1900, just before Egerton arrived, total revenues amounted to £1,153,518 while expenditure totalled £1,131,729 (and this even included £20,000 paid to the RNC as compensation for the Akassa massacre in 1897)[12]. There was no public investment coming from London. Southern Nigeria, therefore, offered a perfect test-tube for the Swettenham doctrine in the hands of the capable Egerton: because by 1903 the Protectorate was already a 'profitable' enterprise, generating surplus revenue from customs duties on ever-increasing trade volumes to cover all its administrative expenses with cash remaining in the bank. By 1908, Egerton was sufficiently confident about his policy to respond to the Colonial Office when charged with extravagance that; 'I attribute the rapid development of Southern Nigeria in great part to the large expenditure on extraordinary works; it is an example of the adage: money makes money.'[13] In simple terms, following the initial armed conquests, British rule in the Southern protectorate was enforced and expanded less through violence and more through the reinvestment of its revenues in the creation of modern economic infrastructure: vessels, railways, roads, wharves, telegraph but also customs organisation and internal security forces.

From the perspective of the native traditional and westernised elite in the protectorate during the very short period of Egertonian government which ended in 1912, British rule was an undesirable intrusion, even if it brought with it unprecedented opportunities for economic prosperity. And prosper they did, in trade, the professions, finance, artisan work and manual labour as we have seen with many examples across our narrative. It was the manifestation of Clapham Sect doctrine, but without the deliberate focus on native agency. For his sins, Egerton was opposed every step of the way by his masters at the Colonial Office in London, with every deficit budget he presented being queried, resisted, and protested. Egerton had less resistance from London about some of his much less intelligent political policies, such as the continued confused appointment and empowerment of inept and corrupt so-called Warrant Chiefs of no traditional provenance or authority in Igboland. Even his more liberal policies were not resisted as much, such as the acceptance of Abeokuta's semi-independence under the Egba United Government following the Egba Jurisdiction Ordinance of 1903.

Egba Independence and its Aftermath

The latter decision is worth discussing in a bit more detail, given its implications for the unravelling of Egertonian governance in Southern Nigeria. Our story has already come across the travails of the Saro former tailor 'Reversible' G.W. Johnson, who attempted and failed woefully to streamline and westernise the unwieldy Abeokuta ruling elite through the Egba United Board of Management (EUBM). Beyond the many letters and triggering the Ifole ('Housebreaking') uprising which chased most Europeans out of Egba in 1867, Johnson was unable to achieve much and died a disappointed man. However, this was not before partially de-anglicising his name to Oshokale Tejumade Johnson in 1885.

The feat that the departed Johnson failed to achieve organically at Abeokuta was later brokered into being by external military and diplomatic means in 1898 by a White man named McCallum, then British Governor of Lagos. McCallum convinced the Egba that it was in their best interests to form a centralised government called the 'Egba National Council', under the titular leadership of the Alake. This Council would exist under the executive management of another de-anglicised Saro Reverend named Adegboyega Edun, whose birth name in Sierra Leone had been Jacob Henryson Samuel. As secretary of a nascent Egba government with responsibility for an area measured at nearly 2,000 square miles, Reverend Edun would become one of the most important personalities in the historical evolution of southern Nigeria. It was Edun's leadership that received official British sanction in the 1903 ordinance, following the spectacular reduction of Ijebu by force of arms in the Imagbon War. Under Secretary Edun, this nominally independent enclave, smack in the middle of the new British Southern Nigeria, would make gallant efforts to maintain its political autonomy when surrounded by such a powerful new regional hegemon.

In the end, it would be the internal political disharmony

among the various chiefs and factions as much as the external risk factor of British influence that triggered the demise of Egba independence. The first outward sign of trouble in Egba revealed itself in 1907 when Edun attempted to exert his official power over a very old, small-town chief named Odugbemi Ariwo, at a place called *Ikija*. The secretary was on a field trip away from the capital, along with the British resident and other officers, and stopped at Ikija for some official reason. Ariwo refused to acknowledge the visiting Secretary Edun, who was not a duly constituted authority as far as most of the Egba country was concerned. Even the Alake himself was considered by the locals to have limited jurisdiction, never mind his Saro secretary. Attempting to extract by force the respect for his position that was not offered peacefully, Edun and his armed contingent violently arrested Baba Ariwo, who was killed in the process. Popular outrage followed, with many Ogboni chiefs demanding the removal of Edun from office by Alake Gbadebo.

But the Alake flatly refused. Gbadebo was a pro-British royal who had visited London with Edun in 1904 and even managed via the CMS to secure a conference with Victoria's successor King Edward VII. The Egba ruler owed his traditionally unconstitutional pre-eminence among his colleagues of Egba paramount chiefs to two factors. One was favouritism by Europeans, and the other was the historical accident of the great Balogun Sodeke having been from the Ake section of Abeokuta. For all his efforts to match the developmental strides of Egerton in the 1903 to 1914 era of rapid infrastructural development and trade expansion in southern Nigeria, Edun would be met with a great deal of unpopularity at Abeokuta among the disempowered Ogboni and other sectional chiefs opposed to Ake's pre-eminence. We will return shortly to the consequences of that unpopularity and internal discord for Egba independence in the post-Egerton era. While the Egba feuded, the thinking was changing in Britain again. Egerton's excellent forward investment strategy, being proposed by the government of an area that was fiscally sound, would lose out to another concept. The new idea was a fiscally conservative imperial accountant's simplistic but hare-brained proposal. The Southern Protectorate was to be merged with its much less financially buoyant and landlocked Northern neighbour. This was considered especially shrewd by the penny-pinchers in London, given the high cost of achieving and maintaining military conquest in that country. In the minds of these unthinking (or perhaps small thinking) bean counters, all that mattered was the happy compromise of utilising surplus customs revenues collected at the coast to develop the entire contiguous territory. A most important decision for the future country had been reached, without reference to the facts on the ground, or to the views and ideas of the people that would be most affected by it. The moment of Formation had arrived, the future political and economic character of Nigeria was about to be cast in stone.

Lugard Returns to Lagos

Once this decision was made, there was little doubt in the minds of British officialdom as to who the best man for the job of merging the two young administrations would be. It just had to be Frederick Lugard, resilient conqueror of East Africa and the Caliphate. Lugard had been carefully manoeuvred into the position of best-known and most respected African field officer in British colonial circles. His new boss was to be Lord Lewis Vernon Harcourt, a known sexual predator who killed himself when his attempt to have sex with a 12-year-old boy was about to be published in the papers. Harcourt made the call appointing Lugard to the job, in his capacity as the reigning Secretary of State for the Colonies since 1910, under Liberal Prime Minister Herbert Henry Asquith. Lugard eagerly accepted the challenge. He had been bored and dissatisfied with life in Hong Kong, where there were not many walls to breach and no empires to crush. Soon after his appointment, the former 'King in the North' returned to London in 1911 to commence planning for the amalgamation of Nigeria. This time, Lugard would be returning to Nigeria without Flora but with his younger brother, Major Edward ('Ned') Lugard as his secretary.

Flora's initial stay in Nigeria with Lugard had not been a pleasant one. She was frequently ill and lonely with her husband working long days. She also found her usually convivial social life curtailed in the isolated but rapidly expanding Zungeru. She complained that putting together a meal for a handful of guests tasked all her resourcefulness. One time while arranging for such a feast, a hyena found its way into her kitchen, having been attracted by the smell of chicken. 'Everything is much further away from civilisation than I expected. Zungeru is a little town looking rather like a pretty English suburb' she had written to her niece, Hilda Brackenbury, the Suffragette, in August 1902. In the end, she lasted less than six months before returning to Britain to recuperate, on the orders of her doctor, where she continued to campaign for the work Lugard was doing in Nigeria[14]. She would carry on writing articles and campaigning for various good causes. In 1905, she wrote her critically acclaimed book *A Tropical Mandate* which was praised by Nnamdi Azikiwe, who posited that the book supported the idea of African independence since it showed that Africans had governed themselves perfectly fine in the past and were thus able to do so again. On Lugard's 71st birthday in January 1929, Flora took ill with pneumonia and was dead three days later on 25th January at the age of 76. At her passing, Lugard described her death as a 'Blow that fell on me which can never be healed'[15].

On 3 October 1912, the now balding but still energetic 54-year-old Sir Frederick Lugard arrived at Apapa wharf and crossed the new bridge across the Lagoon. The new bridge had been built only in 1901 and was named after former Governor Carter, conqueror of the Ijebu. The new ruler of Nigeria had been knighted in 1901 but would not be elevated to the peerage until 1928 when he became 'Lord' Lugard as he is now best remembered. A few days after his arrival, the new Governor-General departed Lagos by train for Zungeru, crossing the river by a combination of rail-bridge and rail-ferry at Jebba island. This transformational infrastructure investment had been sanctioned while Lugard was away in Asia, after much negotiation and contention between Egerton, Moor, Girouard, Churchill and other denizens of the Colonial Office in London. Lugard continued from Zungeru up to see his former enemies and now loyal subjects in the Sokoto Caliphate. A grand durbar was hosted in his honour before he returned down the river for a tour of the Niger delta. It was on this trip that he approved the selection of the site for a new seaport in Okrika country, which he obsequiously named 'Port Harcourt' after his new boss.

At Calabar, he met with the famed Mary Slessor, a red-haired Scottish Presbyterian woman missionary who by this time had lived among the Efik people of the inland Niger delta for more than 30 years since her first arrival in 1876 at 28 years old. Slessor had become so embedded among the native people that she was appointed vice-consul of her town, Okoyong in 1892 and had managed to spread enlightenment about Christianity, Western education, non-slave trade, and the discontinuance of numerous superstitions including the one which previously led to the killing of twins. The saintly Slessor would die of Malaria about two years after meeting with Lugard on his tour of the country. Flags were flown at half-mast across the country to mourn her and in 1997, Slessor was honoured in Scotland with a now withdrawn 'Famous Scots' issue of the £10 Clydesdale Bank note[16].

Friends and Opponents: Carr versus Macaulay

By the time of his arrival on this second coming, Lugard was already very well-known and detested among the local traditional and intellectual elite in southern Nigeria, particularly among the educated Saro and Yoruba at Lagos. His exploits, most especially his tax policies, in the north were well-known, as was his autocratic and self-promoting behaviour, in direct contrast to the more collaborative and collegial approach of the Egerton era. Prominent journalists and publishers in the flourishing newspaper trade like

Kitoye Ajasa (*Nigerian Pioneer*), James Bright Davies (*Times of Nigeria*), George Williams (*Lagos Standard*), John Payne and later his son and successor Horatio Jackson (*Lagos Weekly Record*) held attitudes ranging from healthy scepticism to outright hostility towards the King in the North. At 48 years old, not much younger than Governor-General Lugard himself, Herbert Macaulay, grandson of Bishop Crowther and son of T.B. Macaulay (founder of CMS Grammar School), would become the chief antagonist and leading opposition figure to Lugard in his reincarnation at Lagos. Sadly, for Macaulay, his activism would be hampered by his rather tarnished career copybook by this point in his life.

Born at Lagos in 1864, the same year that Domingo Martinez the great slave-trader died at Porto Novo; Macaulay was the first blueblood of a new generation of Nigerians free from the evil of slavery. Clothed from birth in the institutional privilege that came with the societal status of his grandparents and parents, Macaulay attended CMS Grammar School and chose to immediately join the Lagos Colonial civil service upon graduation, at 17 years old in 1881. Rising rapidly, Macaulay was sent by the government in 1890 to be educated as a land surveyor and engineer under a prominent professional in the field named G.D. Bellamy at Plymouth, England. Returning three years later, the rising star was immediately appointed a Colonial Surveyor of Crown Lands; a high office from which he would have to resign in questionable circumstances only five years later in 1898.

Accused by the government of inappropriate dealings and conflicts of interest, he was nonetheless able to obtain a license to practice privately and commence a career in political opposition to the British government in Nigeria. Perhaps due to that vocal and eloquent opposition - most famously illustrated in the so-called Eleko Affair, Macaulay was a much loved and prominent local figure. The Eleko Affair was a multi-year saga that began when Oba Eshugbayi Eleko of Lagos spoke against a proposed tax by Egerton for a pipe-borne water infrastructure project, leading to protests and riots in the city. As a result of this, Oba Eleko would be temporarily exiled and removed from office many years later in 1925. But as the Oba's chief spokesman from the start of the affair, Macaulay was a marked man politically.

In 1913, just a year after Lugard arrived on his second coming, an opportunity arose for the Bishop's grandson to be dealt with. Macaulay was accused of financial misappropriation by the beneficiaries of a private fund, which was part of the estate of a departed wealthy notable and to which he had been appointed trustee and executor. The case was enthusiastically taken up by the government and prosecuted vigorously. Macaulay was found guilty, banned perpetually from holding public elected office and sentenced to two years in prison, earning for himself the unfortunate sobriquet 'Ex-Convict' - an appellation that would be happily added to all future written references to Herbert Macaulay by Lugard and the rest of his colonial officers. The enmity between Lugard and Macaulay was therefore personal, and the partisan supporters of either man would come to play major roles in the evolution of British rule in Nigeria.

One of the most prominent of these partisans among the local elite was the impeccably well-spoken Henry Rawlingson Carr. Also born in Lagos of Saro parents, Carr was a great friend and supporter of Lugard and British rule, providing the perfect foil to Herbert Macaulay. Born around the same time, Carr attended the Wesleyan schools in Lagos and Freetown, Fourah Bay College (same as Bishop Crowther), trained in maths, physics and the law in England; and taught at CMS Grammar School (founded by Macaulay's father). In short, Carr came from the same pedigree as the bishop's grandson, and unlike his arch-rival, enjoyed an unblemished career in the British colonial service - rising as high as director of Education and Acting Administrator of Lagos Colony for a time. The political rivalry between the two men would come to assume legendary proportions, with salacious rumours and vicious press attacks to the bargain. In all, Henry Carr would hold his head high, a truly remarkable citizen of nineteenth-century Nigeria, and the first of many British educated Nigerians who would embrace Western knowledge and culture without losing their traditional grounding, 'an admirable fusion of African and European intellect' as Sylvia Leith-Ross the ever perceptive contemporary observer described him. Henry Carr's collection of nearly 20,000 books would be acquired by the colonial government to form the core of the University College Library at Ibadan, when it was later established.

For his part, Lugard did not cover himself in glory at Lagos, demonstrating a complete lack of self-awareness and naivete as to the political potency of the unarmed indigenous elite. A military man - more used to succinct proclamations backed by Maxim guns, heavy artillery, well-drilled troops and properly stocked garrisons - Lugard was not prepared for a contest based on constitutional political action, newspaper articles, native pressure groups and the judicial infrastructure provided by his very own British government. On the other hand, the Lagos elite of the early twentieth century (many of them legally British subjects by virtue of descent or birth in the colony) were already well versed in the business of contending with the foreign power now ruling their homeland, on entirely non-militaristic terms. In the ensuing contest, Lugard's imperial megalomania would meet its political match in the countervailing resistance of the Lagos intellectual elite. Unexpectedly, the outbreak of a much more important military contest far away from the scene of this scheming on the tiny Lagos island would provide the supporting background for Lugard's defeat.

The Great War Tests the White Man

On June 28, 1914, Gavrilo Princip ignited the seminal catastrophe when he assassinated Archduke Franz Ferdinand in Sarajevo, firing the shot that kicked off the First World War. War had been brewing for years, and much of the intense imperial activity in Africa during the late nineteenth century was partly the strategic accumulation of resources and positioning, ahead of the feared conflict to come. The Great War was nowhere, a bloody battle intended to settle finally among mostly European contestants, the hierarchy of imperial powers on the globe. All the recently collected new overseas territories were now required to support their respective overlords.

Lasting until November 1918, the First World War put a freeze on any intentional economic development aspect to British colonial rule in Nigeria. Austerity ensued, and any infrastructure developed in this period would be strictly to meet the demands of the war both internationally and in Africa itself, starting with nearby Cameroon, a German possession. A significant proportion of the military-age British population in Nigeria departed to enlist in various war fronts globally, and even Nigerian troops were corralled into action overseas. Thus, within six months of accomplishing the amalgamation of Northern and Southern Nigeria on the first of January 1914, Lugard lost his much-treasured monopoly on organised, large-scale violence across the country. Worse still, the leading Muslim country in the world, the Turkish Caliphate (comprising the remaining rump of the Ottoman Empire) soon entered the Great War *against* Britain, on the side of Germany, putting the loyalty of the Islamic Sokoto Caliphate potentially in doubt for the first time since its subjugation.

It was a critical moment for British rule in Nigeria, and the native population seized the moment eagerly. Armed revolts began to spring up across the country, each ostensibly for easily identifiable local reasons, but in reality, a collective response to the impaired ability of the British rulers to enforce civil order under their new laws. Abeokuta took the lead as usual, with a full-scale riot erupting following a nearly identical situation to the Odugbemi Ariwo affair, again involving the unpopular Secretary Adegboyega Edun.

This time, the trigger was an octogenarian named Ponlade Shobiyi, who remained stubbornly opposed (like many Egba) to what appeared to them as the British-backed government of Alake

Gbadebo. Though merely a minor chief of a place called *Ijemo*, Edun had ordered the arrest of the old man for insubordination, and he died in police custody. Once the news broke, Abeokuta was on the edge - spoiling for war against the ruling elite. The tense situation was exacerbated beyond control when an inexperienced and unthinking British lieutenant named Wilson (commanding troops from Kaduna) arrived on the scene and applied indiscriminate force in attempting to disperse a public gathering at Ijemo. Between 40 and 60 people were killed in the Ijemo Massacre - depending on the version of reports accepted with many more wounded. With riots against British interests now raging, the Alake essentially lost control of his nominally independent country and was required by the British Commissioner P.C.V. Young to forfeit Egba independence if he wanted British armed support to put down the riots. Young had already been directed by Lugard to do this and was grateful when the opportunity presented itself. Seeking to protect his position, the Alake accepted Lugard's Faustian bargain. Therefore, on 16 September, Lugard arrived in Egba by train to sign a new treaty in which the last Yoruba holdouts finally accepted British protectorate status. Abeokuta, the beam of Sunshine in the Tropics, became the only part of Southern Nigeria that lost its independence to Lugard.

But Egba was just the start of the violent opposition to colonial rule during the Great War. Throughout the rest of 1914, armed and popular revolts broke out sporadically in Warri Province (around present-day Kwale) in the Niger delta, as well as across several townships in the Igbo country. Much of this agitation and uprising was against the fundamental idea of British rule, or its manifestation in corruptly managed native administrations, but in all cases, the people were acting at this very moment in the belief that Britain was losing in the Great War and would soon be forced out of the country. These ideas were encouraged by German traders still active in Nigeria. By 1913, German merchants originated up to 50 per cent of the export trade from Nigeria, and they did their best to fuel such rumours in favour of their country. By November, substantial German commercial interests - collectively responsible for £4 million of the value of trade in Nigeria, or more than £400 million in present-day money - were expropriated by the British government, and all citizens of the enemy country interred as prisoners of war.

The following year, 1915, saw fighting commence across the border in Cameroon against German forces, resulting in the capture of Douala by sea and subsequently the rest of the country. Meanwhile, the Senussi revolution across French West Africa - from Timbuktu to Lake Chad - erupted, sparked by unhappiness with French colonial rule and particularly with the forced recruitment of young men in those countries as French fighters in the Great War. This revolution would spill over into the security situation in the Northern Emirates, which nonetheless remained loyal to Lugard and the British Empire for the duration of the war, resisting the Turkish temptation.

Across the river, 1915 saw more armed revolts at Owerri province, which was yet to be fully subjected to British rule. In Udi district, where coal had been discovered and a colliery dug, an uprising broke out which led to all British police forces being driven away for a time. It would take the efforts of a volunteer force of Europeans to put down this particularly bloody uprising, in which more than 250 armed locals were killed. The state of crisis continued into 1916 when another revolt broke out at Okeiho in the old Oyo country, led by some former war chiefs. They were irate at Lugard's version of indirect rule, which supplanted their former dominance with that of a new class of native institutions (primarily, civil courts).

Over 200 people were killed in the ensuing fighting to put down this uprising, which had developed into a full-scale insurgency when war chiefs from Iseyin and other towns joined in the revolt. Colonial edicts regarding potable water, sanitary inspections and direct taxation were the most potent sources of discontent which triggered political crises. But direct taxation would prove the single most significant source of discontent in colonial Southern Nigeria. Direct taxes acted as the primary catalyst for the tragic Aba women's war and the Egba women's revolt against British Indirect Rule, under Olufunmilayo Ransome-Kuti's leadership at Abeokuta a few decades later. For the moment, the Eleko Affair at Lagos also erupted again in 1916 over the introduction of a water rate and a new Criminal Code by Lugard. This was considered especially egregious because it was the same code used in Northern Nigeria. More than 2,000 people were involved in the serious protests and 27 were arrested after the homes and property of known government supporters were vandalised. This time, Oba Eleko's stipend was suspended, and the 'ex-convict' Macaulay was again at the forefront of defending the monarch against the government all the way to London, much to the embarrassment of Lugard.

Pioneer Patriots and Nationalists

In the same year, James Bright Davies, the venerable Saro newspaper publisher was arrested and prosecuted in Lagos for libel on account of several articles, including one in which he labelled the thin-skinned Lugard a 'negrophobist.' This was a term that appears to be a colourful early twentieth-century euphemism for the simpler and now more commonly used term 'racist'. Davies contended that Lugard was implementing 'iniquitous measures and laws that hampered the genuine progress of the country.' The old man was convicted and sentenced to pay a fine of £100, a substantial sum, worth more than £10,000 in present-day money. Yet this irrepressible activist wrote even more articles, including one in which he suggested that Africans would prefer that Germany prevailed in the war. This was on account of the unpopular wartime monopoly enjoyed by British traders led by the UAC, the commercial rump of the former Royal Niger Company. This was a step too far for the colonial government and this time Davies was sentenced to 6 months in prison, after being convicted for sedition. With the benefit of hindsight, the jeremiads of J.B. Davies were the most prominent early warning signal to Lugard and the Colonial Office of the deep underlying currents of native feeling and opposition to his attempted enthronement in the South of his Northern version of Indirect Rule. Had this warning been heeded and responded to actively, much might have been different in the historical evolution of Nigeria over the next century.

James Bright Davies was not the only western-educated newspaper publisher speaking loudly against the 'Brutish' rule of Lugard at Lagos. There was another venerable newspaperman in the business. Originally a Liberian, his father migrated to that country from Maryland in the United States. This publisher was a perhaps even louder canary in the coal mine, propagating the native African viewpoint. Forced out of the palm oil trade on the river by the monopoly of Goldie in the late Clapham-Sect era, John Payne Jackson founded *The Lagos Weekly Record* in 1891 and published the newspaper until his death and succession by his son, Horatio in 1915. J.P. Jackson would lend the megaphone of his widely circulating broadsheet to prominent cases like the British sacking of Ijebu (in 1892, which he supported) and the removal of Nana Olomu from the Benin River (in 1894 as we have seen already), which he campaigned against. Together, Jackson, Macaulay and Davies (whatever their political and personal differences) would form a troika of vocal opposition not so much to British rule itself, but to any colonial policy in Nigeria that was formed without what they considered to be due weight and concern for the native African viewpoint. This intrepid trio would fight Lugard to the finish, in direct contrast to the conservative party among the educated local elite. The latter group was led by Kitoye (later, Sir) Ajasa, the newspaper publisher, an England-educated lawyer and father of future prominent feminist Lady Oyinkan Abayomi. Ajasa had been named Edmund Macaulay at birth, although he was not a relative of the Bishop's grandson. Henry Carr, whom we have met already was a friend of Lugard, and a prominent supporter of official policy.

Carr and Ajasa would lead the local elite support for the former King in the North, who in any event was not a man to rely on public opinion for decision making.

Direct Taxation and Other Discontents

By 1917, the clouds of war appeared to be clearing in Nigeria, with the United States emerging as a replacement for Germany in terms of produce exports, leading to a record year for the newly amalgamated colony. At the height of the economic crisis during the war, a significant shortage in shipping capacity from Lagos had resulted in a glut of produce at the ports and railways in 1915, depressing local prices for farmers and creating volatile trading conditions. British concerns like UAC and Lever Brothers had been the major ultimate beneficiaries, but the arrival of the Americans into the war and the local market was a welcome development. In this atmosphere of record exports and a seeming return of British dominance in internal security affairs, the resolute Lugard determined that this was an appropriate moment to introduce his long-desired goal of direct taxation in Southern Nigeria, starting with the Yoruba country. The Yoruba, like most people in Southern Nigeria, and unlike the denizens of the Islamic Caliphate, had never paid regular direct taxes in their history. Customs duties and road tolls were the accepted means by which government revenues were levied in times of peace, and in any event, there was in historical times no substantial standing government budget or expansive infrastructure development to finance.

The king, his main chief and the other leading officers of the government in most Yoruba states were typically also traders and merchants and earned their keep either from tolls and excise duties or directly via preferred trading access, rather than through general taxation and salaries drawn from the public purse. However, in direct contrast, Lugard had successfully implemented in his Caliphate, a system of Native Administration funded by direct taxes, a public purse, and permanent government officials. Thanks to duties on healthy trade flows, the British government of Southern Nigeria had never seriously suffered from insufficient funds to meet its impressive infrastructure development goals. Lugard however arrived and held that direct taxation was a *cardinal concept* in responsible African government, quite apart from any revenue implications, which were anyway not expected to be significant in the first instance. It was a matter of political *principle*, more than a matter of economics. Local advisers at Lagos had advised against it as a hare-brained idea. Even his overlords at the wartime Colonial Office had vetoed the proposal several times as a bad idea since there were not sufficient armed forces available if implementation led to riots. Eventually however, London succumbed to Lugard's persistence.

The Governor-General himself knew very well what the local people of the South felt about taxes, as it had come up time and again during his tour of the country. Opinion leaders among both the traditional and westernised elite had made it known to him that they had heard about his tax policies in the north and wanted none of it in the south. For their sins, Lugard developed a particularly strong and deeply personal dislike for the many educated elites - men like Macaulay, the so-called 'trousered natives' in the derogatory words of his brother, Ned. Lugard's preferred philosophy for native education was the one faithfully practiced in Northern Nigeria by a prominent, Swiss-born, fluent Hausa-speaking Afrophile named (later, Sir) Hanns Vischer, who served as Lugard's Director of Education until 1916. Popular in Northern Nigeria as Dan Hausa or 'Son of Hausa,' Vischer departed during the Great War to serve in the British army as an Intelligence Officer, under criticism from the Lagos media[17]. But long before that, he had joined Lugard's Northern Nigeria Administrative Service in 1903, having arrived in the country for the first time two years prior, as a CMS missionary. Prior to this, he studied Modern Languages at Cambridge. Eventually one of the most important educators in British Africa, Hanns Vischer's preferred approach to native education was one that focused its emphasis on 'traditional' rather than 'Western' learning, in direct contrast with the more liberal-minded Lagos educated elite. In his own words, the erudite Vischer stated that: 'Native education should develop the national and racial characteristics of the natives on such lines that will enable them to use their own moral and physical forces to the best advantage, widen their mental horizon without destroying their respect for race and parentage'[18].

In any event, the opposition of the Lagos educated elite to Lugard's taxation policy was disregarded, and the Governor-General marched forward. After a perfunctory sensitisation exercise, the new tax was rolled out across Yorubaland - starting at Oyo in 1916, with the intention to do the same in the other parts of the south. It would be the final miscalculation of Lugard's brief career in Nigeria and would lead directly to his removal from the country.

The Egba Revolt Sacks Lugard

The Egba remained restless under British rule. Their unceremonious annexation in 1914 had never settled well among a people whose entire historical foundation and indeed, the raison d'etre for their city-state was an ode to freedom and independence. The descendants of Sodeke and numerous elite baloguns over the decades, the Egba had successfully resisted the fearsome Ghezo and his horde of vicious Mino, and they believed that they could remove the British from their country too. Lugard's misguided roll-out of his direct tax was the last straw in a multiple decade-long contest between modernity and traditional rule in Egba. The Ogboni chiefs who previously held much of whatever direct taxation powers existed in Egba viewed a struggle against direct colonial taxation in existential terms. Thus, a quixotic but carefully planned Egba war of independence was conceived of and launched. The idea was to cut Egba off from British influence by destroying the railway, the telegraph lines and every other piece of connecting infrastructure, including all local supporters (like the Alake and Secretary Edun). The Adubi War as it came to be known was viciously contested on multiple fronts starting in June 1918[19].

Luckily for Lugard, the Nigerian troops of the West African Service Brigade (WASB) which had been involved in fighting the Great War for Britain in East Africa had just returned from the front and were not yet demobilised. Therefore, the Governor-General had an unusually large force of well-trained and combat-ready troops at his disposal. As always, this was his preferred starting point for any policy discussion. More than 600 Egba men were killed in this conflict, which required 70 European officers and nearly 3,000 Nigerian troops to subdue the disaffected local rebellion against British rule. Property valued at more than £55,000 (or nearly £3 million in present-day money) was destroyed, and the Osile of Egba, an important chief on the same level as the Alake in pre-British Abeokuta, was beheaded by armed partisans. It was a bloodbath of unprecedented proportions, and even though the slippery Lugard tried his best to lay it elsewhere, the entire blame for it was placed squarely on his stubborn head. An extensive enquiry was commissioned into the Adubi War, which produced a scathing report, the excellent recommendations of which were predictably never acted upon by the British.

But Lugard's position at Lagos was no longer politically tenable. At the earliest excuse, he offered his resignation, which was not only enthusiastically accepted but also interpreted as retirement from the Colonial Service entirely. Thus, the unfortunate but brave Egba martyrs of the Adubi War had achieved the same outcome as the victorious Satiru horde of the previous decade - the removal from their country of a most undesirable British ruler. Lugard would be replaced by British leaders with the more appropriate temperaments and skill sets for colonial development work. For his part, history would be exceedingly kind to the public relations savvy Lugard, who was jealously protected until her death by his personal publicist, the clever newspaperwoman Flora Shaw. His most popular tome *The Dual Mandate in British Tropical Africa* was published in 1922, well after his disastrous exit from Nigeria and it would surpass even *The Rise of Our East African Empire* in popularity, cementing the hard-headed conqueror's dubious place of honour as his generation's leading British influencer on matters of sub-Saharan African development. With the end of the Great War, the colonial project in Nigeria would continue from where it stopped, under the guidance of stronger and better-suited leaders like Sir Hugh Clifford, the highly experienced successor to Lugard.

From Revolution to Amalgamation

The still-evolving country had come a long way from the opening shots of Dan Fodio's revolution, which had heralded the first of many series of forced combinations, snowballing into the eventual formal emergence of a single political entity called Nigeria on January 1, 1914. Along the way, several consistent themes had shone through: the outsized influence of outside forces on domestic affairs, the inability except for a few notable exceptions of the local elite (both traditional and westernised) to form sustainable political compromises, the unfortunate and remarkable sacrifice of life, treasure and expertise by many heroes foreign and domestic during the century it took to assemble the country.

The consistent use of violence and military force to resolve political crises or disagreements, and to maintain economic hegemony by both domestic and foreign powers was another unfortunate factor throughout the period, which would leave deep cultural imprints. The fundamental character of Nigeria was formed in these one hundred year-long crucibles and has proven resiliently unalterable since then, mutating and evolving in tune to the newest outside forces, the latest internal domestic elite squabble and the most recent tools of violent economic subjugation. From Jihad to Lugard, a chaotic combination was brought to life through a haphazard series of actions by extraneous forces, to which the forever quarrelling and self-interested incumbent leadership often had no effective answer, with both devastating and transformational consequences for the contemporary ordinary citizen.

1. Johnson S. *The History of the Yorubas: From the Earliest Times to the Beginning of the British Protectorate*. Cambridge University Press; 1921.

2. Stone RH, Stone RH. *In Africa's Forest and Jungle: Six Years Among the Yorubas*. University of Alabama Press; 2010.

3. *Ibid*.

4. Leith-Ross S. *Stepping-stones: Memoirs of Colonial Nigeria, 1907-1960*. P. Owen; 1983.

5. Orr CWJ. *The Making of Northern Nigeria*. Macmillan and Company, Limited; 1911.

6. *Ibid*.

7. Perham MF. *Lugard: The Years of Authority, 1898-1945*. Collins; 1960.

8. The Times Newspapers Archive - The Rising in Sokoto 1906/2/22 1906 (Available online)

9. Lovejoy PE, Hogendorn JS. Revolutionary Mahdism and Resistance to Colonial Rule in the Sokoto Caliphate, 1905–6. *Journal of African History*. 1990;31(2):217-244.

10. *Daily Trust Newspapers*, Nigeria - Satiru: A Community Frozen by a Curse. 2009/9/27 2009; (Available online)

11. Carland JM. *The Colonial Office and Nigeria, 1898-1914*. Hoover Press; 1985.

12. Robinson RE, Gallagher J, Denny A. *Africa and the Victorians: The Official Mind of Imperialism*. Macmillan; 1961.

13. Carland JM. *The Colonial Office and Nigeria, 1898-1914*. Hoover Press; 1985.

14. Scharrer J. *The Journalist: The Jameson Raid, the Klondike Gold Rush, the Anglo Boer War, the Founding of Nigeria: Flora Shaw was there*. CreateSpace Independent Publishing Platform; 2014.

15. O'Grady R. *The Passionate Imperialists*. Conrad Press; 2018.

16. The Committee of Scottish Bankers (CSCB) - £10 Famous Scots Series -

Withdrawn. Scotsbank.org

17. Whitehead C. *Colonial Educators: The British Indian and Colonial Education Service 1858-1983*. Bloomsbury Academic; 2003.

18. Graham SF. *Government and Mission Education in Northern Nigeria: 1900-1919; With Special Reference to the Work of Hanns Vischer*. Ibadan University Press; 1966.

19. Gailey HA. *Lugard and the Abeokuta Uprising: The Demise of Egba Independence*. Routledge; 2014.

Bibliography

Ade Ajayi JF. *Christian Missions in Nigeria, 1841-1891; The Making of a New Elite*. Longmans; 1965.

Anene JC. *Southern Nigeria in Transition 1885-1906: Theory and Practice in a Colonial Protectorate*. Cambridge University Press; 1966.

Baba, Smith MF. *Baba of Karo: A Woman of the Moslem Hausa*. New York, Praeger; 1964.

Bacon R. *Benin, the City of Blood*. Creative Media Partners, LLC; 2018

Baikie WB. *Narrative of an Exploring Voyage up the Rivers Kwóra and Bínue (commonly known as the Niger and Tsádda) in 1854. With a Map and Appendices. Pub. with the Sanction of Her Majesty's Government*. J. Murray; 1856.

Baker GL. *Trade Winds On the Niger: The Saga of the Royal Niger Company 1830-1971*. Tauris Academic Studies; 1996.

Barth H. *Travels and Discoveries in North and Central Africa: Being a Journal of an Expedition Undertaken Under the Auspices of H. B. M.'s Government, in the Years 1849-1855*. 1857.

Basden GT. *Among the Ibos of Nigeria*. Seeley, Service & Co.; 1921.

Bashir Abubakar MM. Muslim Responses to British Colonialism in Northern Nigeria as Expressed in Fulfulde Poems. *Islamic Africa*. 2013/6/3 2013;4(1):1-14.

Bello M. *Infaḵul maisuri*. Northern Nigeria Publishing Company; 1974.

Biobaku SO. *The Egba and Their Neighbours, 1842-1872*. Clarendon Press; 1957.

Boyd J. *The Caliph's Sister: Nana Asma'u, 1793-1865, Teacher, Poet and Islamic Leader*. Routledge; 2013.

Bulwer HL. *The Life of Henry John Temple, Viscount Palmerston: With Selections from His Speeches and Correspondence*. Adegi Graphics LLC; 1871.

Buxton C. *Memoirs of Sir Thomas Fowell Buxton, Baronet: With Selections from His Correspondence*. H. Longstreth; 1849.

Carland JM. *The Colonial Office and Nigeria, 1898-1914*. Hoover Press; 1985.

Churchill WS. *The River War: An Account of the Reconquest of the Sudan*. Library of Alexandria; 1933.

Cook AN. *British Enterprise in Nigeria*. University of Pennsylvania Press; 1943.

Cookey SJS. *King Jaja of the Niger Delta: His Life and Times, 1821-1891*. UGR publishing; 2005.

Crosby TL. *Joseph Chamberlain: A Most Radical Imperialist*. I.B.Tauris; 2011.

Crowder M. *The Story of Nigeria*. Faber; 1973.

Crowther S, Taylor JC. *The Gospel on the Banks of the Niger: Journals and Notices of the Native Missionaries Accompanying the Niger Expedition of 1857-1859*. Cambridge University Press; 2010.

Daily Trust Newspapers, Nigeria - Meet the Royal Ndayakos of Bida. 2018/7/28 2018; (Available online)

Daily Trust Newspapers, Nigeria - Satiru: A Community Frozen by a Curse. 2009/9/27 2009; (Available online)

Daily Trust Newspapers, Nigeria - The Baikies: Hausa Christians with European background. 2018/2/17 2018; (Available online)

De Gramont S. *The Strong Brown God: The Story of the Niger River*. Houghton Mifflin; 1975.

de St Croix FW. *The Fulani of Northern Nigeria: Some General Notes*. Gregg International Publishers Limited; 1972.

Denham D, Clapperton H, Oudney W. *Narrative of Travels and Discoveries in Northern and Central Africa: In the Years 1822, 1823, and 1824*. 1828.

Dike KO. *Trade and Politics in the Niger Delta, 1803-1885: An Introduction to the Economic and Political History of Nigeria*. Oxford University Press; 1956.

Diouf SA. *Servants of Allah: African Muslims Enslaved in the Americas*. NYU Press; 1998.

Dusgate RH. *The Conquest of Northern Nigeria*. F. Cass; 1985.

Elebute A. *The Life of James Pinson Labulo Davies: A Colossus of Victorian Lagos*. Kachifo; 2013.

Equiano O. *The Interesting Narrative of the Life of Olaudah Equiano Or Gustavus Vassa, the African*. G. Vassa; 1794.

Falola T, Heaton MM. *A History of Nigeria*. Cambridge University Press; 2008.

Falola T, Jennings C. *Sources and Methods in African History: Spoken, Written, Unearthed*. University Rochester Press; 2004.

Flint JE. *Sir George Goldie and the Making of Nigeria*. Oxford University Press; 1960.

Flint JE. *The Cambridge History of Africa*. Oxford University Press; 1978.

Forbes FE. *Dahomey and the Dahomans: Being the Journals of Two Missions to the King of Dahomey, and Residence at His Capital, in the Years 1849 and*

1850. Longman; 1851.

Gailey HA. *Lugard and the Abeokuta Uprising: The Demise of Egba Independence*. Routledge; 2014.

Glover JH. *The Voyage of the Dayspring: Being the Journal of the Late Sir John Hawley Glover, R. N., G. C. M. G., Together with Some Account of the Expedition Up the Niger River in 1857*. J. Lane; 1926.

Graham SF. *Government and Mission Education in Northern Nigeria: 1900-1919; With Special Reference to the Work of Hanns Vischer*. Ibadan University Press; 1966.

Hallett R. *The Niger Journal of Richard and John Lander*. Routledge; 1966.

Hansard - CLASS II. 1895/8/22 1895;

Hansard - COLONIAL SERVICES (SUPPLEMENTARY). 1898/2/24 1898;

Hansard - Nigeria Protectorate-Aro Expedition. 1902/11/20 1902;

Hansard - SLAVE TRADE ABOLITION BILL. 1807/2/23 1807

Hansard - Slave Trade. 1850/3/19 1850;

Hansard - Sokoto. 1902/12/9 1902;

Harunah HB. SODEKE: Hero and Statesman of the Egba. *Journal of the Historical Society of Nigeria*. 1983 1983;12(1/2):109-131.

Headrick DR, Professor of Social S, History Daniel RH. *The Tools of Empire: Technology and European Imperialism in the Nineteenth Century*. Oxford University Press; 1981.

Hiskett M. Kitāb Al-Farq: A Work on the Habe Kingdoms Attributed to 'Uthmān Dan Fodio. *Bulletin of the School of Oriental and African Studies*. 1960 1960;23(3):558-579.

Hiskett M. Material Relating to the State of Learning among the Fulani before Their Jihād. *Bulletin of the School of Oriental and African Studies*. 1957 1957;19(3):550-578.

Hiskett M. *Tazyin al-Waraqat by Abdullah ibn Muhammad*. University Press Ibadan; 1963.

Hiskett M. *The Sword of Truth: The Life and Times of the Shehu Usuman dan Fodio*. Oxford University Press; 1973.

Hurston ZN. *Barracoon: The Story of the Last "Black Cargo"*. HarperCollins; 2018.

Ibn-Ḥaldūn '-A-RI-M, Khaldūn I. *The Muqaddimah : An Introduction to History*. Princeton University Press; 1967.

Idrees AA. Collaboration and the British Conquest of Bida in 1798: The

Role and Achievement of the Indigenous Interest Groups. *African Study Monographs*. 1989/8 1989;10(2):69-82.

Idrees AA. *Domination and Reaction in Nupeland, Central Nigeria: The Kyadya Revolt, 1857-1905*. E. Mellen Press; 1996.

Idrees AA. Gogo Habiba of Bida: The Rise and Demise of a nineteenth Century Nupe Merchant Princess and Politician. *African Study Monographs*. 1991 1991;12(1):1-9.

Iliffe J. *Africans: The History of a Continent*. Cambridge University Press; 2007.

Jenkins R. *Gladstone: A Biography*. Random House; 1997.

Jeppie S, Diagne SB. *The Meanings of Timbuktu*. HSRC Press, 2008.

Johnson S. *The History of the Yorubas: From the Earliest Times to the Beginning of the British Protectorate*. Cambridge University Press; 1921.

Johnston HAS. *The Fulani Empire of Sokoto*. Oxford University Press; 1967.

Kemper S. *A Labyrinth of Kingdoms: 10,000 Miles through Islamic Africa*. W. W. Norton & Company; 2012

Kirk J. *Report by Sir John Kirk on the disturbances at Brass*. H.M. Stationery Office; 1896.

Knowles C. Ascent of the Niger in September and October, 1864. *Proceedings of the Royal Geographical Society of London*. 1864 1864;9(2):72-75.

Last M. *The Sokoto Caliphate*. Harlow: Longmans; 1967.

Law R. *The Oyo Empire, C.1600-c.1836: A West African Imperialism in the Era of the Atlantic Slave Trade*. Clarendon Press; 1977.

Leith-Ross S. *Stepping-stones: Memoirs of Colonial Nigeria, 1907-1960*. P. Owen; 1983.

Lovejoy PE, Hogendorn JS. Revolutionary Mahdism and Resistance to Colonial Rule in the Sokoto Caliphate, 1905–6. *Journal of African History*. 1990;31(2):217-244.

Lovejoy PE. *Jihād in West Africa during the Age of Revolutions*. Ohio University Press; 2016.

Mann K. *Slavery and the Birth of an African City: Lagos, 1760--1900*. Indiana University Press; 2007.

Martin BG. *Muslim Brotherhoods in Nineteenth-Century Africa*. Cambridge University Press; 1978.

Mason M. Captive and Client Labour and the Economy of the Bida Emirate: 1857-1901. *Journal of African history*. 1973 1973;14(3):453-471.

Medical History of the Expedition to the Niger during the Years 1841-2,

Comprising an Account of the Fever Which Led to Its Abrupt Termination. *Edinburgh Medical and Surgical Journal.* 1845/4/1 1845;63(163):415-454.

Mockler-Ferryman AF. *Up the Niger: Narrative of Major Claude MacDonald's Mission to the Niger and Benue Rivers, West Africa (Classic Reprint).* Fb&c Limited; 2018.

Muffett DJM. *Concerning Brave Captains: Being a History of the British Occupation of Kano and Sokoto and of the Last Stand of the Fulani Forces.* A. Deutsch; 1964.

Nadel SF. *A Black Byzantium: The Kingdom of Nupe in Nigeria.* LIT Verlag Münster; 1996.

Newell S. Remembering J. M. Stuart-Young of Onitsha, Colonial Nigeria: Memoirs, Obituaries and Names. *Africa: Journal of the International African Institute.* 2003 2003;73(4):505-530.

Nigerian Tribune Newspapers - Tambuwal allocates land for proposed Nana Asma'u University in Sokoto. 2019/10/15 2019; (Available online)

Niven CR. *A Short History of Nigeria.* Longmans of Nigeria; 1962.

O'Grady R. *The Passionate Imperialists.* Conrad Press; 2018.

Orr CWJ. *The Making of Northern Nigeria.* Macmillan and Company, Limited; 1911.

Park M. *Travels in the interior districts of Africa: performed in the years 1795, 1796, and 1797 by Mungo Park ..., with an account of his susequent mission to that country in 1805.* vol 2. Murray; 1815.

Perham MF. *Lugard: The Years of Authority, 1898-1945.* Collins; 1960.

Philips JE. Causes of the Jihad of Usman 'Dan Fodio: A Historiographical Review. *Journal for Islamic Studies.* 2017 2017;36(1):18-58.

Robinson CH. *Hausaland Or Fifteen Hundred Miles Through the Central Soudan.* Sampson Low, Marston & Co.; 1897.

Robinson RE, Gallagher J, Denny A. *Africa and the Victorians: The Official Mind of Imperialism.* Macmillan; 1961.

Ross DA. The Career of Domingo Martinez in the Bight of Benin 1833–64. *J Afr Hist.* 1965 1965;6(1):79-90.

Scharrer J. *The Journalist : the Jameson Raid, the Klondike Gold Rush, the Anglo Boer War, the Founding of Nigeria : Flora Shaw was there.* CreateSpace Independent Publishing Platform; 2014.

Spencer Trimingham J. *A History of Islam in West Africa.* vol 8. Oxford University Press; 1963.

Spencer Trimingham J. *The Sufi Orders in Islam*. Oxford University Press; 1998.

Sperl S. *Classical Traditions and Modern Meanings*. BRILL; 1996.

State of the Nation 1806. (Available online)

Stone RH, Stone RH. *In Africa's Forest and Jungle: Six Years Among the Yorubas*. University of Alabama Press; 2010.

Storey G, Dickens C. *Dickens: Bleak House*. Cambridge University Press; 1987.

Sulaiman I. *A Revolution in History: The Jihad of Usman Dan Fodio*. Mansell; 1986.

Temple CL. *Notes on the Tribes, Provinces, Emirates and States of the Northern Provinces of Nigeria*. Cass; 1965.

The Committee of Scottish Bankers (CSCB) - £10 Famous Scots Series - Withdrawn. Scotsbank.org

The Spectator Archive - The Battle of Bida. 1897/2/13 1897; (Available online)

The Times Newspapers Archive - Shaw F. Captain Lugard's Book. 1893/11/22 1893;

The Times Newspapers Archive - The Rising in Sokoto 1906/2/22 1906 (Available online)

Theresa May – 2016 Speech to Launch Leadership Campaign – UKPOL. CO.UK. (Available online)

Thomas H. *The Slave Trade*. Hachette UK; 2015.

Tombs R. *The English and their History: The First Thirteen Centuries*. Penguin UK; 2014.

Ubah CN. Suppression of the Slave Trade in the Nigerian Emirates. *Journal of African History*. 1991 1991;32(3):447-470.

Untold stories: Birmingham, the British Empire and Bangladeshi curry 2017/12/7 https://advisor.museumsandheritage.com/features/untold-stories-birmingham-british-empire-bangladeshi-curry/.

Vandervort B. *Wars of Imperial Conquest In Africa*. Routledge; 1998.

Walker FD. *The Romance of the Black River: The Story of the C.M.S. Nigeria Mission*. Church Missionary Society; 1938.

Watts MJ. *Silent Violence: Food, Famine, and Peasantry in Northern Nigeria*. University of Georgia Press; 2013.

Whitehead C. *Colonial Educators: The British Indian and Colonial Education Service 1858-1983*. Bloomsbury Academic; 2003.

Willcocks J. *The Romance of Soldiering and Sport*. Cassell & Co.; 1925.

ACKNOWLEDGMENTS

Feyi Fawehinmi

To my wife, Adenike, and my two boys who have been invaluable while I was writing this book - I thank them immensely for their support. My two boys in particular have provided very early critical reviews even before reading a word of the book, a useful way to keep one grounded.

In writing this book, we stood on the shoulders of giants who have done the heavy lifting of researching countless documents and papers. We have tried to reference as many of them as possible, especially Nigerian historians who often do not get the recognition they deserve. We owe them a debt for making the writing of this book possible.

My friends in 'The Cabal' who continue to provide a safe space to test out ideas and thoughts without judgement. The Whatsapp groups I belong to who have unwittingly helped me refine a lot of the ideas and thoughts that you will encounter in this book. By providing an outlet for daily vigorous debates about Nigeria, iron sharpens iron and if nothing else, I come away realising how much I do not know. I learnt to write in public.

To Tunde Leye and Elnathan John for the regular twitter debates and discussions we have about Nigeria's history. They played no small part in making me realise there was an interesting story to tell about Nigerian history and to lose my fear of telling it.

To my Nigerian Ogas - Akin Dawodu's discussion of even the most niche bit of history has been incredibly infectious. He unwittingly set the standard for the kind of book I realised I had to write. Mallam Abba Kyari's encouragement and pointers were very much appreciated. I regret that he did not live to read the book. Dele Olojede who I was fortunate enough to work with a few years ago as my introduction to collaborating with a truly talented writer and editor. What I learnt in that year and some with him would cost a King's ransom to acquire on the open market. Ambassador Yusuf Tuggar's effortless brilliance and deep knowledge of Nigerian history has been of incredible value. Dr. Kingsley Obiora who has been incredibly kind and who was one of the first people to tell me I had a book in me. Tope Owolabi might never know how valuable her freely given advice was when this book was no more than a document sitting on our computers looking for where to go. I am deeply grateful to all of them.

My mother Florence did the heavy lifting of raising me. To her I owe more than I can ever repay.

Lastly, I could not have asked for a better co-author than Fola. From being able to handle big stories so easily to synthesising complex ideas that ensured we could tell a coherent and interesting story. I pay him my tribute by saying this will not be the last book we write together.

ACKNOWLEDGMENTS

Fola Fagbule

Writing *Formation* was not my idea. Talking to Feyi regularly about Nigeria for a few years led to an entirely unexpected invitation to co-author a book about Nigeria. Once we started, it took only a short period of time for me to rediscover my love for writing, especially about a subject that is an enduring passion for me. So, my first tribute is to Feyi, who has been an excellent co-conspirator on this project. I tell everyone who will listen that Feyi is the most important thinker currently writing about Nigeria and writing *Formation* has done nothing to remove from that assessment in my mind.

I am thankful to the great historians and writers (living and departed) who have come before us to this story. We were astounded at the trove of historical material that existed about Nigeria's pre-colonial period, thanks to the dedication of so many important writers, foreign and indigenous. We could not have written this book without them. Special thanks to Wiebe Boer, a true Nigerian patriot, who heard about our project fortuitously, and took it upon himself to become a supporter. Wiebe, your guidance, early support and introductions were invaluable. Thanks also to Akin Oyebode who introduced us to Bibi Bakare-Yusuf. Bibi has been the most important person other than Feyi and I in bringing this book to life. We are forever indebted.

Over the years, my family and friends have become used to my busy lifestyle and general unavailability. Writing a book has not made it any easier. To my aunties, uncles, siblings, cousins, nieces, and nephews: I love you all very much and thank you for your support and unconditional love. Also, to my closest friends, with whom I have had endless discussions about how Nigeria can be made better, this book is also for you. I believe that we can make a big difference in our lifetime, and understanding our history is a small first step in the direction of contributing towards that different and better future.

In the writing process itself, I have been grateful to work for an organisation that provides me with the means to afford the numerous expensive and rare books without which the writing of *Formation* would have been impossible, and for that, I am grateful. My long-time mentor and friend, Andrew Alli is worth a special mention - not least because at the time of writing, he had purchased (as gifts) more copies of *Formation* than any other single individual. Thank you, Andrew.

My original love for words and writing came from my parents, who spared little expense or consideration in supporting my passion for literature from as early as I can remember. They both departed too early, but I am certain they would be proud of everything I have achieved. And to Ayshatu, from whom I have learnt about love and faith and spirituality in ways that I did not previously know was possible, thank you darling.

INDEX

Support *Formation*

We hope you enjoyed reading this book. If you think more people should read it, here's how you can support:

1. **Recommend it.** Don't keep the enjoyment of this book to yourself; spread the word to your friends and family.

2. **Review, review review**. Your opinion is powerful and a positive review from you can generate new sales. Spare a minute to leave a short review on Amazon, GoodReads, our website and other book buying sites.

3. **Join the conversation.** Hearing somebody you trust talk about a book with passion and excitement is one of the most powerful ways to get people to engage with it. If you like this book, talk about it, Facebook it, Tweet it, Blog it, Instagram it. Take pictures of the book and quote or highlight from your favourite passage. You could even add a link so others know where to purchase the book from.

4. **Buy the book as gifts for others.** Buying a gift is a regular activity for most of us – birthdays, anniversaries, holidays, special days or just a nice present for a loved one for no reason… If you love this book and you think it might resonate with others, then please buy extra copies!

5. **Get your local bookshop or library to stock it.** Sometimes bookshops and libraries only order books that they have heard about. If you loved this book, why not ask your librarian or bookshop to order it in. If enough people request a title, the bookshop or library will take note and

will order a few copies for their shelves.

6. **Recommend a book to your book club.** Persuade your book club to read this book and discuss why you enjoyed it in the company of others. This is a wonderful way to share what you like and help us to boost the sales.

7. **Attend a book reading.** There are lots of opportunities to hear writers talk about their work. Support them by attending their book events online and offline. Get your friends, colleagues and families to a reading and show an author your support.

Thank you!

Stay up to date with the latest books, special offers and exclusive content with our monthly newsletter.
Sign up on our website:
www.cassavarepublic.biz

Twitter: @cassavarepublic
Instagram: @cassavarepublicpress
Facebook: facebook.com/CassavaRepublic
Hashtag: #FormationNG #ReadCassava
#ReadingAfrica #ReadAfrica

SUPPORTERS

A. Adesanya

Abba Ibrahim

Abdul Adawudi

Abdulazeez Ajibola

Abdulhafeez Balogun

Abdul-Jalil Surajo

Abdulwahab Oseni

Abigail Mshelbwala

Abiodun Adetona

Abioye Ayeni

Abraham Elegbede

Abubakar Ahmed

Abubakar Bello

Abubakar Suleiman

Adaku Uche Ekpo

Adamu Ibrahim Tijjani

Adebanke Equagoo

Adebayo Adeola

Adebayo Babalola

Adebayo Onigbanjo

Adebola Adeyemo

Adebola Akapo

Adebowale Asiru

Adedamola Adepetu

Adedayo Daini

Adedayo Ajiboye

Adedayo Balogun Adeola

Adedayo Fagade

Adetayo Balogun

Adedeji Awodele

Adefunke Ajala

Adegboyega Odubiyi

Adekunle Adebiyi

Adekunle Adesoji

Ademola Hassan

Adeniranyusuf Abdullateef

Adeniyi Ajiboye

Aderinsola Adebayo Endeavor

Aderonke Nedd

Adetola Onayemi

Adetomiwa Aladekomo

Adewale Jinadu

Adewale Yemi-Sofumade

Adewole Ayoade

Adeyemi Adedokun

Adeyinka Adewole

Afolabi   Ajao

Ahmed Dasuki

Ahmed   Maccido

Ahmed Rufai   Isah

Aigboje Aig-Imoukhuede

Ajibola Adigun

Ajibola Oyekunle

Ajibola Olayemi

Ajuma Fawehinmi

Akin Fatunke

Akin Akintayo

Akin Dawodu

Akin Adigun

Akinade Aderele

Akinbayo

Akintunde Oyebode

Akinwale Akinmusire

Akpanke Utande

Alexander Sewell

Alhaji Garba Galadima

Alhaji Aliyu Datti

Alice Usanase

Allen Akinkunle

Allen Ogedengbe

Amaka Ezike

Amole Taokeek

Amy Jadesimi

Andrew Esezobor

Andrew Mccabe

Andrew Alli

Anita Mudiaga

Anna Frain

Anne Harte

Anthony Ekene

Arinola Bello

Arogundade Moshood

Asmau Dahiru

Atedo Peterside

Ayo Ogunlade

Ayo Alli

Ayobami Aladeloye

Ayodeji Akinselure

Ayodele Ademosu

Ayotunde Adeyemi

Aysha Abba

Babaranti Familusi

Babatunde Amoo

Babatunde Dada

Babatunde Osibodu

Babatunde Adama

Bade Ayanbule

Bashir Ibrahim T.

Bashirat Balogun

Bayo Adebiyi

Bayo Odunlami

Bayo Adeola

Bekeme Masade

Bibi Bakare-Yusuf

Bimbo Oyedokun

Bimbola Bukoye

Bimpe Bucknor

Blessed Edem

Blessing Oladunjoye

Blessing Mikairu

Bode Pedro

Bode Agusto

Bola Akapo

Bolaji Aluko

Bolaji Balogun

Bolaji Kekere-Ekun

Busola K-Moradeyo

Caleb Uzuegbunam

Carlson Oseghale

Charles Banigo

Cheta Nwanze

Chibueze Oriji

Chibueze Emenike

Chibuzor Nwaezeapu

Chidinma Adeniyi

Chigozie Aja

Chinenye Okechukwu

Chioma Onyenwe

Chris Akpakwu

Christopher Ibru

Chuks Anugwom

Clare Cummings

D. O

Damilola Alawode

Daniel Obidiegwu

Daniel Aideyan Omorogbe

David Adebiyi

Dayo Mofikoya

Deji Haastrup

Delmwa Deshi Kura

Deo Alagbe

Deola Kamson

Desola Ilori

Dewumi Ogunsanya

Dilys Iyalla-Harry

Dolapo Adelana

Doyin Ogun

Dozie Anyaegbunam

Dr. Kayode Fayemi

Dupe Killa-Kafidipe

Ebenezer Seun Oyajumo

Ebere Nkoro

Ebisse Rouw

Efosa Ojomo

Efremfon Eduo

Egghead Odewale

Ekanem Ukpong

Ekpedeme Inyang

Elizabeth Plumptre

Eloho Omame

Emeka Ogri

Emike Kanabe

Emma Shercliff

Emmanuel Obute

Emmanuel-Francis Nwaolisa

Eniola Bolarin

Eniola Fawehinmi

Enitan Benson

Enitan Shonibare

Ererhe Okparavero

Ernest Ndukwe

Eromosele OAriosh

Esther Jones

Evan Procknow

Eyitayo Garbson

Eyitope Owolabi

Ezeibe Francis

Fahd Isa

Faiza Attah

Fatu Ogwuche

Femi Adebayo

Femi Fowora

Feranmi Akinlade

Ferdi Moolman

Fola Oluwehinmi

Fola Laoye

Fola Adeola

Folahanmi Fagbule

Folake Erogbogbo

Folorunsho Atteh

Foluwaso Adebobiyi

Frank Nwosu

Funke Opeke

Funlola Seriki

Funsho Fagbalu

Gafar Alli

Gbemi Adekoya

'Gbenga Sesan

Gbolahan Adenuga

Gboyega Bamgboye

Gideon   Mshelbwala

Godfrey Orji

Godman Akinlabi

Godwin Obaseki

Graeme   Burton

Hadeel   Ibrahim

Halima   Dangote

Hammed Amusa

Harrison Yinfaowei

Hassan Taiwo Yahaya

Hauwa Datti-Garba

Hayatudeen Mohammed

Hope Adodo

Ibrahim Adams

Ifeanyi Onwuka

Ifeoluwa Goriola

Ighodalo Ifada

Igwe Ndukwe

Igwegbe Victor

Ikenna Ogbue

Ikwulono Unobe

Imoni Akpofure

Ireti Bakare-Yusuf

Ishola Oyewo

Iyinoluwa Aboyeji

Jaime Raybin

Jaiyeola A Vincent

Jameel Ahmed

James Nwankwo

Jamiu Niniola

Jason Njoku

Jayve Montgomery

Jeffrey Sgay Lawal

Jeremiah Angai

Jesutooni Ajiboye

Jide Olanlokun

Jide Ogundare

Johnpaul Iwu

Jola Ayeye

Jolaoluwa Ladipo

Jonah Dienye

Joshua Ojo

Jubril Olambiwonnu

Jubril Saba

Jubril Sadiq

Kabir Shittu

Kabir Lawal

Kayode Adewuyi

Kayode Khalidson

Kehinde Daodu

353

Kofoworola Okunola

L A

Ladebi Victor

Ladi Ani-Mumuney

Lai Yahaya

Lailah Gumbi

'Lamide Young

Lanre Irewole

Lanre Shasore

Laolu Owolabi

Laolu Thomas

Lawal Akus

Lawal Lawal

Lawrence Gbadamosi

Layla Mohamed

Linda Ojo

Lotanna Igwe Odunze

Lynette Lisk

Mabe Adejoh

Major General (Rtd) Akintunde Akinkunmi

Maria-Goretti Ndunwere Debiyi

Martha Eleyinma

Mary Ogunremi

Matthew Page

Mayowa Olaleye

Mayowa Omogbenigun

Mazi Chima Amadi

Meredith Startz

Meyene Ibanga

Mfonobong Nsehe

Michael Imeh

Michael Erigha

Michael Harte

Mobolaji Taiwo

Mogbekeloluwa Koye-Ladele

Mohammed Adamu

Mohammed Ibrahim Tijjani

Moje Ikpeme

Morris John

Mutiat Adeyemo

Nana Nwachukwu

Nanfa Pennap

Nathaniel Okwoli

Nicky Fawehinmi

Niki Igbaroola

Niyi Akinsulere

Nkechi Usani

Nnadozie Asinobi

Nnaemeka Ijioma

Nnaemeka Nwachukwu

Nonso Obikili

Nurudeen Akande

Obaro Ikoh

Obinnaya Egbe

Ochiagha Ananaba

Odion Oriaifo

Odunoluwa Longe

Ofofonono Umoren

Ogochukwu Okafor

Ojoma Ochai

Ola Babatolu

Oladele Balogun

Oladimeji Edwards

Olaiwola Bolaji

Olajide Bello

Olalekan Otubu

Olalekan Abiola

Olamide Aina

Olanrewaju Shasore

Olanrewaju Rufai

Olanrewaju Ajakaiye

Olaolu Oluro

Olatomiwa Lasebikan

Olatunde Okeowo

Olatunde Makanjuola

Olatunde Olagunju

Olatunde Ganiy

Olatunji Alao

Olawale Atanda

Olawale Oguntoye

Olayinka Babalola

Oliver Andrews

Ologunde Oluwaseun

Olufemi Awoyemi

Olufunso Fasetire

Olukayode Odeyinde

Olukayode Taiwo

Olumide Akinkugbe

Olumuyiwa Saka

Olusegun Tinubu

Olusola John

Olusola Adesanwo

Olutomi Oladipo

Oluwafemi Abanishe

Oluwagbemileke Alabi-Isama

Oluwasegun Oyekan

Oluwaseun Onayiga

Oluwaseun Smith

Oluwaseyi Adebayo

Oluwatomisin Numbere

Oluwatosin Alagbe

Oluwatosin Folagbade

Oluwatosin Alagbe

Oluwatoyosi Akinrelere

Omobola Johnson

Omobolanle Jinadu

Omoefe Shaire

Omoluke Tugbobo

Omotola Abimbola

Omowonuola Banjo

Onomakpome Edore

Onyi Ugorji

Oo Nwoye

Opemipo Aikomo

Opeyemi Ajao

Opeyemi Adamolekun

Opeyemi Kolawole

Opeyemi Ibrahim

Osazemwinde Osunde

Otiga Alih

Ovonlen Ebhohimhen

Oyekunle Olaoye

Oyewale Oyewo

Oyinlola Adewoyin

Panashe Chigumadzi

P.O. Bamikole

Paul Adaja

Paul Odunayo Adetipe

Perkins Abaje

Peter Gana

Peter Adesokan

Phillips Oduoza

Philip Oke Naij

Rabi'Atu Tanimu

Ralph Mupita

Rasaq Adeola

Raymond Ononiwu

Rayyan Umar

Richard Okojevoh

Richard Grob

Rofem Egbe

Rosemary Adejoh

Rotimi Ajayi

Sam Adeyemi

Samaila Zubairu

Samson Toromade

Samuel Arua

Samuel Chukwu

Samuel Amegavi

Samuel Kayode Asoro

Sanjeev Gupta

Sanusi Ismaila

Sarah Ozo-Irabor

Sarah Ladipo Manyika

Saude Amina Atoyebi

Sele Inegbedion

Seni Sulyman

Serah Ugbabe

Seun Awoyele

Seyi Laja

Shadrach Saddih

Shakirudeen Taiwo

Shamsuddeen Saleh

Sheba Macham

Shehu Williams

Shehu Yahaya

Simon Lewis

Simon Kolawole

Soala Ekine

Sola Adeduntan

Solomon Quaynor

Solomon Asamoah

Solomon Temison

Stanley Achonu

Sulayman Abu-Bakr

Suleman Sule

Sunday Olumoroti

Tade Durojaiye

Taghogho Emefeke

Taj Onigbanjo

Tams Sokari

Taofik Abdulkareem

TBAKS

Teju Adeyinka

Temi Kujore

Temiloluwa Makanjuola

Temitope Lana

Temitope Owolabi

Temitope Fakile

Theophilus Emuwa

Timi Ajiboye

Tobi Olagoke

Tobi Alli-Balogun

Tobi Lawson

Tokunbo Ishmael

Tokunbo Akerele

Tolu Sokenu

Tolu Ajiboye

Tolu Osinibi

Tolu Obamuroh

Tolulope Olalekan

Tolulope Oguntoyinbo

Tommy Oladeji

Tony Sokan

Tony Elumelu

Tosin Omofoye

Toyin Akinniyi

Tunde Alao-Olaifa

Tunde Sawyerr

Tutu Agyare

Uchechi Ngonadi

Udori Ekpin

Ugo Onyeka

Ugochukwu Obi-Chukwu

Umar Turaki

Uthman Adejumo

Uy Ismaila

Uzoma Nwagba

Victor Olanrewaju

Victor Adegite

Victor Ndukauba

Wale Fapohunda

Wale Okunrinboye

Waziri Adio

Wuraola Fanimokun

Yahaya Maibe

Yemi Adekunle

Yemi Ogunleye

Yemi Osinbajo

Yemisi Ransome-Kuti

Yetunde Erogbogbo

Yinka Adeola

Yinka Sanni

Yvette Dimiri

Yvonne Johnson

Zainab Musa

Zikora Okwor

Ziino Asamaige

Zizoh Anto